IMAGES
of America

NEW MILFORD

IMAGES
of America

NEW MILFORD

Frances L. Smith

ARCADIA
PUBLISHING

ISBN 978-0-7385-0450-6

Published by Arcadia Publishing
Charleston, South Carolina

Printed in the United States of America

Library of Congress Catalog Card Number: 00106461

For all general information contact Arcadia Publishing at:
Telephone 843-853-2070
Fax 843-853-0044
E-mail sales@arcadiapublishing.com
For customer service and orders:
Toll-Free 1-888-313-2665

Visit us on the Internet at www.arcadiapublishing.com

To my sons, Joseph Martin and Raymond Dunbar,
and my granddaughter, Stephanie.

On the cover: Pictured at 39 Old Park Lane are members of the Bostwick family, from left to right, S. Edgar Bostwick, Carrie Bostwick Wallace, Mary Bostwick Berry, Mary Doty Bostwick, and Fred Berry. The family is one of the oldest in town; John Bostwick settled in New Milford in 1707.

Contents

Acknowledgments

It is said, "Men as a whole judge more with their eyes than with their hands." I have gained an even greater appreciation for that proverb during the research and writing of this book. I wish to acknowledge my sincere thanks to each and every one who shared family records, photographs, and innumerable private resources. It has been my endeavor to trace family histories in New Milford and to pass them on to our present and future generations.

I would like to give thanks to the following: the Heacock family; Bette-Lou Emmons, who shared so many photographs of New Milford's first settlers; the Bostwicks; Truman Richmond; Merrill Golden; the New Milford Historical Society; Marilyn Whittlesey, historian, whose time and effort will always be remembered; Roderick Clark, Canterbury School's former headmaster; James Hipp; Maryann Cameron; the Reimeridge family; the Kimberly family; Viola Jones; Robert Stack; Raymond Smith; Stuart Halpin; Rolf Hammer; Sue Noble Kustosz, Classic Photography; Ronald Smith; Patrick Maguire, administrative aide to the mayor; Anna Chapin; Iris Randall; Virginia Decker; Claudia DeLeon; the First Congregational Church; Thomasina Carr; Amy Holding, owner of Office Wizards; and my family, who were a continual source of encouragement in the completion of this work.

—F.L.S.

INTRODUCTION

The Weautenock tribe occupied the land opposite the village of New Milford prior to 1670, when the people of Fairfield and Stratford turned their attention to *Weautenaug*, the Indian name for New Milford, looking for new land for a plantation. The Weautenocks gave the colonists a deed of sale, dated February 8, 1702 or 1703. The first white settler who made New Milford his permanent residence was John Noble Sr. of Westfield, Massachusetts, in 1707. Noble became the first town clerk and surveyor of lands. He died on August 17, 1714. The Noble family were merchants. The second family to settle in New Milford was that of John Bostwick, whose deed was dated December 2, 1707. Bostwick moved to New Milford primarily to go into the tobacco business. He shared in the official work of the plantation and the town. New Milford was incorporated into a colony in 1712.

The Heacock family were descendants of the Pequot and Narragansett tribes. The first black minister of New Milford was Rev. Stephen Heacock. He was involved in the development of New Milford and served on may town committees. The religious leader Rev. Daniel Boardman settled in New Milford in 1715 and established the Congregational church in 1716. The Episcopal church followed. In 1729, civic and educational sites were established at the north end of the town green.

New Milford became a very prosperous business center. It had gristmills, hat and button factories, pottery makers, blacksmiths, and farms, whose main crops were tobacco and wheat. James Hine was the first blacksmith. New Milford Pottery was organized in June 1887, with some 30 residents subscribing to the capital stock. By August 1887, the company had purchased 3 acres of land known as Giddings Mill, where the Robertson Bleachery stands today.

Other places of business included Frederick Boardman's drugstore on the west side of Railroad Street, near the depot; it was stocked with patent medicines of the time. On the south corner of Wall and Railroad Streets was F.G. Bennett and Son furniture store and undertaking business. Daniel Marsh and his son T.T. Marsh ran a coal yard near the depot. Harvey Jennings opened a grocery and confectionery in 1847. Mrs. Stephen Wells was a milliner.

In 1852, Albert S. Hill and Edward Barton built a paper mill on the East Aspetuck River, a mile above Northville; the mill converted straw and rags into straw-board paper that was used for hatboxes and dry goods boxes. Sylvanus Merwin operated a hotel at Gaylord's Ville; at that time, the stop on the railroad was called Merwinsville. Merwin held a contract that required every train to stop at Merwinsville so that passengers might eat or spend the night at his hotel.

Brothers William W. and Edwin S. Wells ran a gristmill on the river. Charles G. Peck was a harness maker. William B. Wright sold stoves, plumbing, and tinware. In the Maryland district, Roswell, Sheldon, and David Northrup operated a foundry and machine shop, making castings to order, iron fences, and machinery.

Bridgewater was a part of New Milford until 1856. Smith and Erwin opened a hat factory in Bridgewater in 1834; they moved their factory to New Milford in 1855. In the the 1880s, the Conetia Wheel Club became popular; residents used bicycles to visit a neighbor or go to the store, but the real fun was in getting a crowd together and going for a spin.

The Fugitive Slave Act of 1850 brought the question of slavery to every mind and resulted in the Underground Railroad, which allowed at least 20,000 Negroes to escape. In New Milford and in nearby Washington, there were active sympathizers for this cause.

The first meeting of the Housatonic Agricultural Society was held in Wright's Hall in 1858. The first fairs in New Milford were held on a lot behind the residence of Dr. James Hine. Later, the Fair Committee rented the grounds of F.S. Richmond, a few miles south of the village, on the west side of the Housatonic River, northwest of the Indian Burying Grounds.

Levi S. Knapp's barbershop on Bank Street was named Topeka Hall for the Kansas-Nebraska troubles of the 1850s. For more than 50 years, the hall was an almost nightly gathering place for the men of the town to play heated games of checkers, interspersed with good talk.

Brothers-in-law Merritt Beach and Alanson Canfield opened the town's first lumberyard; it was located on Elm Street at the former site of St. Francis Xavier Church. One of the few industries in the area at the end of the nineteenth century was the Bridgeport Wood Finishing Company, which was located on the Still River in the Lanesville section of New Milford.

For the past 40 years, the Kimberly-Clark Corporation has been New Milford's largest employer and taxpayer. Selectman E. Paul Martin played a major role in bringing Kimberly-Clark to town. To convince the corporation that New Milford was the place to build a new plant, Martin traveled to company headquarters in Wisconsin with with Gov. Abraham Ribicoff and George DeVoe, president of the New Milford Chamber of Commerce.

As time has gone by, New Milford has developed in new and different ways. However, as you walk or drive by the historic areas and along the country roads, keep in mind the photographs in this book and search for a glimpse of the past from which we came.

—Fran Smith

One

Chief Waraumaug and the First Settlers

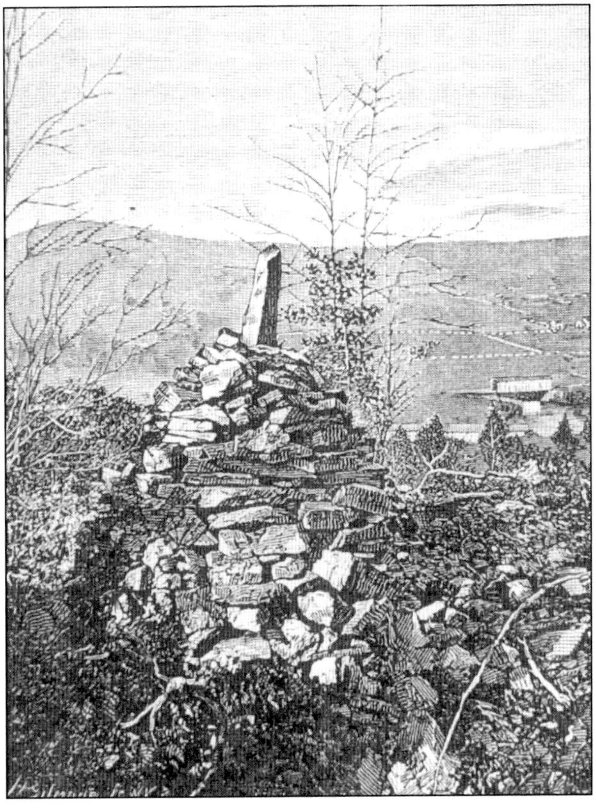

Waraumaug, the last chief of the Weautenock tribe, died *c.* 1735. He was buried on the mountain near the place where he had resided for so long. A pile of stones on an open plot of ground marks the place where his remains repose. The original pile was formed as each of the warriors who belonged to the tribe deposited a stone upon the grave. In the years that followed, members of the tribe continued this custom, placing another stone on the grave each time they visited it. In the 1880s, a family from Bridgeport bought the land and utilized the stones from the monument for the foundation and chimney of a pseudo-castle that was built for them.

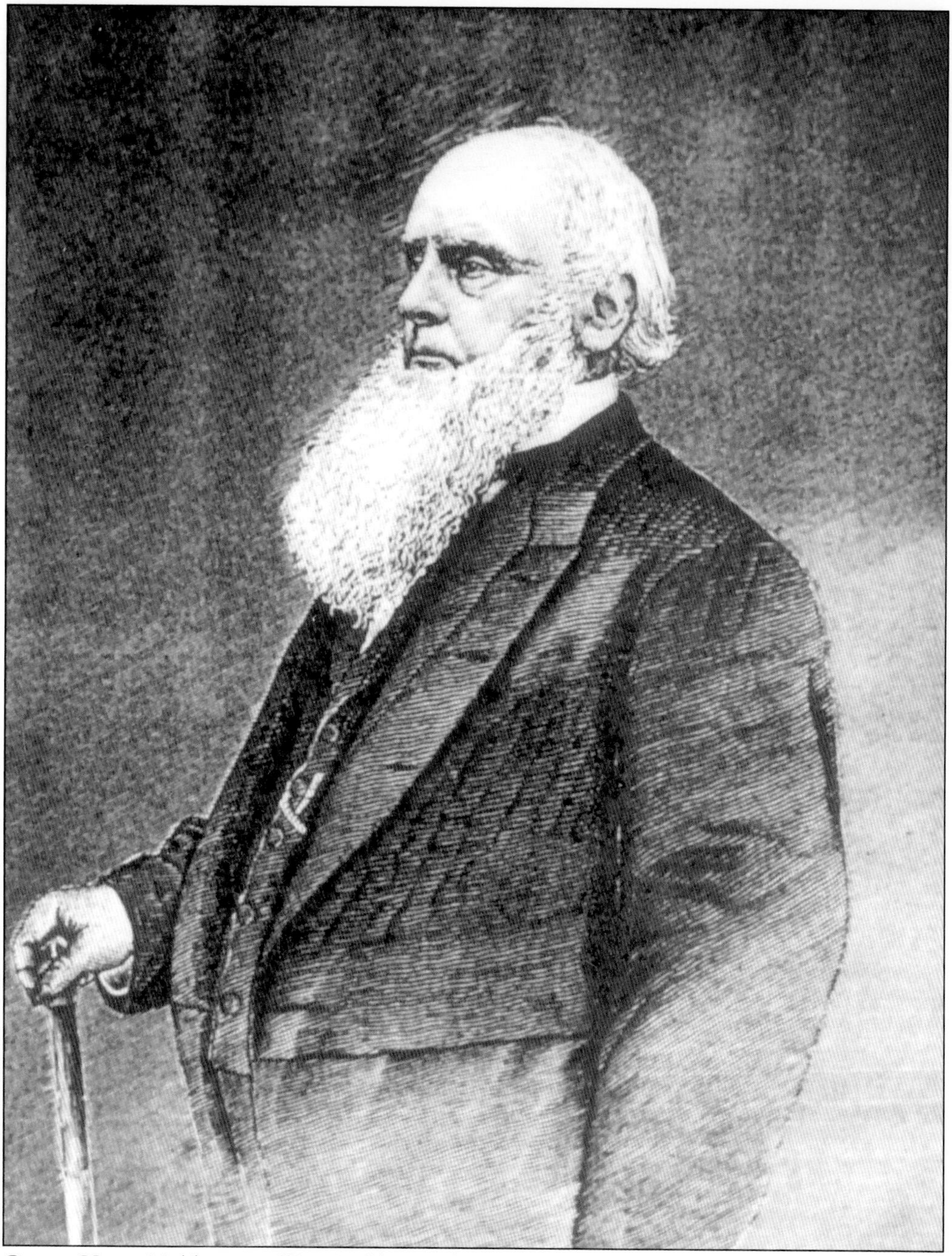

George Henry Noble, son of Ezra Noble, was born in New Milford on March 12, 1814. He was a descendant of New Milford's first settler, John Noble Sr. George Noble served as postmaster from 1853 to 1856 and was a delegate to the national convention that nominated Abraham Lincoln for president in 1860. An influential member of the Congregational church, Noble died on December 10, 1872, at age 58.

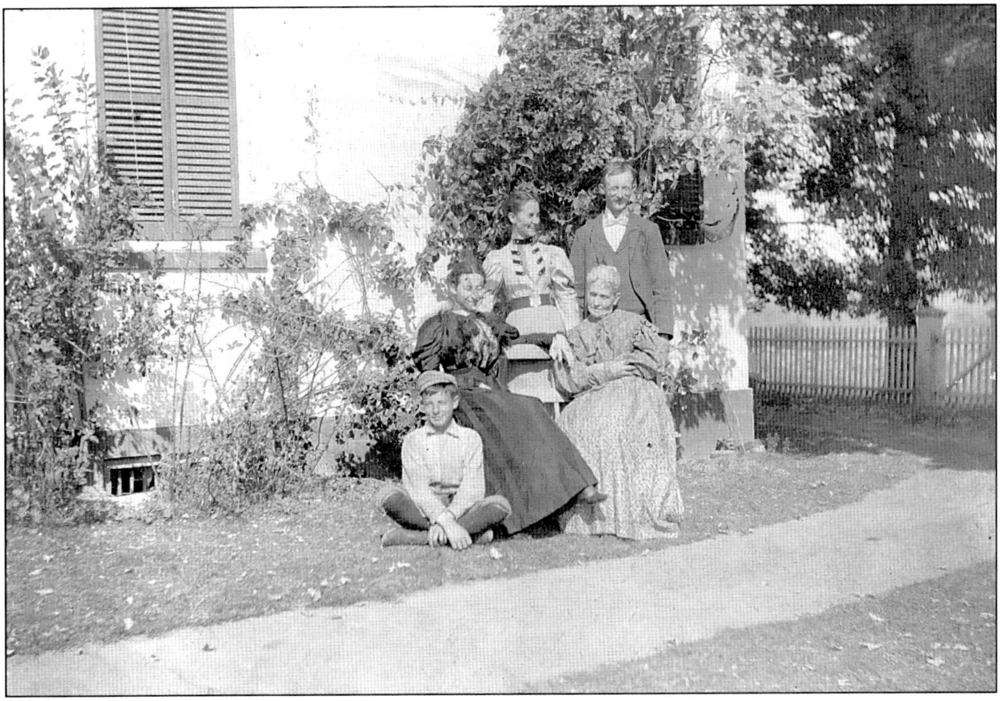

Pictured at 39 Old Park Lane are members of the Bostwick family, from left to right, S. Edgar Bostwick, Carrie Bostwick Wallace, Mary Bostwick Berry, Mary Doty Bostwick, and Fred Berry. The family is one of the oldest in town; John Bostwick settled in New Milford in 1707.

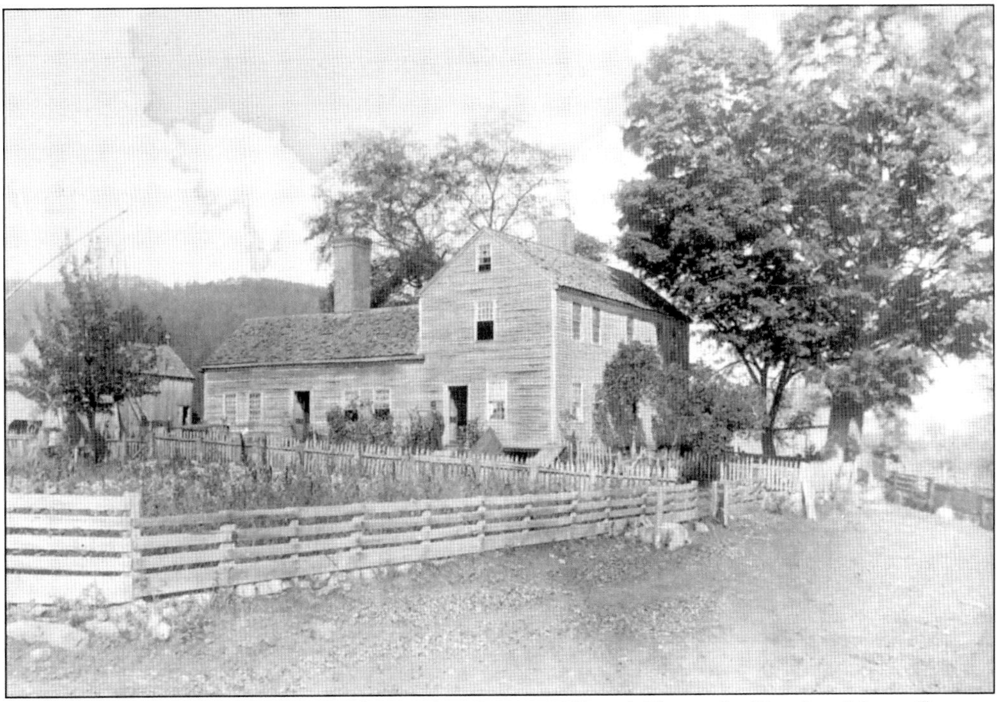

The Benjamin Bostwick farm was located at Squire Hill and Cherniske Road in Merryall.

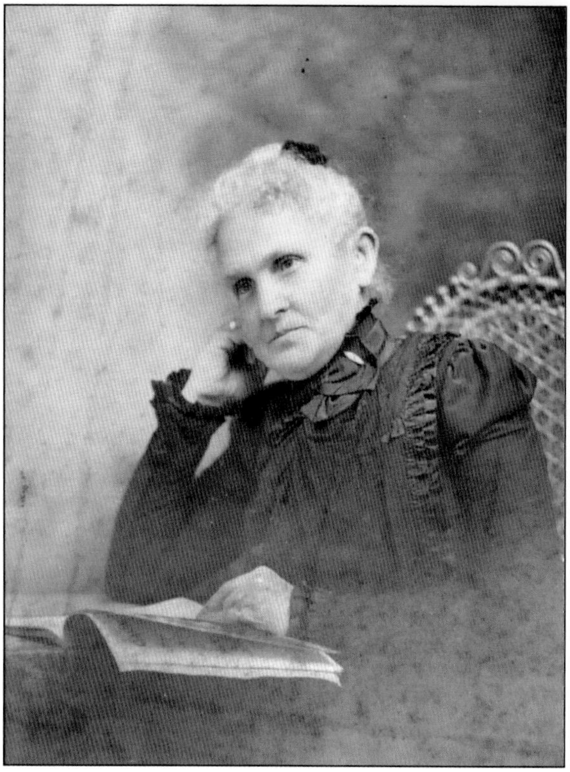

Mary Doty Bostwick leans on her elbow and looks up from the pages in front of her for a moment. She wears a long-sleeved, high-collared dress and an ornament in her hair. A housewife, she was born in 1846 and died in 1919.

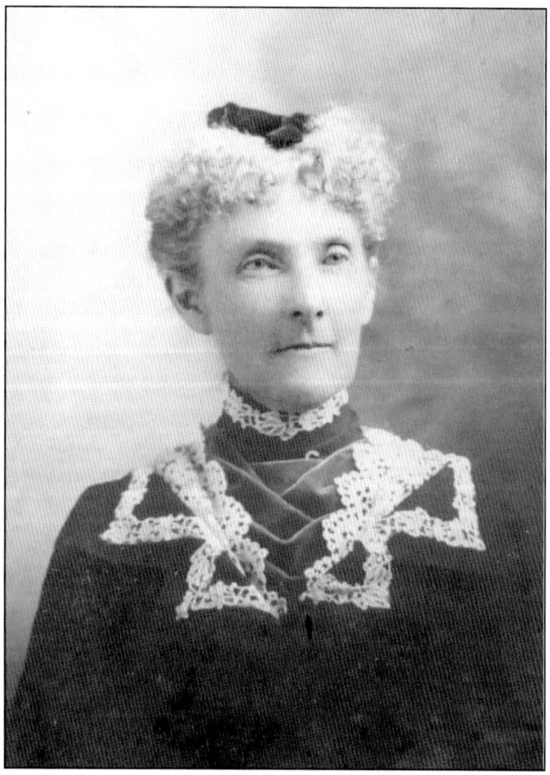

Lile Bostwick was the daughter of Addie Strong. In 1924, she donated her home on Elm Street to the New Milford Hospital. The house had room for 24 patients.

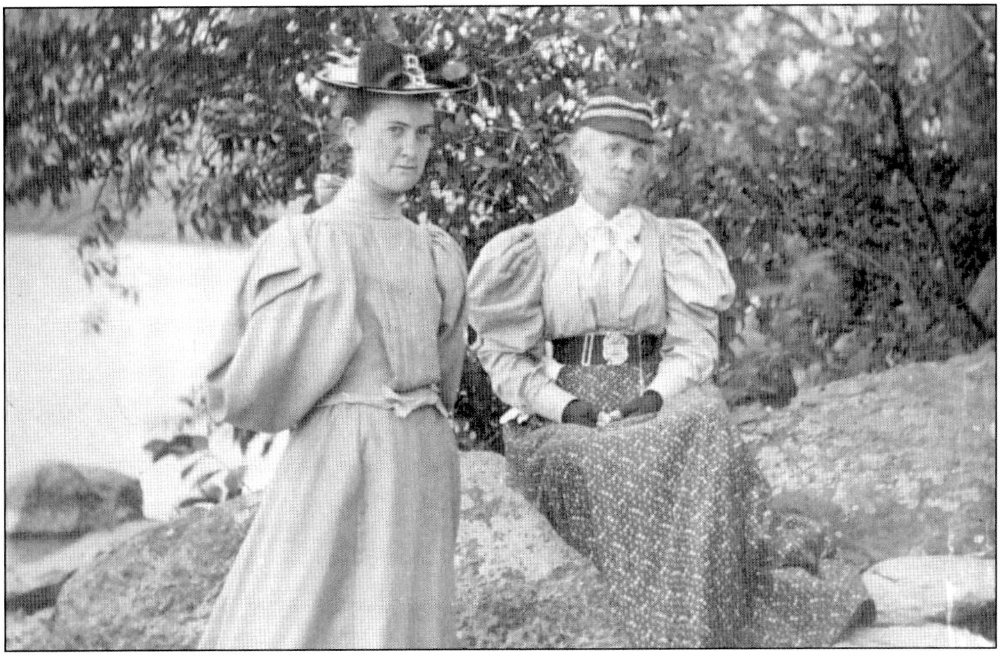

Wearing hats that offer some shade, Mary Bostwick Berry and her mother, Mary Doty Bostwick, share a restful moment at Lake Waraumaug in New Preston. Mary Bostwick Berry was born on August 1, 1873. She married Fred Berry on October 12, 1897. She died on March 25, 1955, at the age of 81.

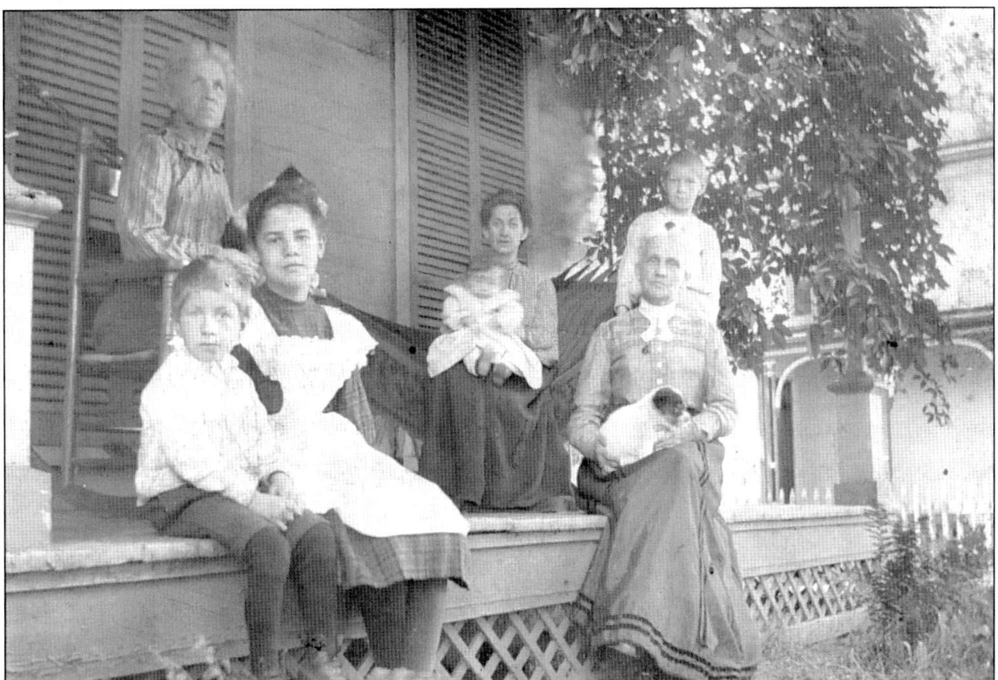

Enjoying the air on the porch c. the 1890s are, from left to right, Martha Stone, three Simpson children, Winnie Simpson, Mary Doty Bostwick holding her dog, and another Simpson boy.

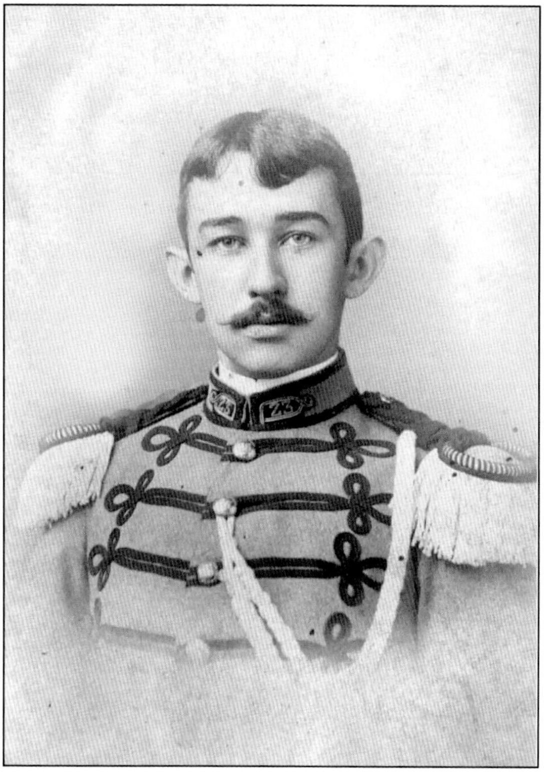

William Bostwick, pictured in uniform at age 18, was born on September 5, 1865, the eldest son of Mary Doty Bostwick. He built the "Bit of Country" house. On October 18, 1893, he married Lottie Root of Bridgeport, and the couple had three children: Lottie May, Raymond William, and Nathan Bostwick. He died on November 14, 1957, at the age of 92.

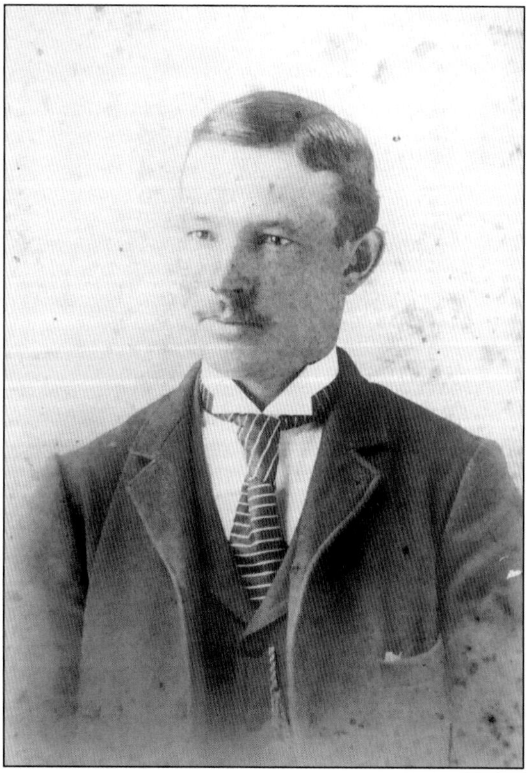

This photograph shows eldest son William Bostwick in his forties. He is still wearing a mustache.

Edward C. Howland (standing) built the house on Old Park Lane where Bette-Lou Emmons now resides. Born in 1877, Howland married Anne Bostwick on September 26, 1900. The couple had two children: Harriet May in 1903 and Jessie L. Howland (Emmons) in 1911. The two seated gentlemen in this late-nineteenth-century photograph could not be identified.

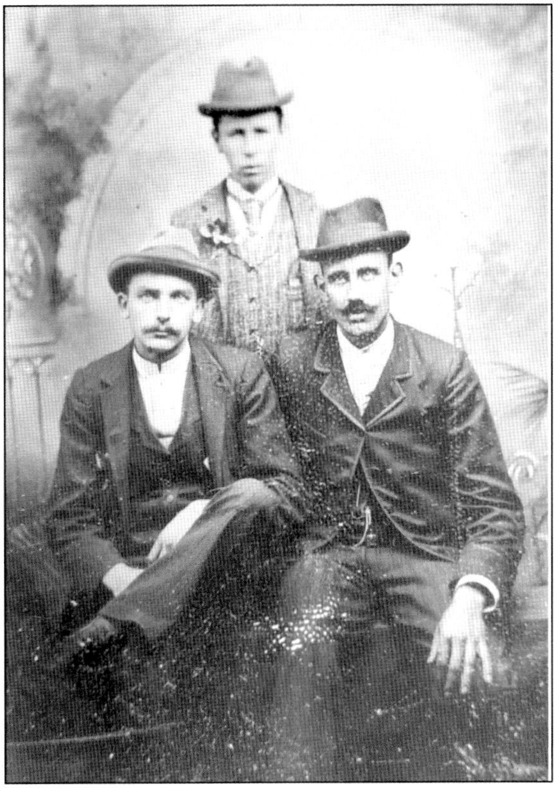

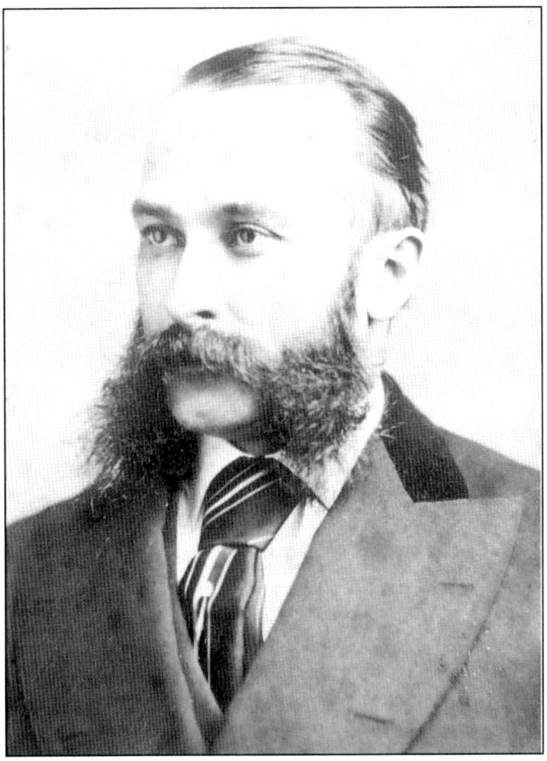

Cyrus Bostwick was another member of the New Milford Bostwick family. Born on May 31, 1836, he left Connecticut to go to Oregon. There, he became involved in the fishing industry and grew very prosperous. He married Sarah Riblet on June 15, 1864. Members of their family still live in Oregon.

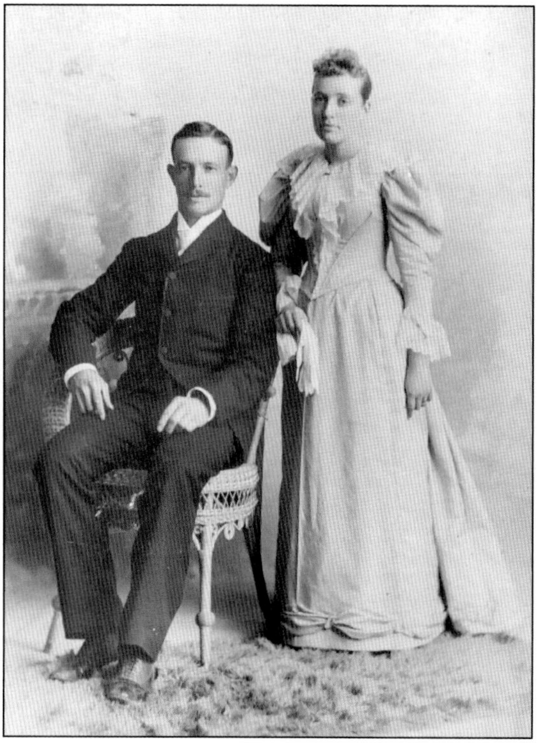

In this mid-1890s view, the husband sits and the wife stands at his side. The couple are William Bostwick and Lottie Root Bostwick. They were married on October 18, 1893.

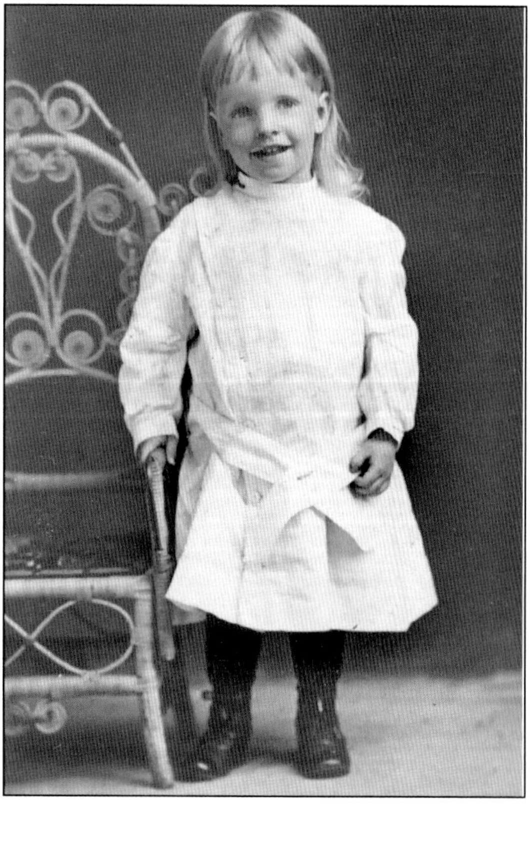

This happy looking two-year-old is Nathan Bostwick, son of William and Lottie Bostwick. He lived in the Bostwick house called "Bit of Country." The photograph dates from *c.* 1905.

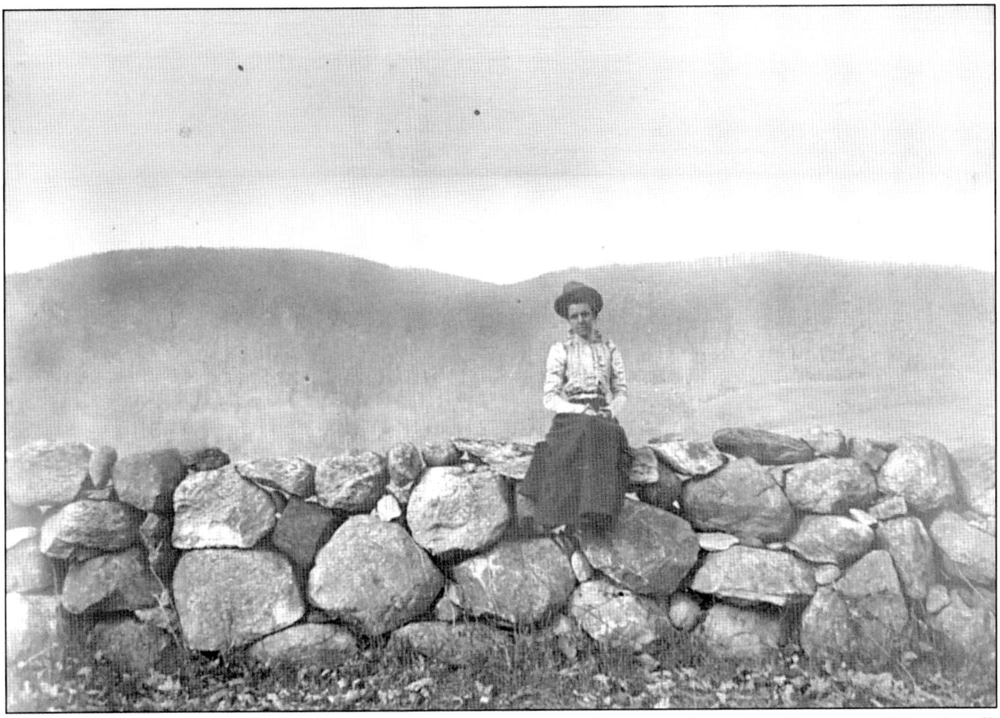

Anne Bostwick Howland, at age 20, sits on a stone wall across from the Emmons (Howland) House on Park Lane. The photograph was taken in 1896. Today, the field remains the same.

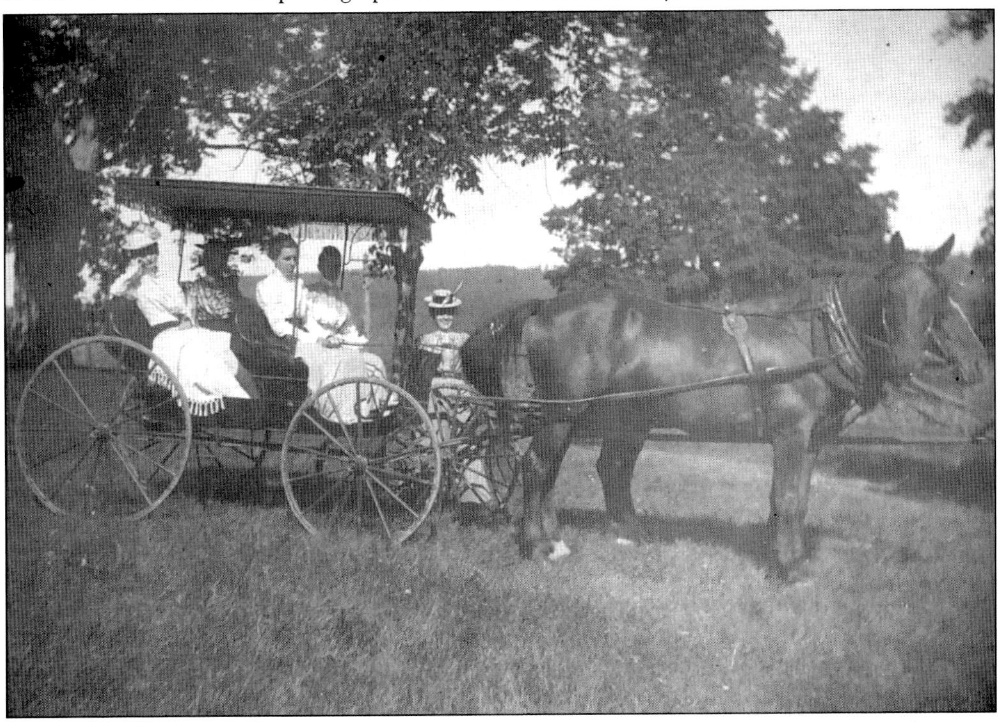

Ready for a carriage ride in 1890 are, from left to right, Mary Jane Angus, Mary Bostwick, Anne Bostwick, Lyla Bostwick, and Em Bostwick.

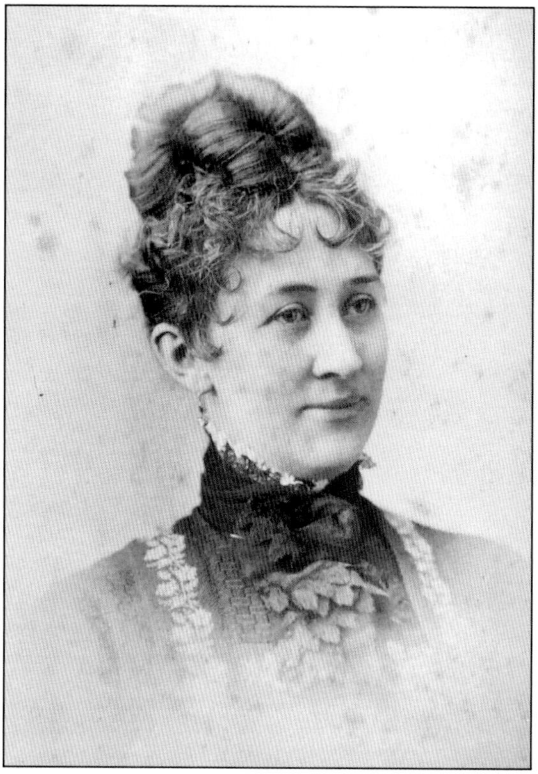

Sarah "Sate" Bostwick married Dr. Frederick King in 1899. The couple lived on Bridge Street in a house that is now the Mini Mart Store.

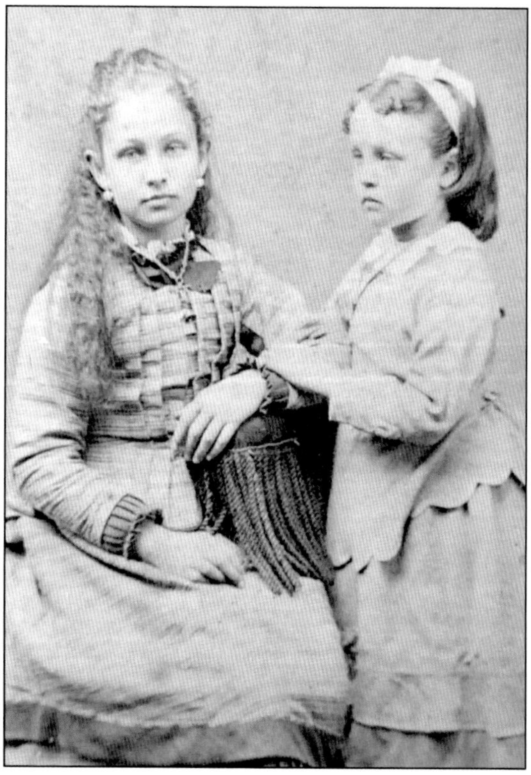

The Bostwick sisters pose for a picture in 1876. On the left at age ten is Sara "Sate" Bostwick. On the right at age seven is Emily Bostwick. Born in July 1869, Emily Bostwick became a Christian Science practitioner in New Milford. She died in 1956.

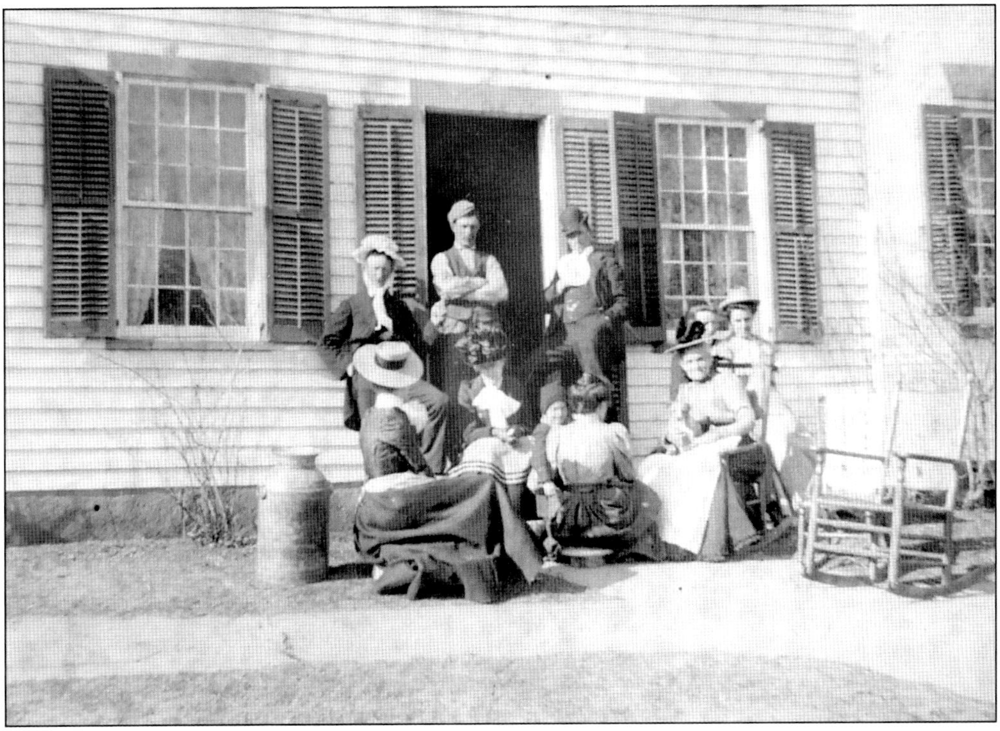

Among the family members pictured outside in the sun at the Bostwick Homestead *c.* 1900 are the following: (front row) Emily Bostwick, Amy Bostwick, and grandmother Mary Doty Bostwick, holding her dog; (back row) Fred Berry, husband of Mary Bostwick, wearing a bonnet; William Bostwick, standing the doorway; and Anne Bostwick. The children are Arthur Bostwick's.

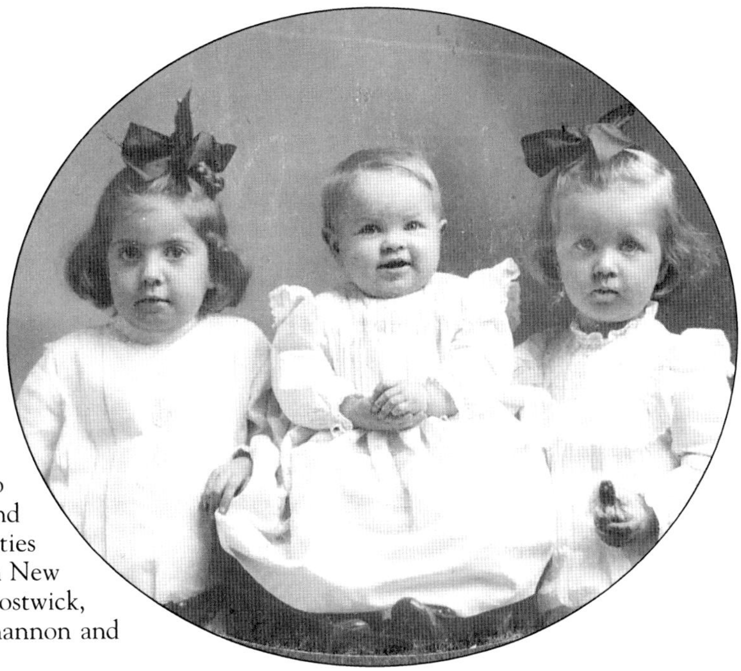

These three sisters are Arthur Bostwick's daughters: from left to right, they are Molly Bostwick, who married David Rogers; Amy Bostwick, who married Mark Howland and is now in her nineties and continues to live in New Milford; and Laura Bostwick, who married Lonnie Shannon and had no children.

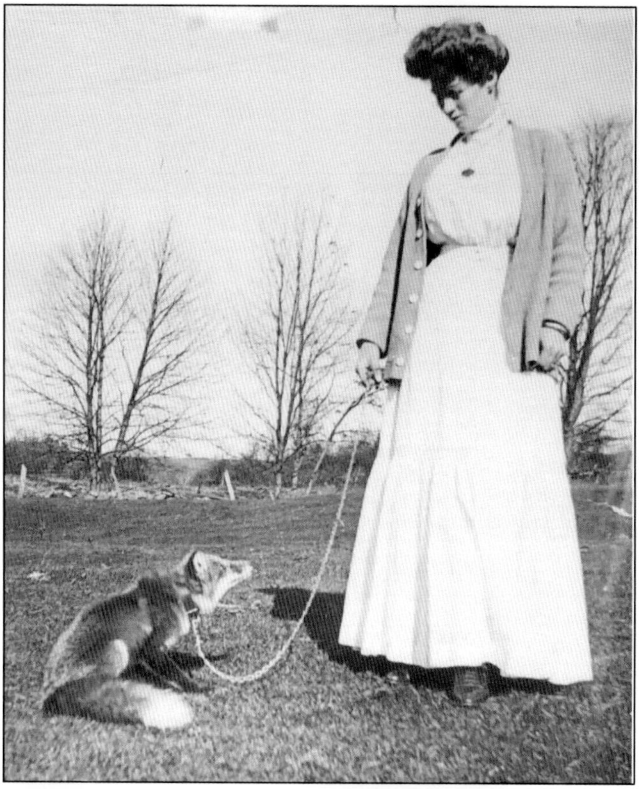

A very attentive fox studies Lillian Turrell, who has the animal on a leash. The fox was caught inside the Turrell home on Old Park Lane *c.* the early 1900s.

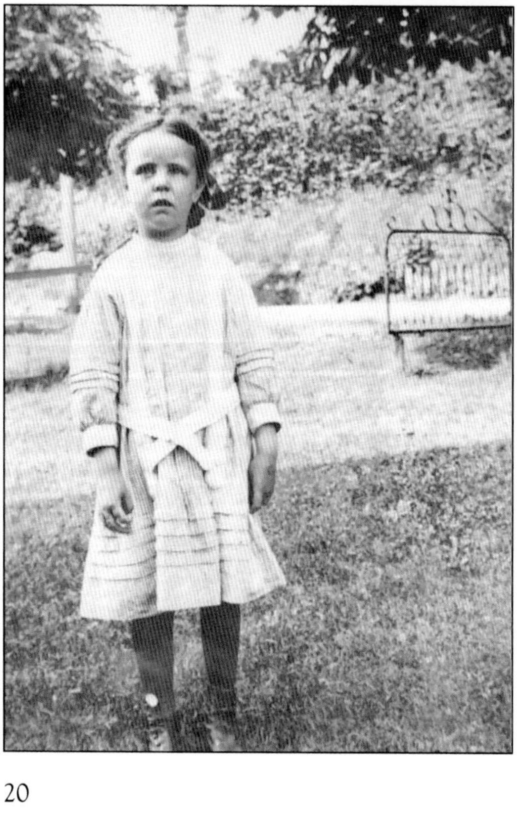

Harriet May Howland is pictured at age five in the yard of her family's home on Wellsville Avenue in 1908. She never married.

These three sisters are the children of Mary Bostwick Berry and Fred Berry, and the granddaughters of Mary Doty Bostwick. Pictured in 1909, from left to right, they are Dorothy, Mary, and Flora Berry.

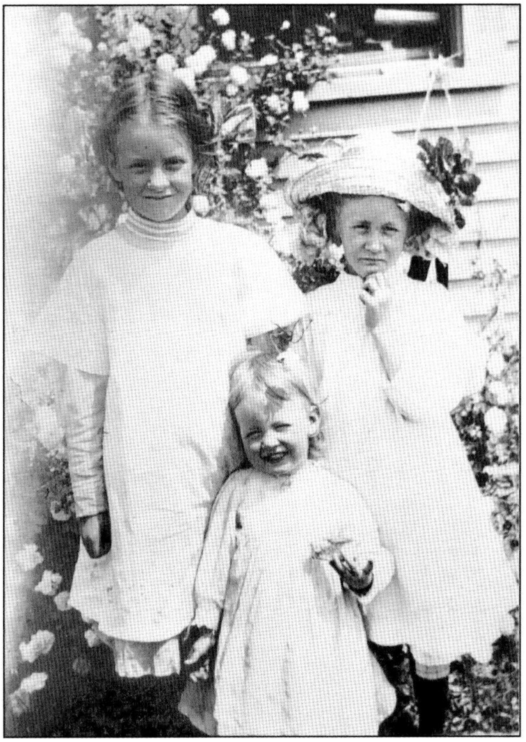

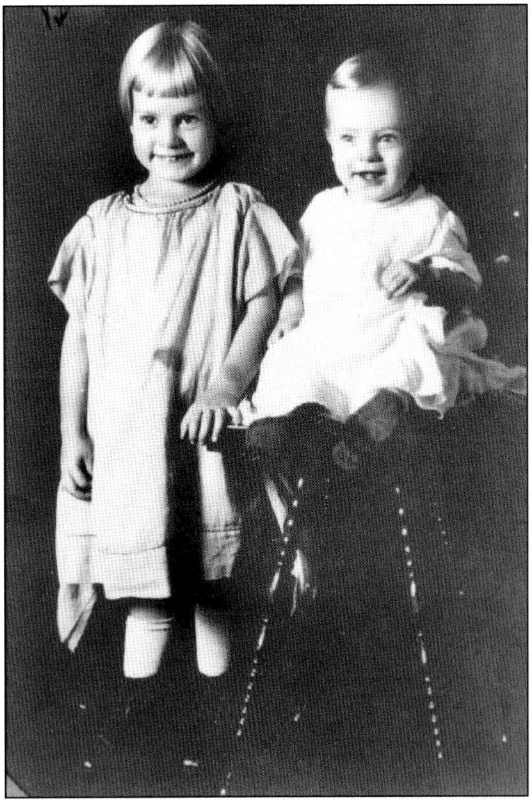

Jean and Raymond "Bud" Bostwick, grandchildren of William Bostwick, smile brightly as their picture is taken. Bud Bostwick, who lived on Crossman Road, died early in the summer of 2000.

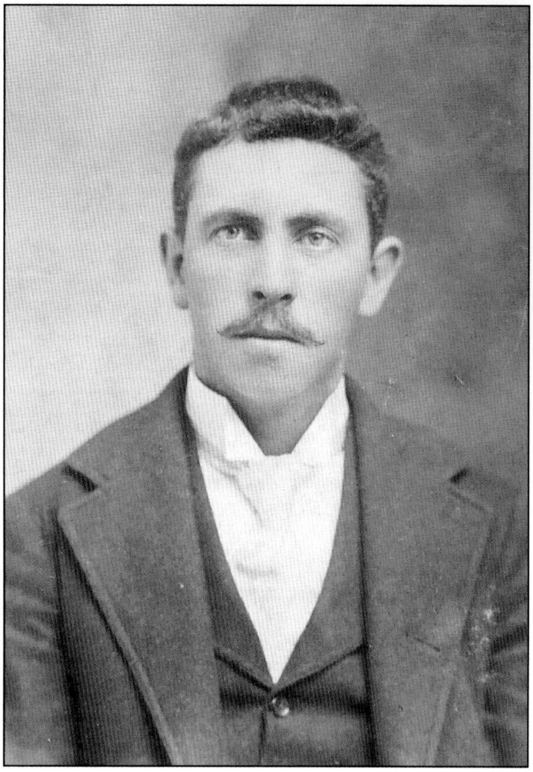

This 1897 photograph shows Arthur Bostwick at age 21. Notice his fancy shirt and tie.

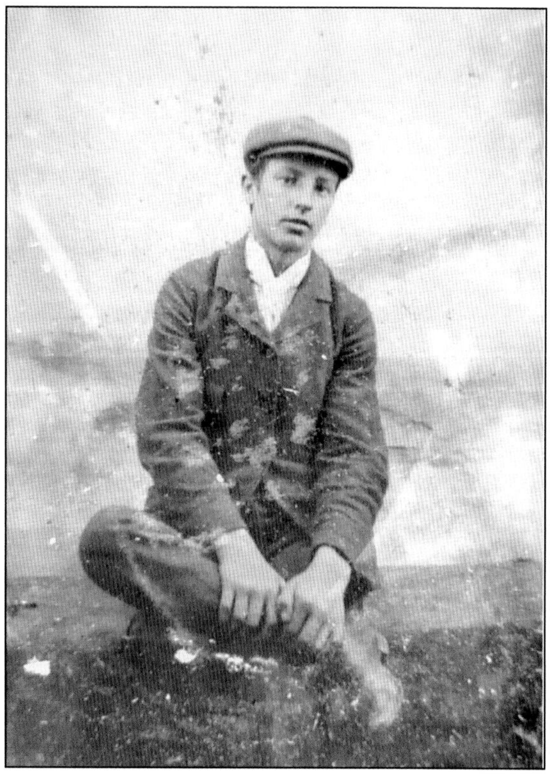

At age 15, Edgar Bostwick sits atop a stone wall *c.* 1898, dressed in his best suit and cap.

Focusing their attention on two different things, the little dog and the little girl remain in place long enough for this photograph to be taken in 1906. The girl is Harriet May Howland, age 3, eldest daughter of Anne Bostwick Howland.

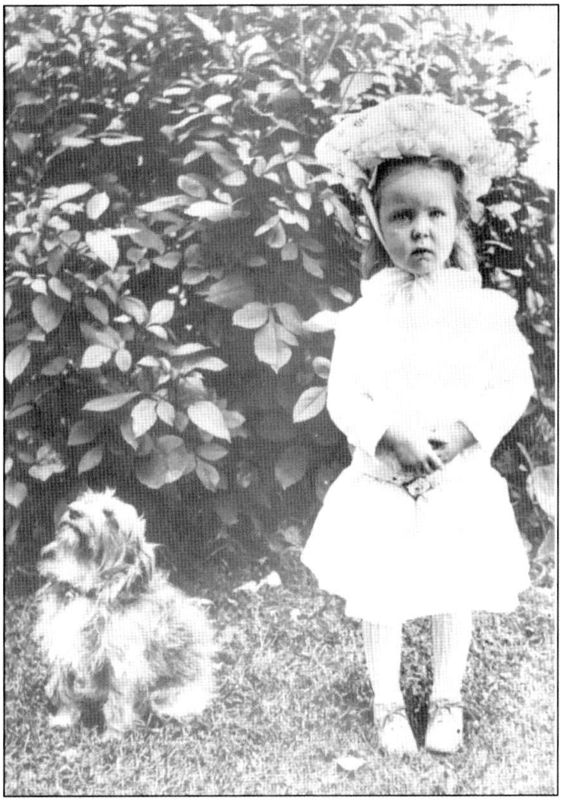

Fancy hats were in vogue for the New Milford Bicentennial Celebration in 1907. Posing on the occasion of the town's 200th anniversary are the following, from left to right: (front row) Minnie Sullivan, Dorothy Berry, Georgia Johnson, Vera Leavenworth, Ruth Sullivan, Lottie May Bostwick, Genevieve Crane, May Bostwick, Esther Carlson, three unidentified young women, Elizabeth Sullivan, unidentified, and Morse Leavensworth; (back row) Ray Bostwick, Dolly Stone, Jerry Northrop, unidentified, Mary Leavenworth, six unidentified young people, Elizabeth Graham, ? Edwards, Eula Dunlap, and George Sullivan.

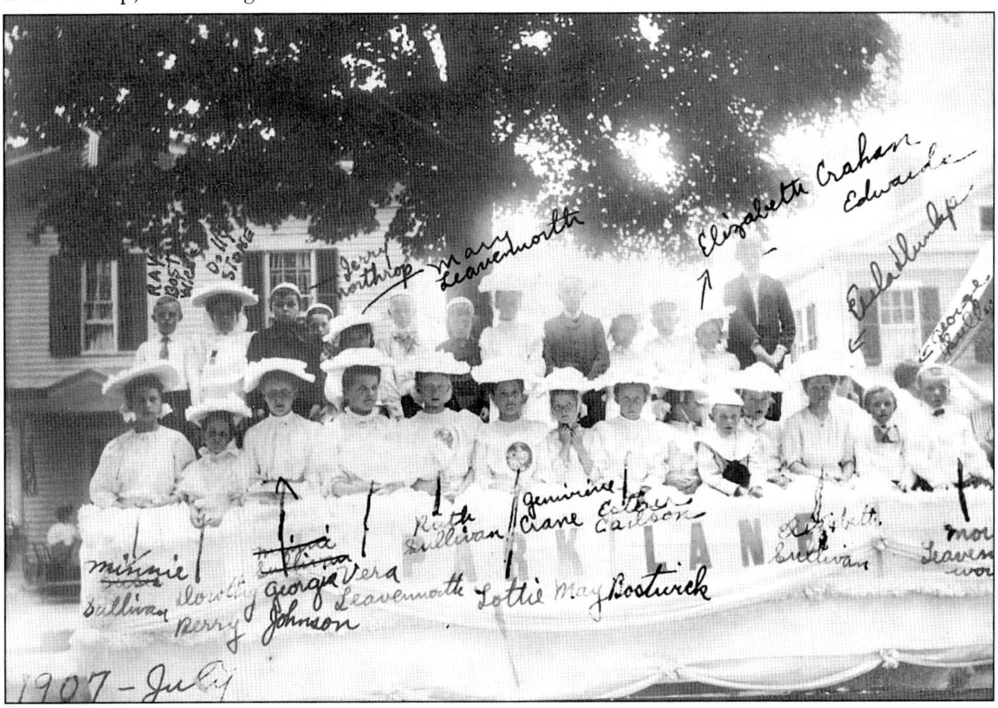

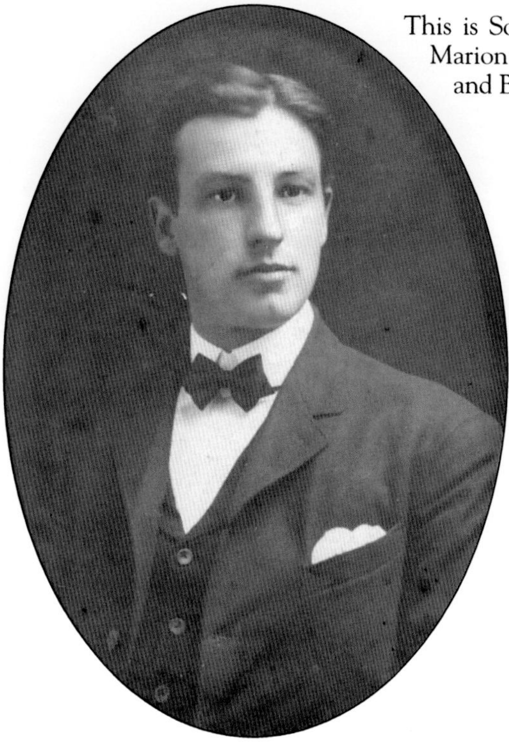

This is Solomon Edgar Bostwick in 1903. He married Marion Wooster, and they had two children, Robert and Betty Bostwick.

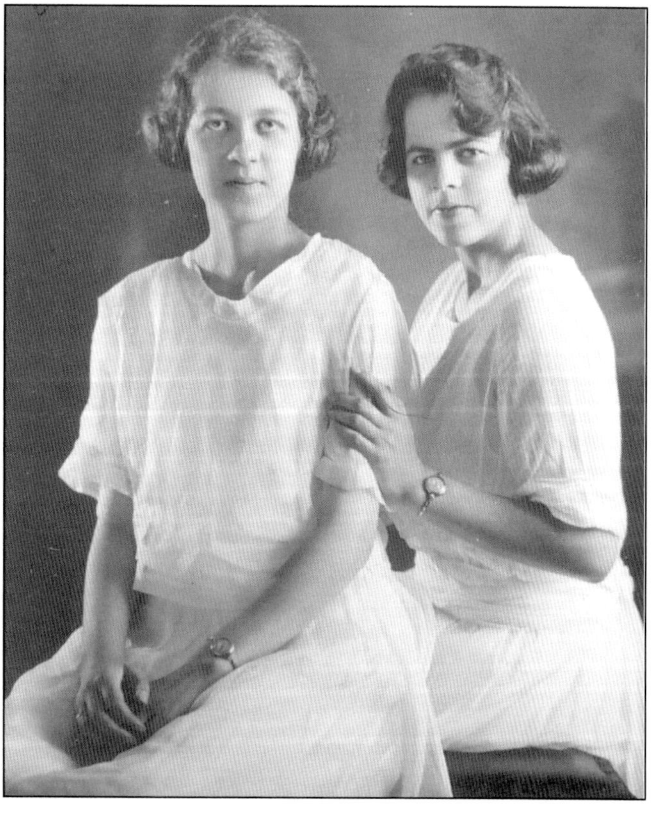

Sisters Laura (left) and Amy Bostwick, daughters of Arthur Bostwick, wear similar dresses, wristwatches, and hairdos.

Two

The Schools

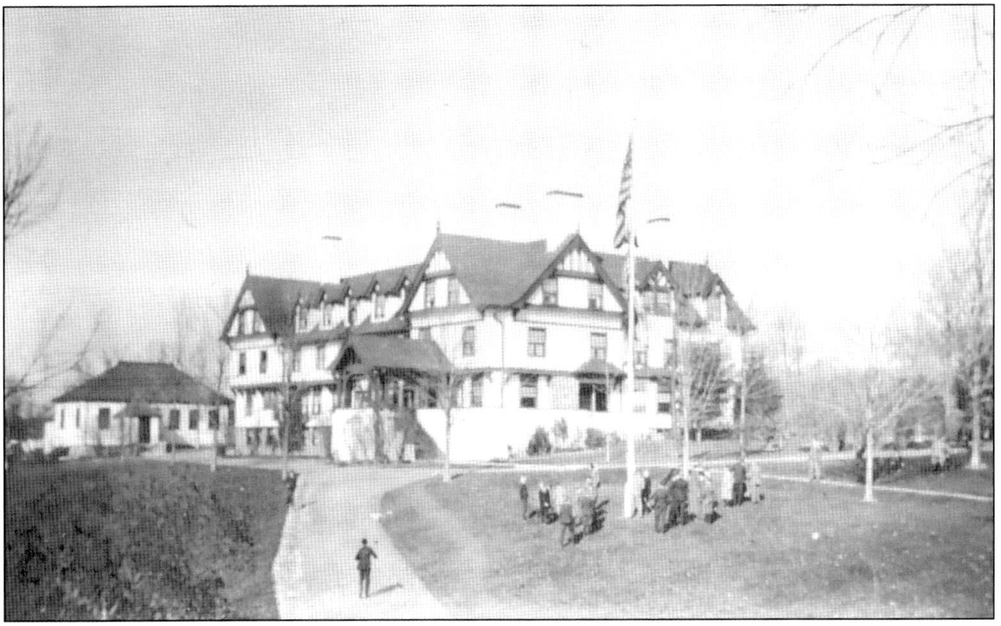

This is the Main House at Canterbury School. Nelson Hume and Henry O. Havemeyer founded the school in 1915. Their vision was an upstart: first, because they wanted a school free of the anti-Catholic prejudice that they had experienced at boarding schools, universities, and other institutions of higher learning; second, because they decided to use laymen as teachers, while keeping the school within the Catholic tradition. Among those who attended Canterbury, with its high standard of learning, are John Carroll, John F. Kennedy, and Mario Cuomo.

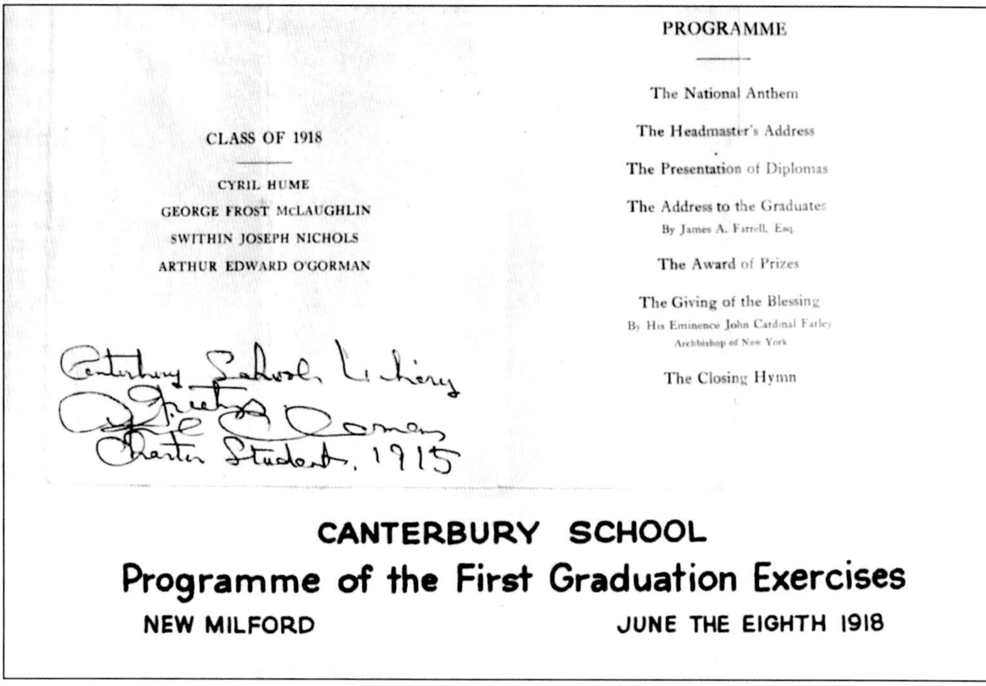

PROGRAMME

The National Anthem

The Headmaster's Address

The Presentation of Diplomas

The Address to the Graduates
By James A. Farrell, Esq.

The Award of Prizes

The Giving of the Blessing
By His Eminence John Cardinal Farley
Archbishop of New York

The Closing Hymn

CLASS OF 1918

CYRIL HUME
GEORGE FROST McLAUGHLIN
SWITHIN JOSEPH NICHOLS
ARTHUR EDWARD O'GORMAN

Canterbury School Library
Gift of A. E. O'Gorman
Charter Student, 1915

CANTERBURY SCHOOL

Programme of the First Graduation Exercises

NEW MILFORD JUNE THE EIGHTH 1918

This is the program for the first graduation exercises at Canterbury School, held on June 8, 1918. Listed as members of the graduating class are Cyril Hume, George Frost McLaughlin, Swithin Joseph Nichols, and Arthur Edward O'Gorman. James A. Farrell, Esq., gave the address to the graduates, and his Eminence John Cardinal Farley, archbishop of New York, gave the blessing.

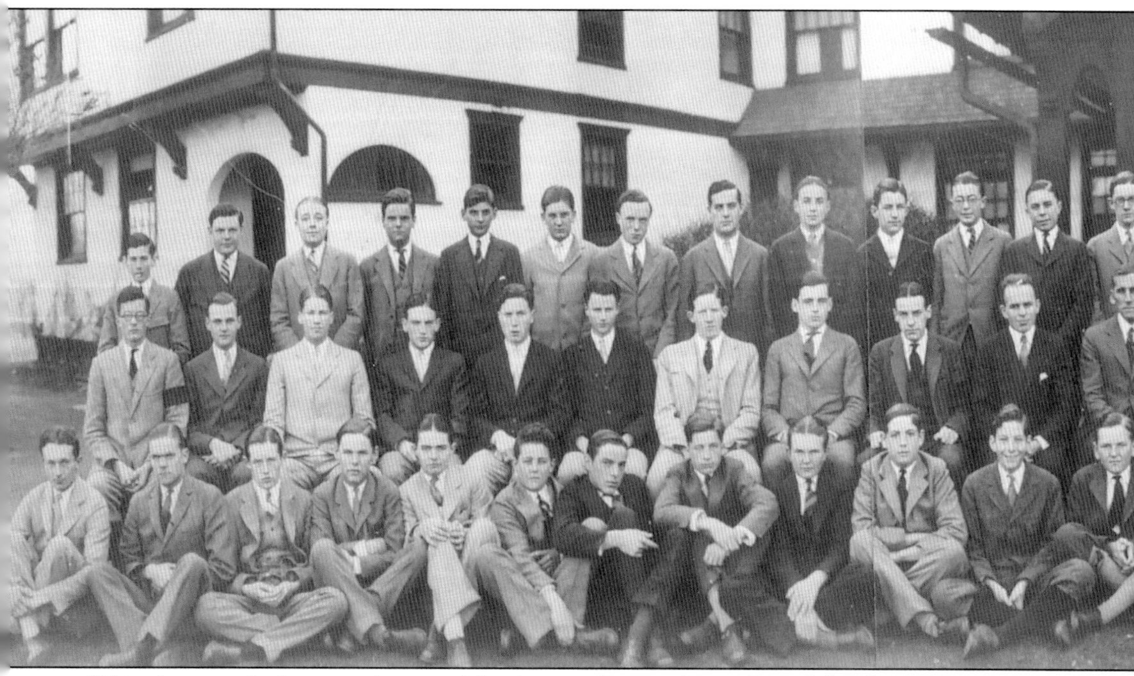

This photograph shows students and faculty members at Canterbury School in 1924, nine years

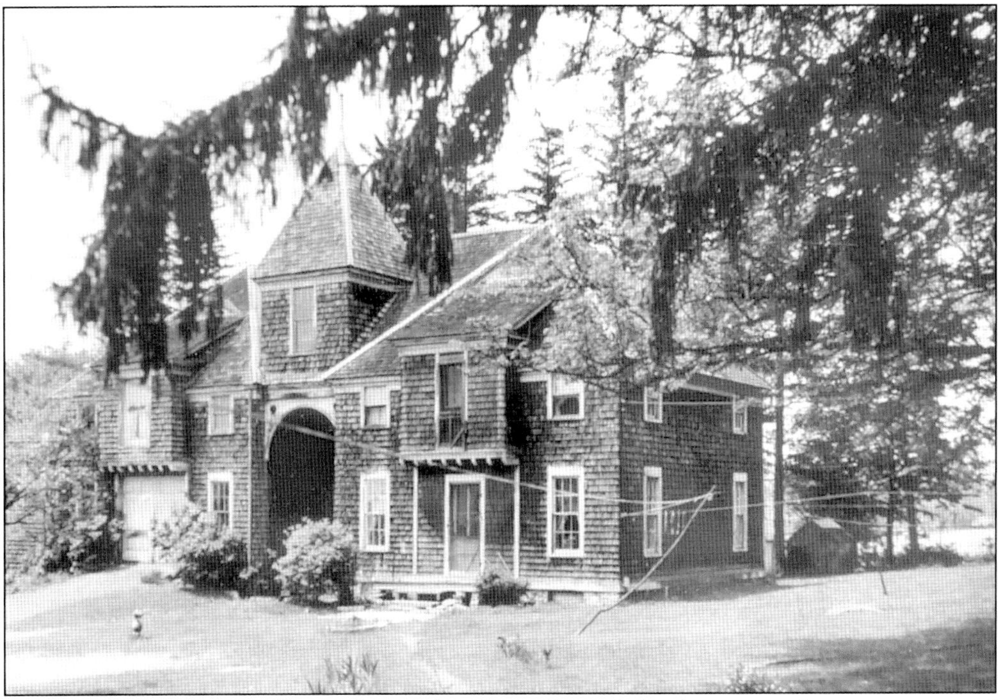

The Carriage House still stands on the Canterbury School campus, but it is in need of repair.

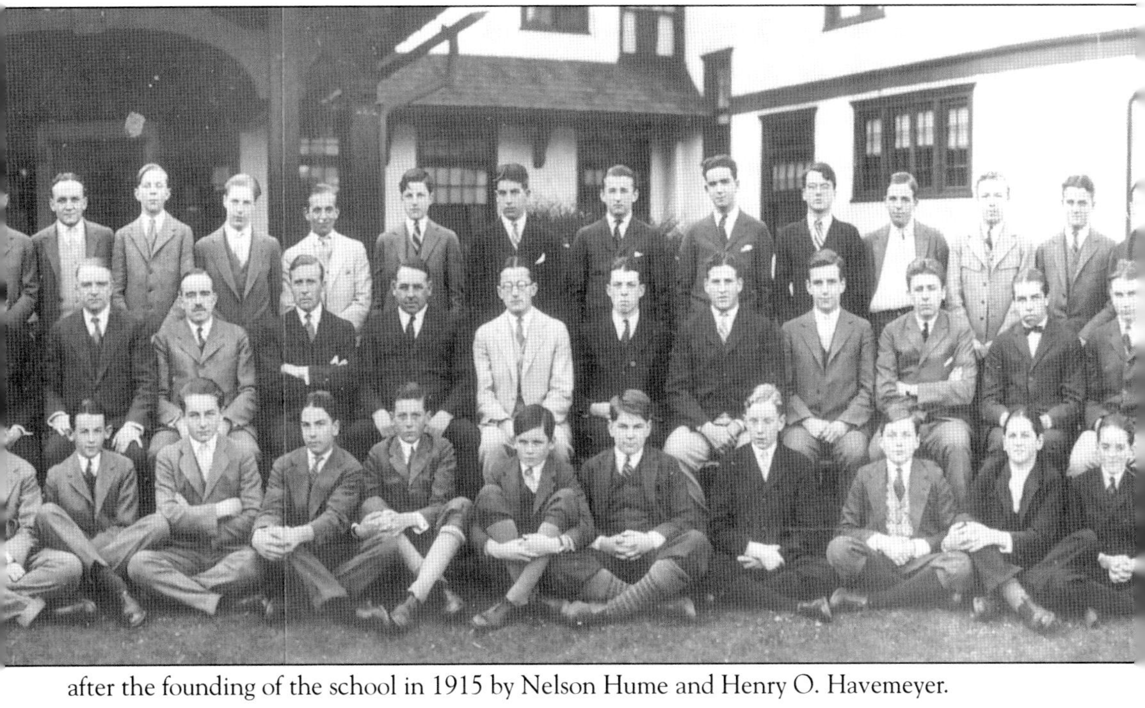

after the founding of the school in 1915 by Nelson Hume and Henry O. Havemeyer.

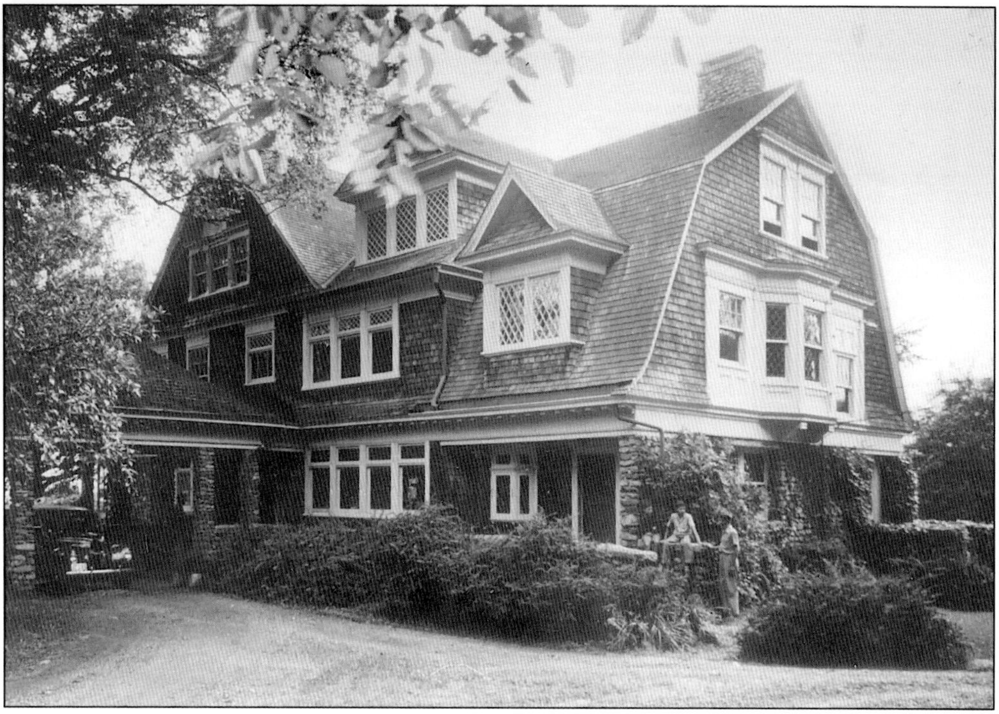

This *c.* 1900s view focuses on the northeast corner of Hickory Hearth at Canterbury School, where two young men are having a conversation.

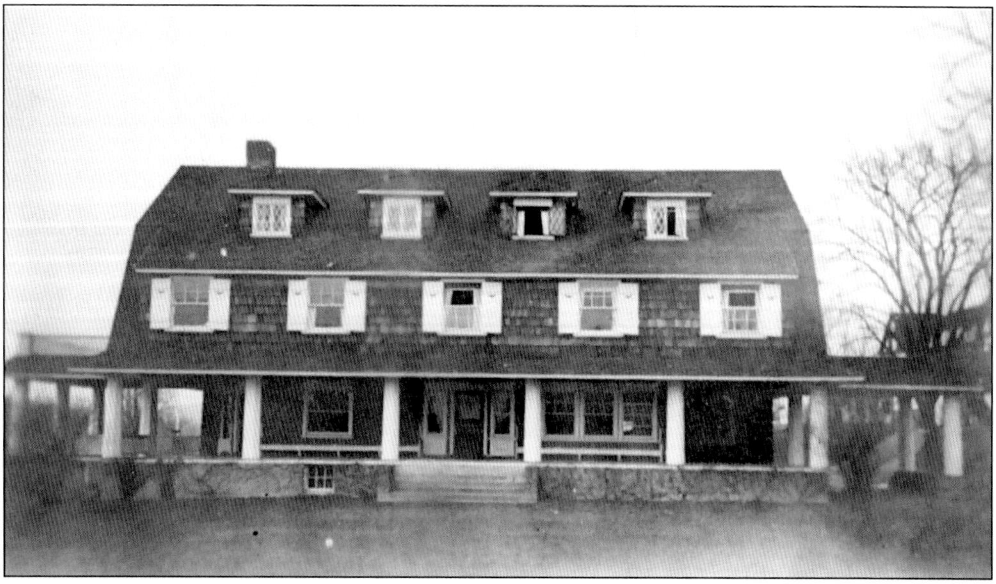

The Bungalow at Canterbury School was used for students and guests. It was destroyed by fire in December 1925.

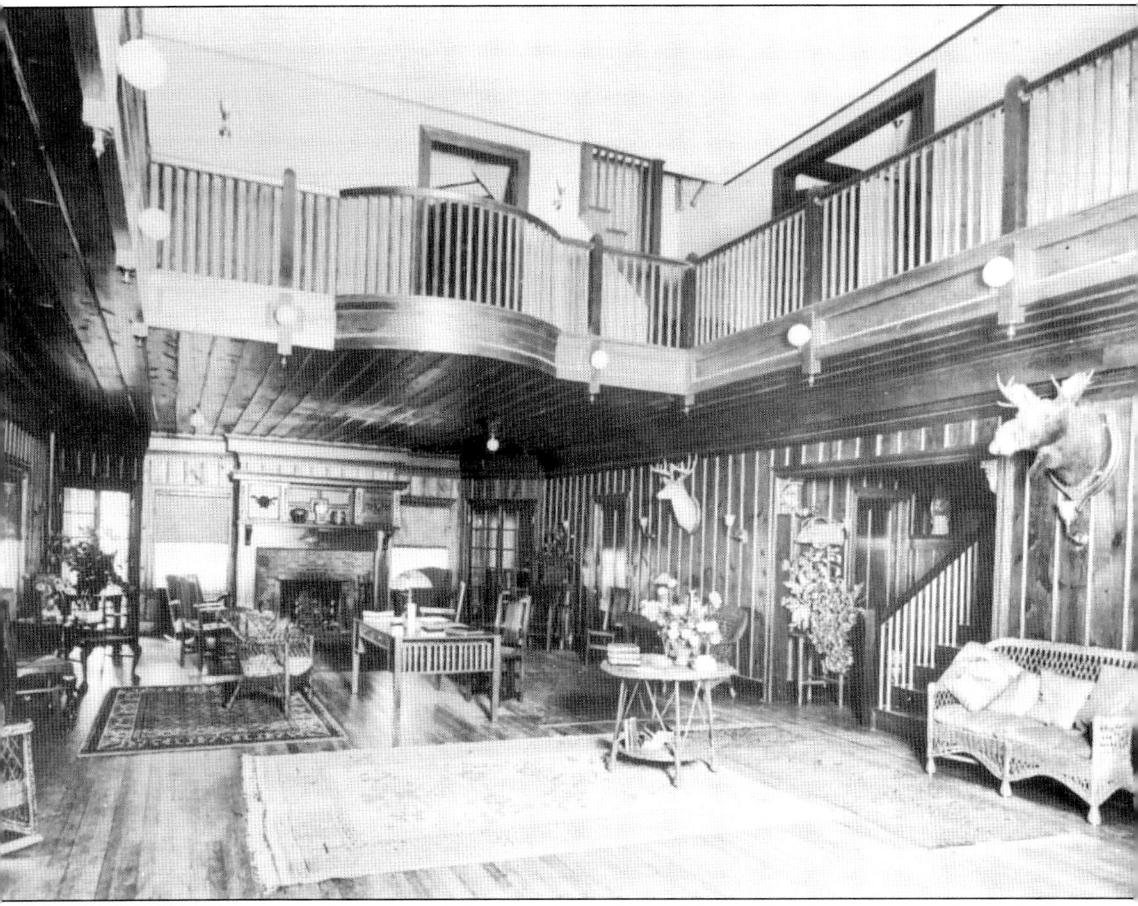

This is an interior view of the Main House at Canterbury School. The house was built in 1915 and was decorated with period pieces. The upstairs floor contained rooms for students and an apartment for guests.

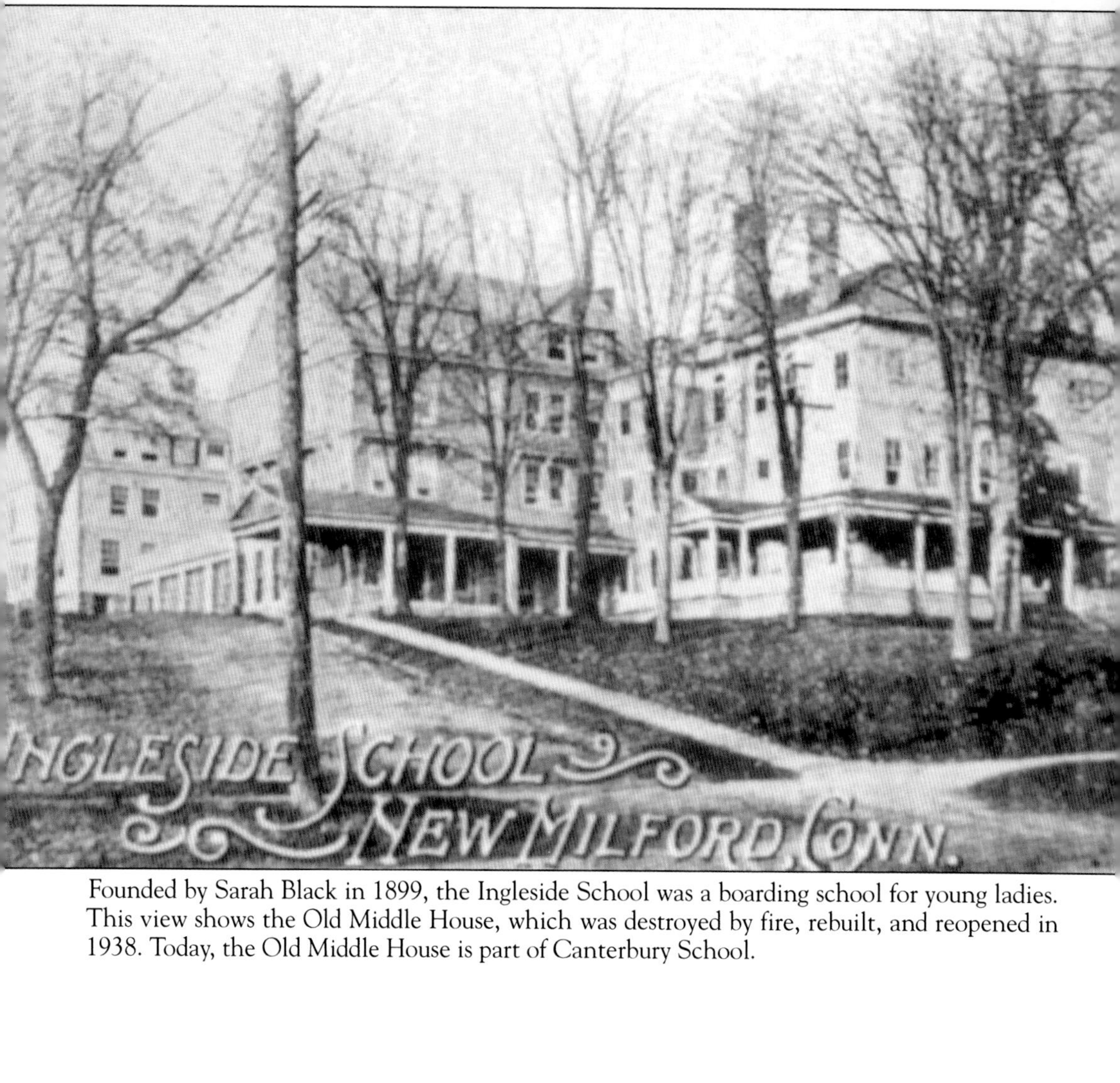

Founded by Sarah Black in 1899, the Ingleside School was a boarding school for young ladies. This view shows the Old Middle House, which was destroyed by fire, rebuilt, and reopened in 1938. Today, the Old Middle House is part of Canterbury School.

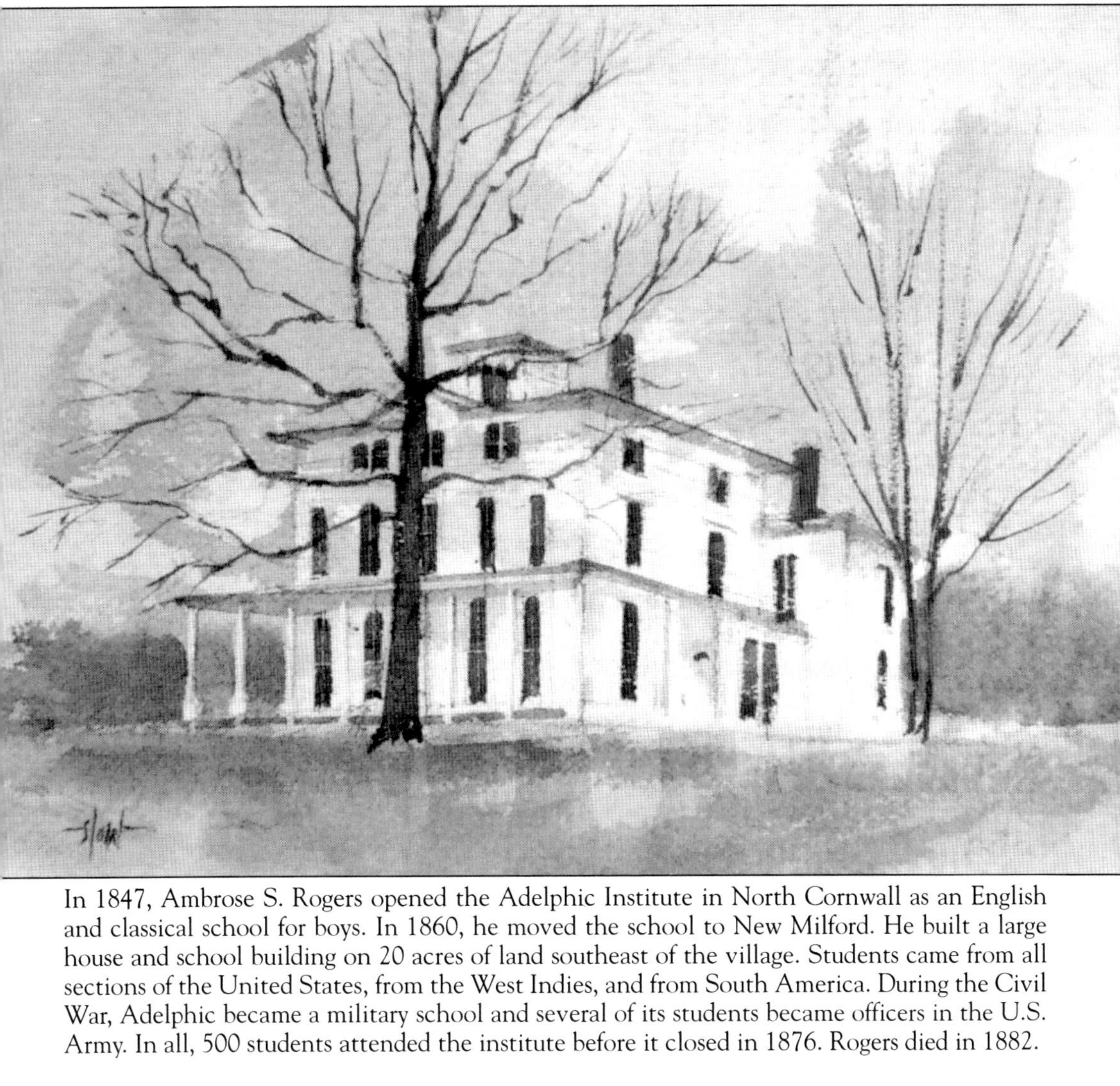

In 1847, Ambrose S. Rogers opened the Adelphic Institute in North Cornwall as an English and classical school for boys. In 1860, he moved the school to New Milford. He built a large house and school building on 20 acres of land southeast of the village. Students came from all sections of the United States, from the West Indies, and from South America. During the Civil War, Adelphic became a military school and several of its students became officers in the U.S. Army. In all, 500 students attended the institute before it closed in 1876. Rogers died in 1882.

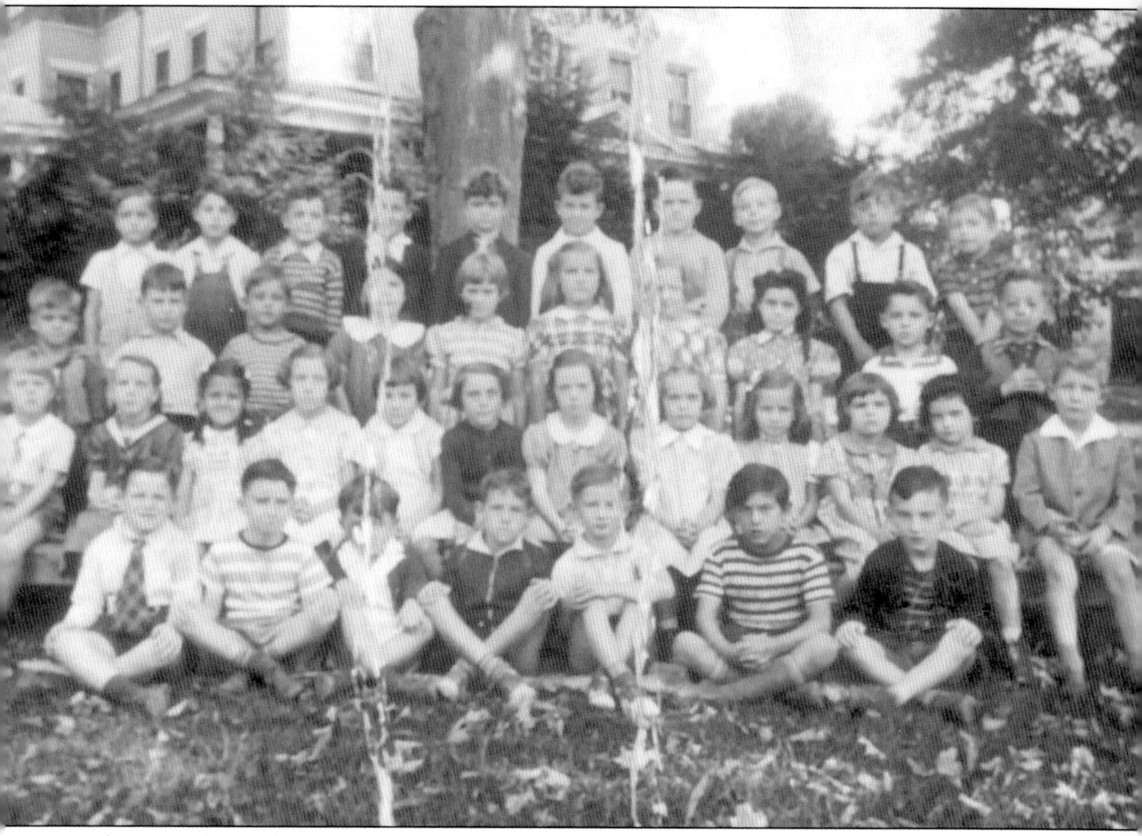

These are the students at St. Francis School in 1938. The students are pictured on the lawn in front of the school.

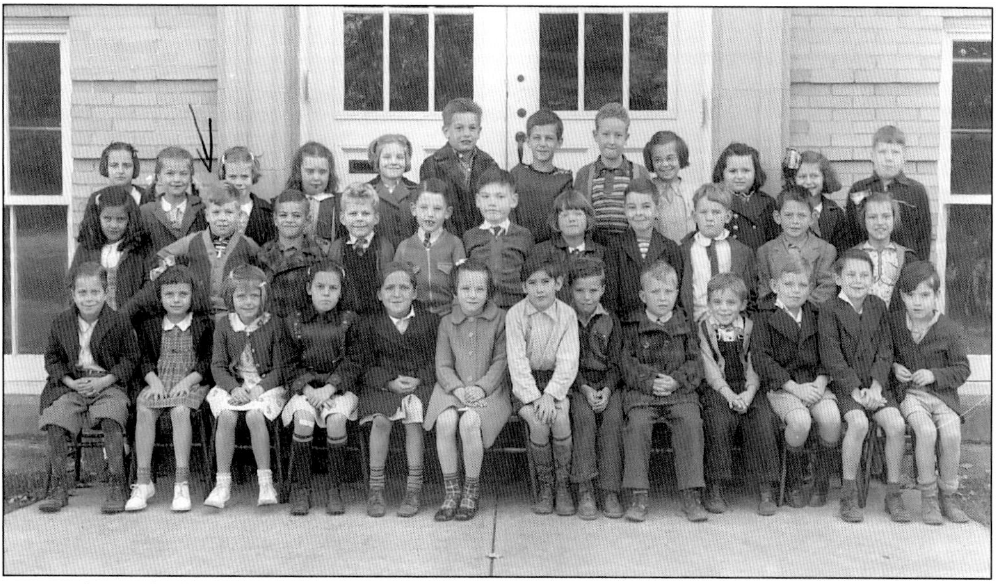

Pictured outside the Main Street School in 1941 is the second-grade class. The boy second from the left in the middle row is Larry Emmons.

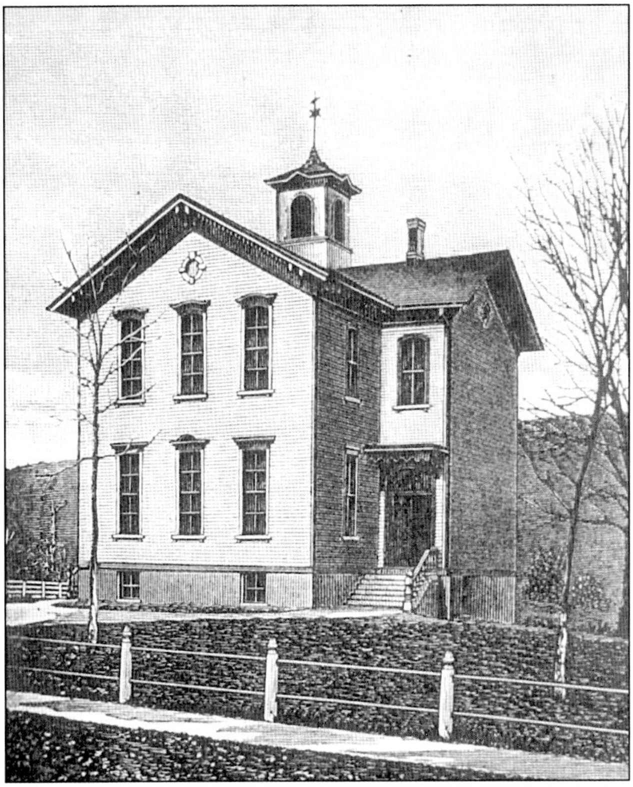

The public schoolhouse was completed in 1876 on East Street. It was organized as a grade school, with four teachers. It had all the modern conveniences, including a library with 600 volumes.

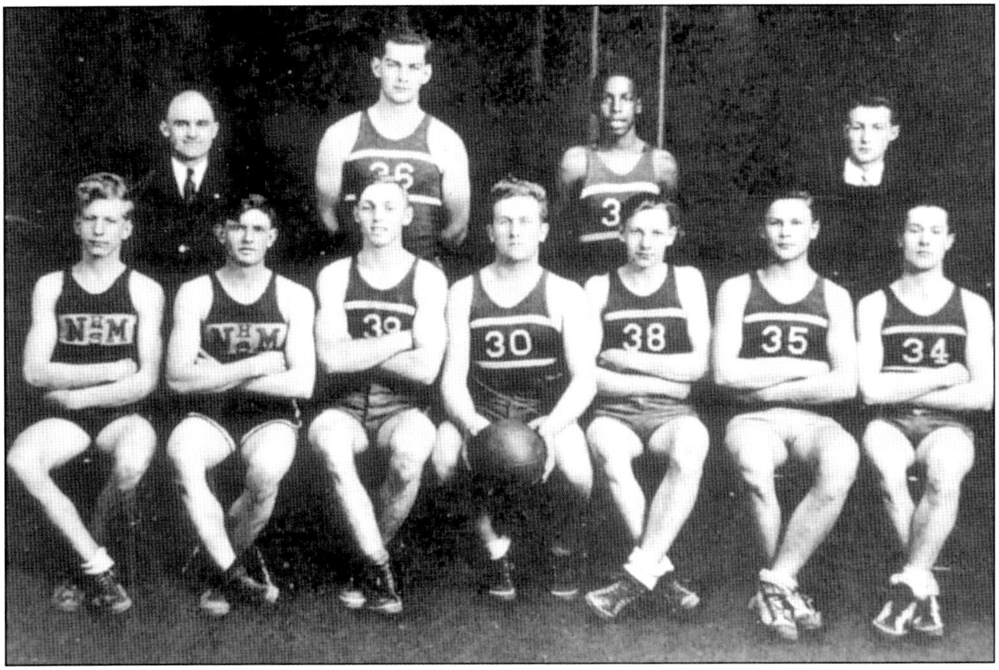

This was a New Milford High School basketball team. The last names of these players are as follows, from left to right: (front row) Straub, Kohne, Leahey, Dorwin, Roscoe, Warner, and Kibbe; (back row) Peagler, Kwasniewski, Tanner, and Lane.

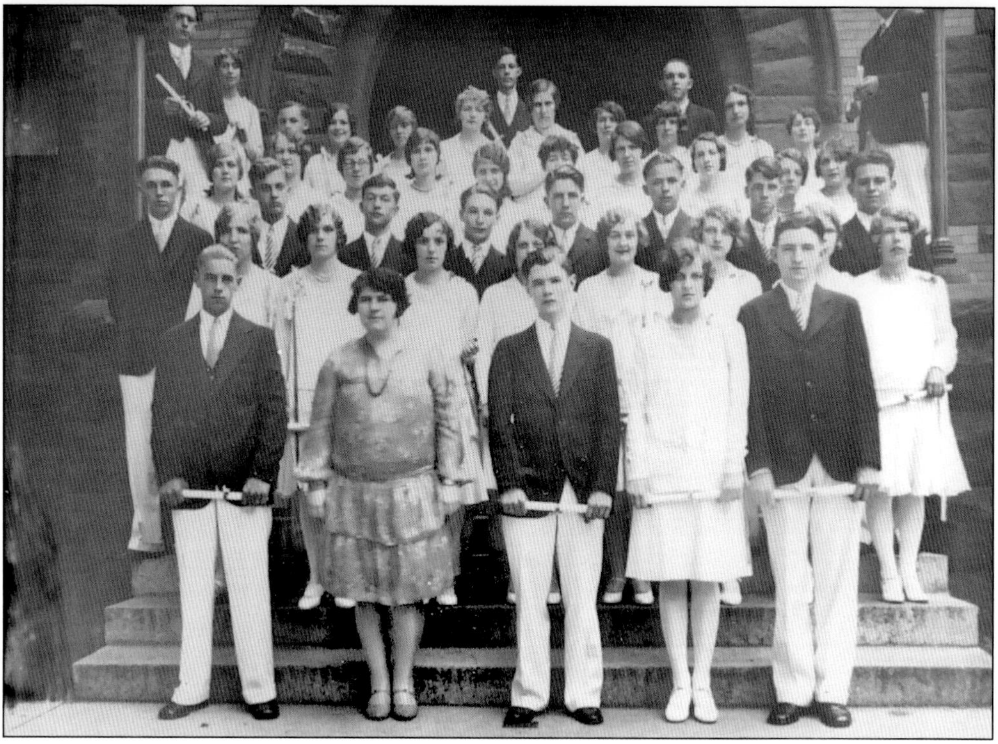

The New Milford High School Class of 1929 started with 83 members. Larry Lillis, shown in the first row on the right, was voted the most popular student.

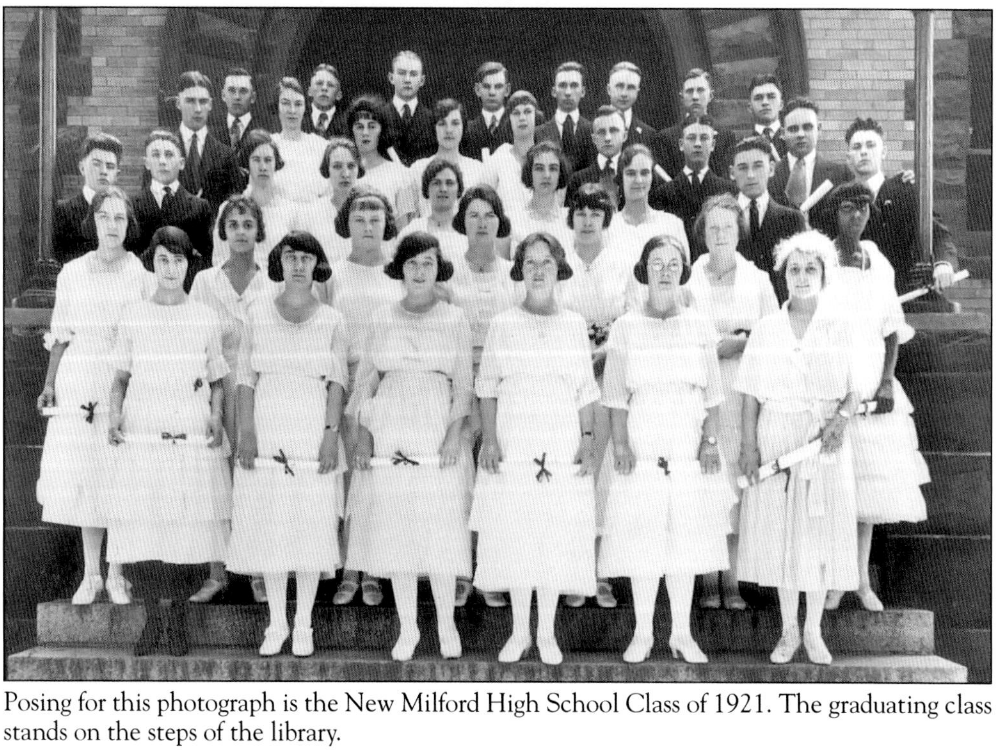

Posing for this photograph is the New Milford High School Class of 1921. The graduating class stands on the steps of the library.

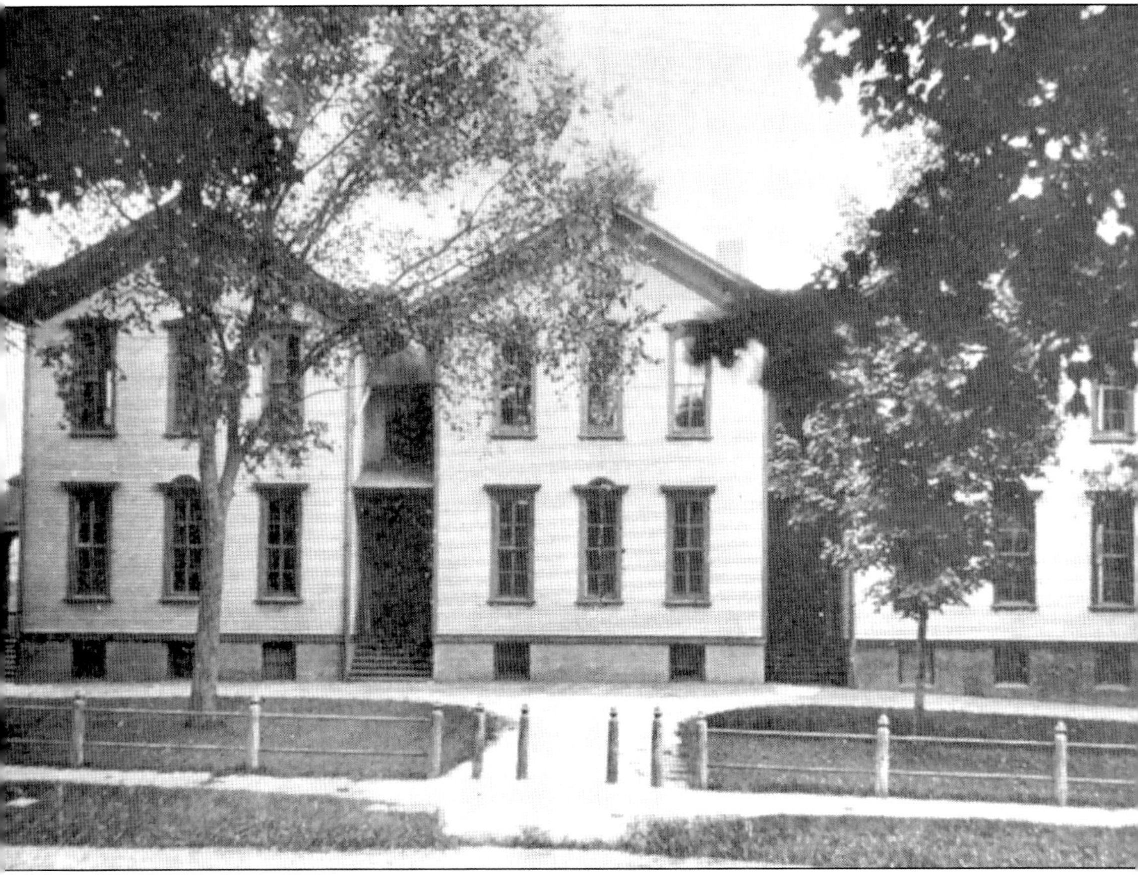

New Milford Center High School was located on Main Street. The original school was attended by Clement H. Noble, Betty Noble, and John Noble, descendants of New Milford's first settler, John Noble Sr. The school became a grade school, for students in first through eighth grades. It was later torn down to make way for Main Street School, which is next to the Congregational church.

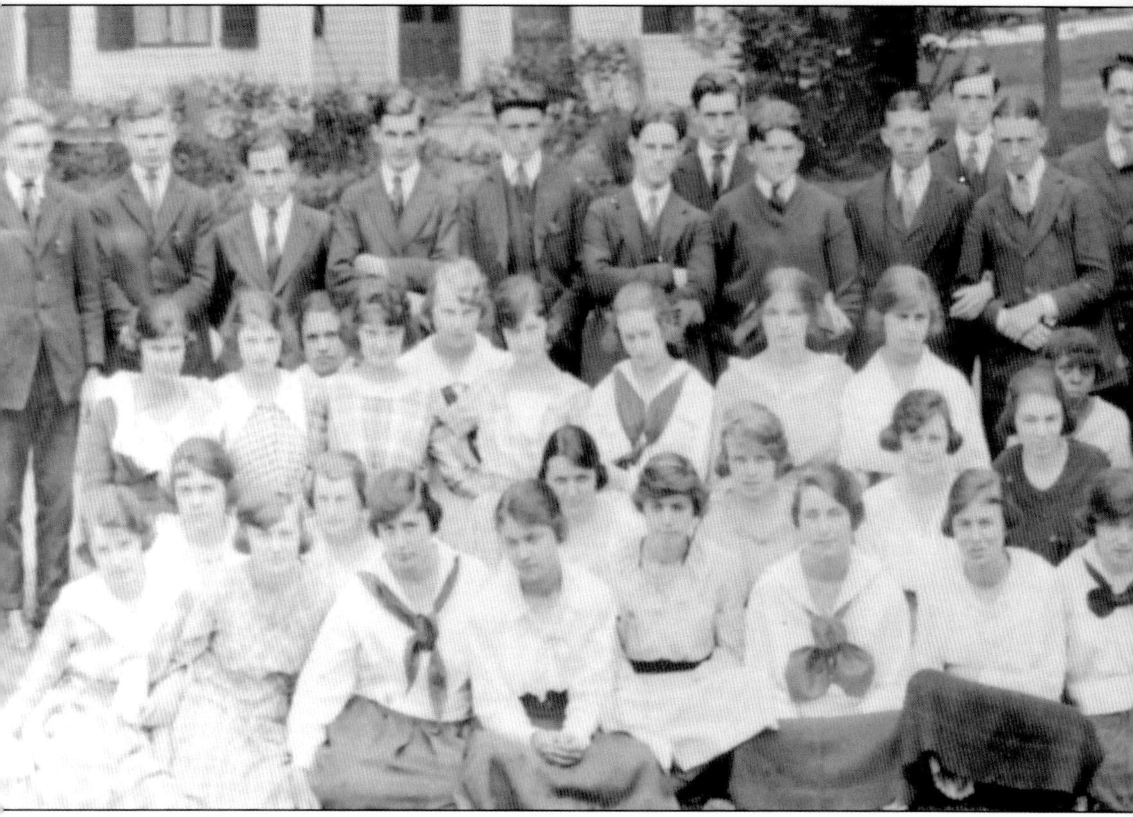

Students and faculty member of New Milford High School gather to have their picture taken outdoors in May 1920. Pictured in the photograph below with his arms folded at the far left is

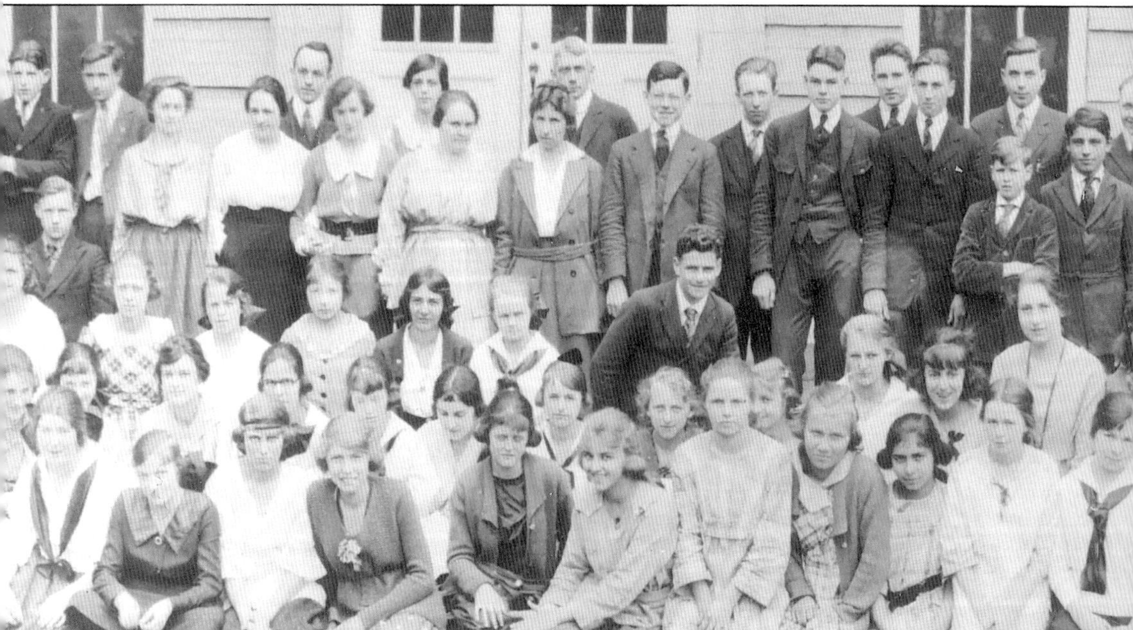

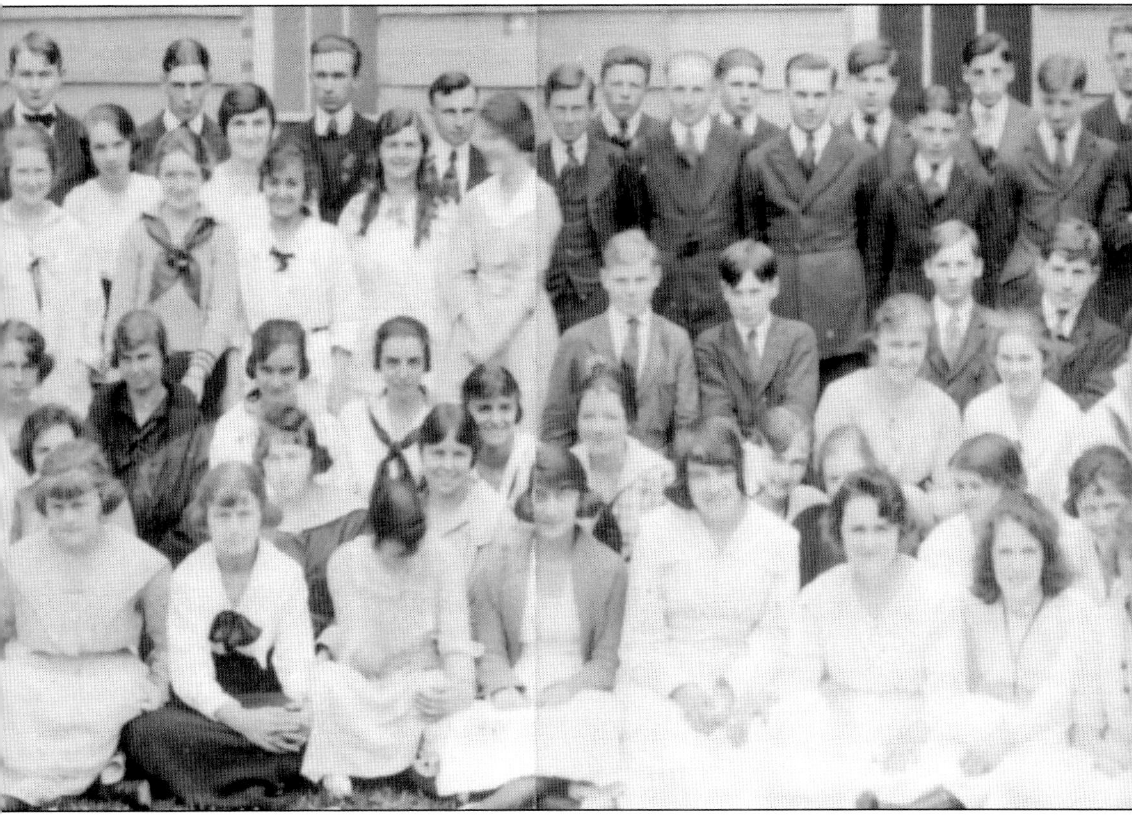

Joe Lillis. The light-haired man standing in front of the doors is John Pettibone.

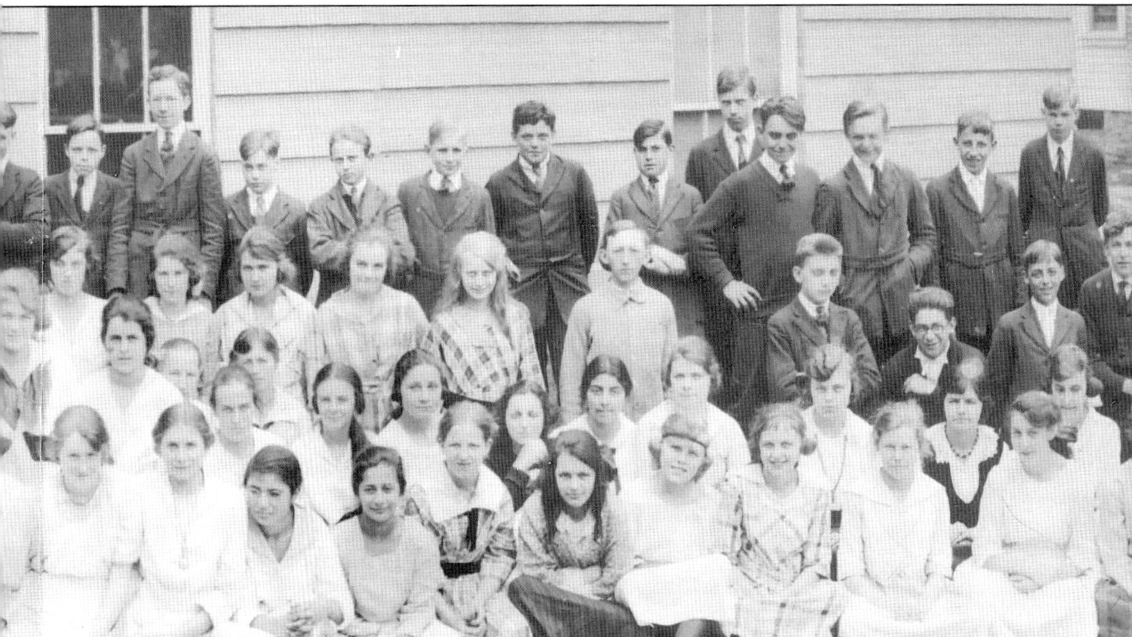

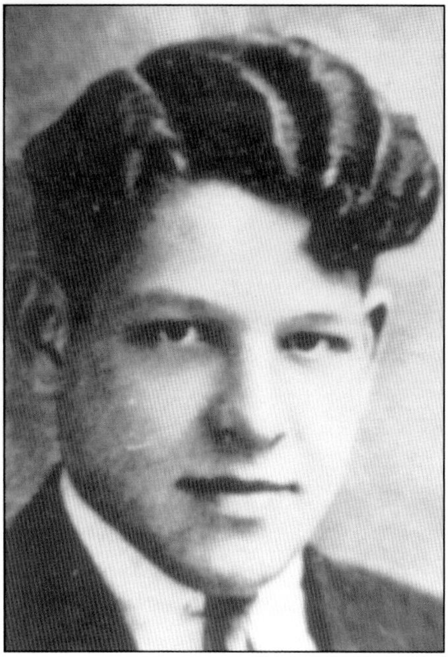

Robert Ohmen was unanimously elected president of the New Milford High School Class of 1931. He was considered the best all-around person in the senior class.

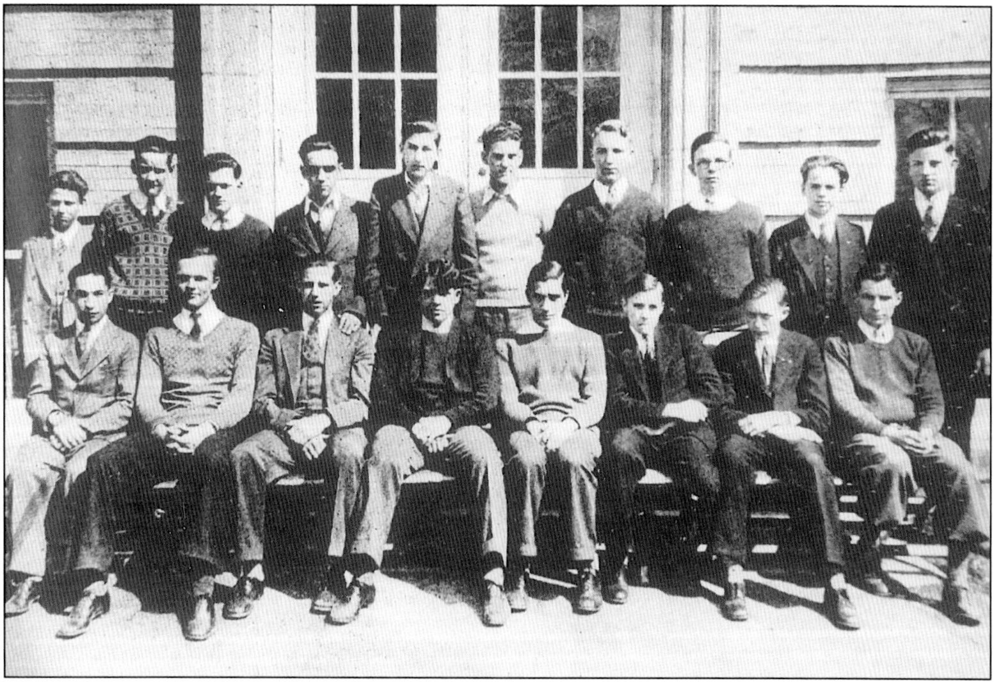

Among the class officers at New Milford High School are four serving the Class of 1931: Robert Ohmen, class president, front row, fourth from left;. Stuart Lathrop, vice president; Clifford Kiefer, secretary; and Reginald Taylor, treasurer.

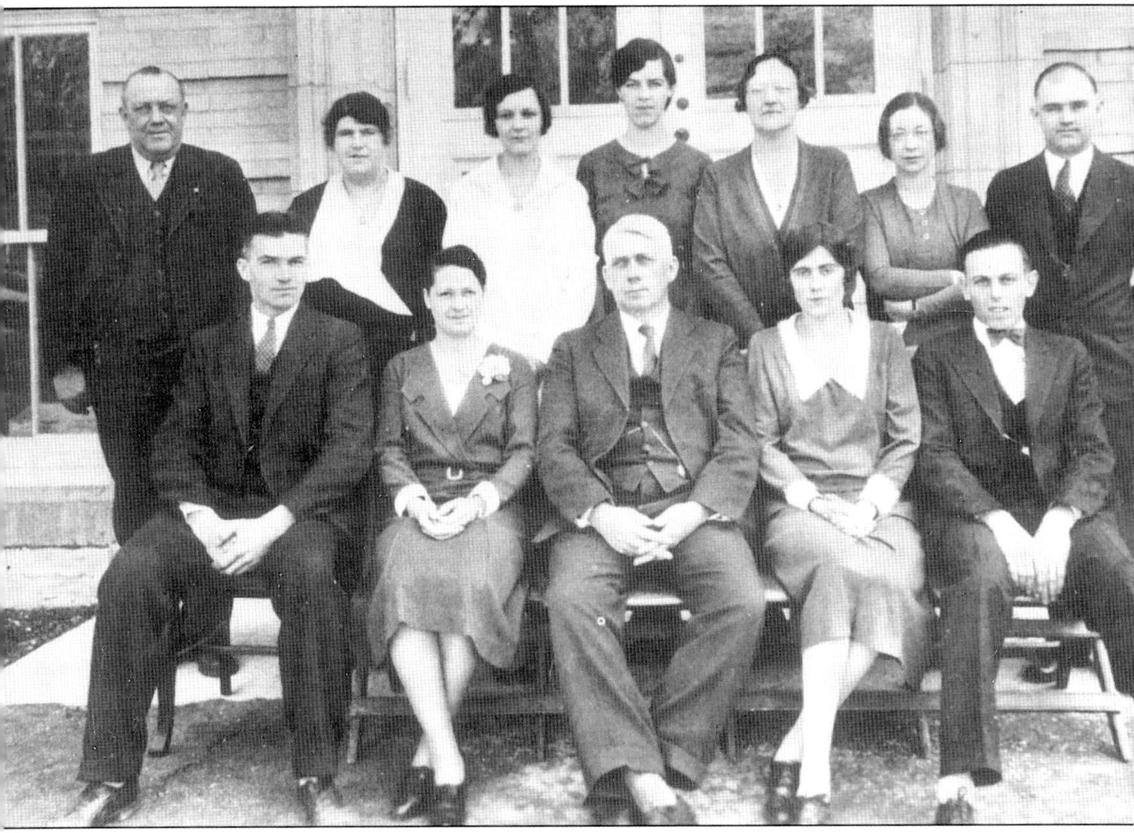

This photograph shows the administration and faculty of New Milford High School in 1931. Pictured, from left to right, are the following, with only last names given: (front row) Wells, Bousquet, Pettibone, Couch, and Knox; (back row) Erwin, Sullivan, Tonkin, Millane, Perry, Campbell, and Lumley.

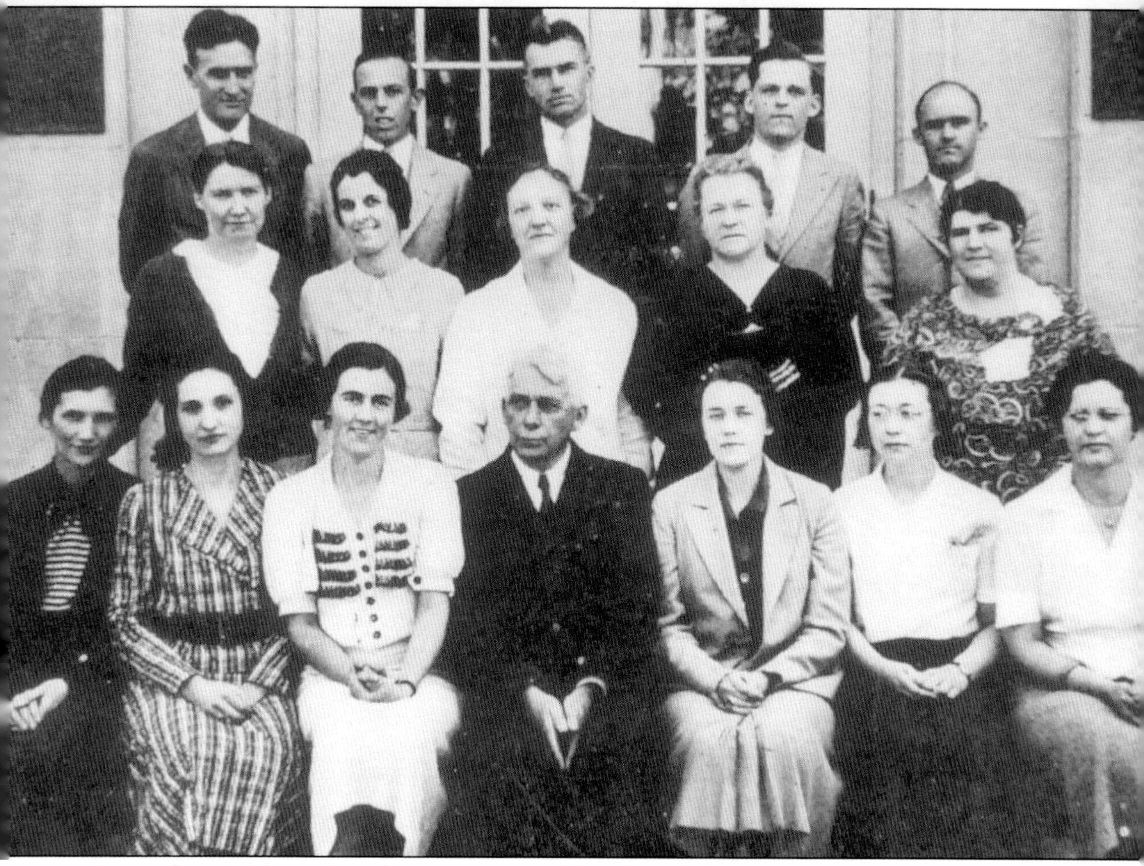

Pictured in 1934 are the administration and faculty of New Milford High School. The last names of the members shown, from left to right, are as follows: (front row) Haas, Merwin, Couch, Pettibone, Welsh, Campbell, and Myers; (middle row) Lynch, Lillis, Perry, Carney, and Sullivan; (back row) Hunt, Knox, Wells, Neidel, and Lamiey.

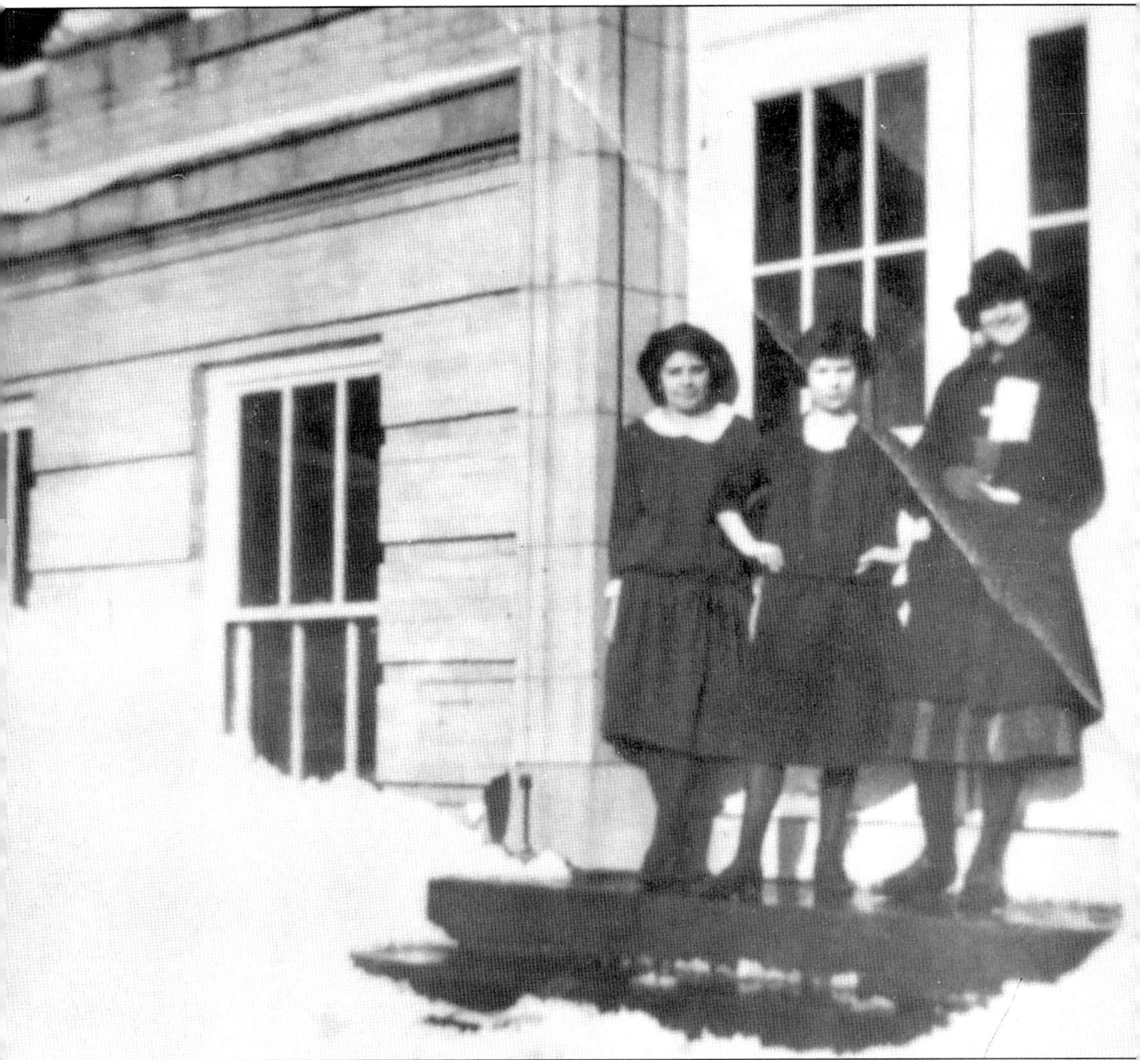

Standing in the doorway with two other young ladies is Catherine Lillis, left, who served as vice principal of the John Pettibone School. Note the large amount of snow still on the ground. Today, this building is called the Richmond Center.

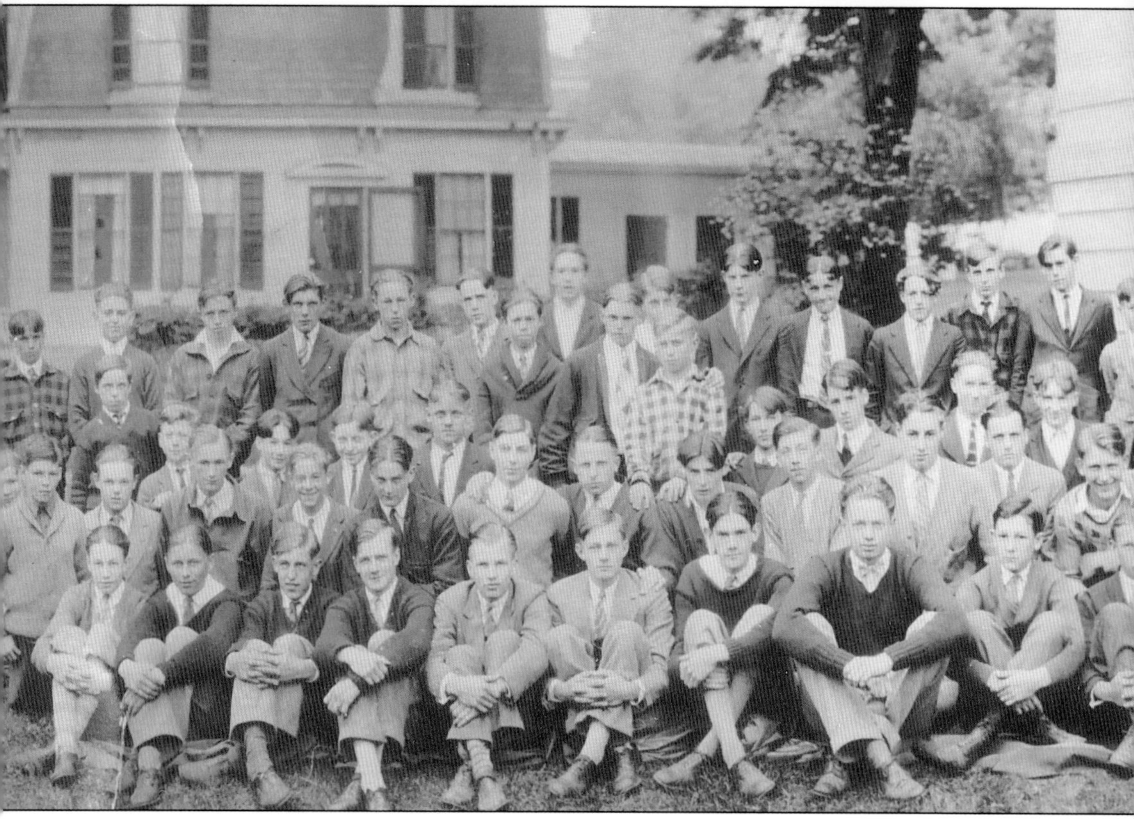

Students and faculty of New Milford High School assemble for a photograph in 1926. The

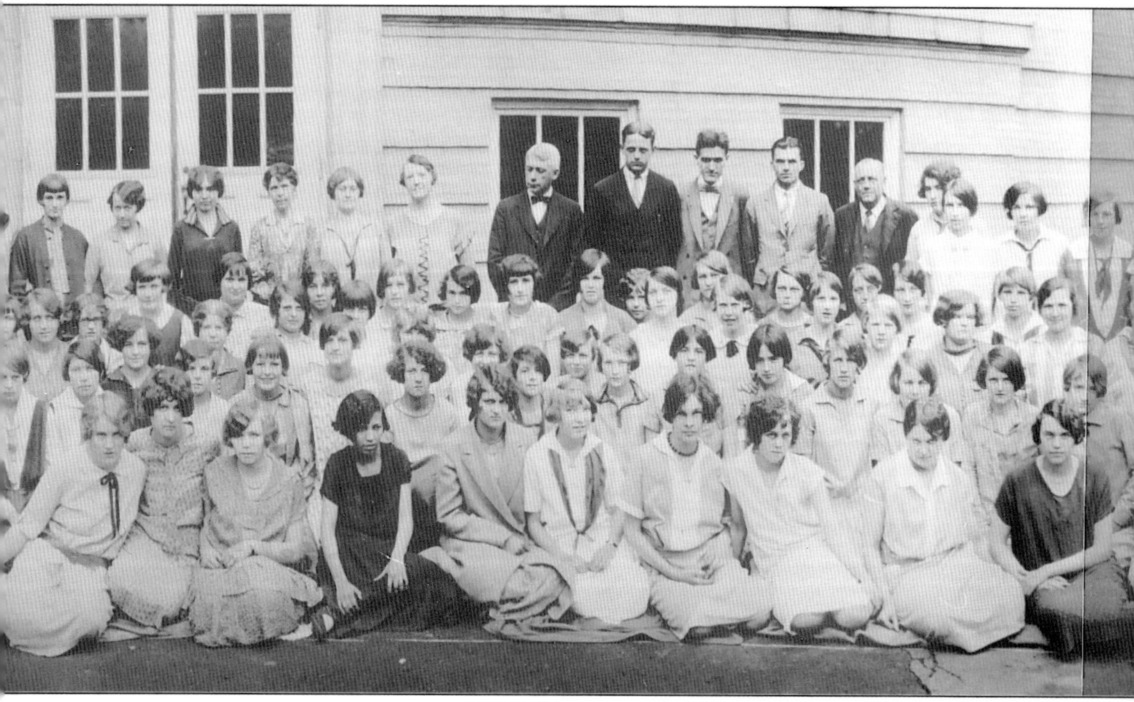

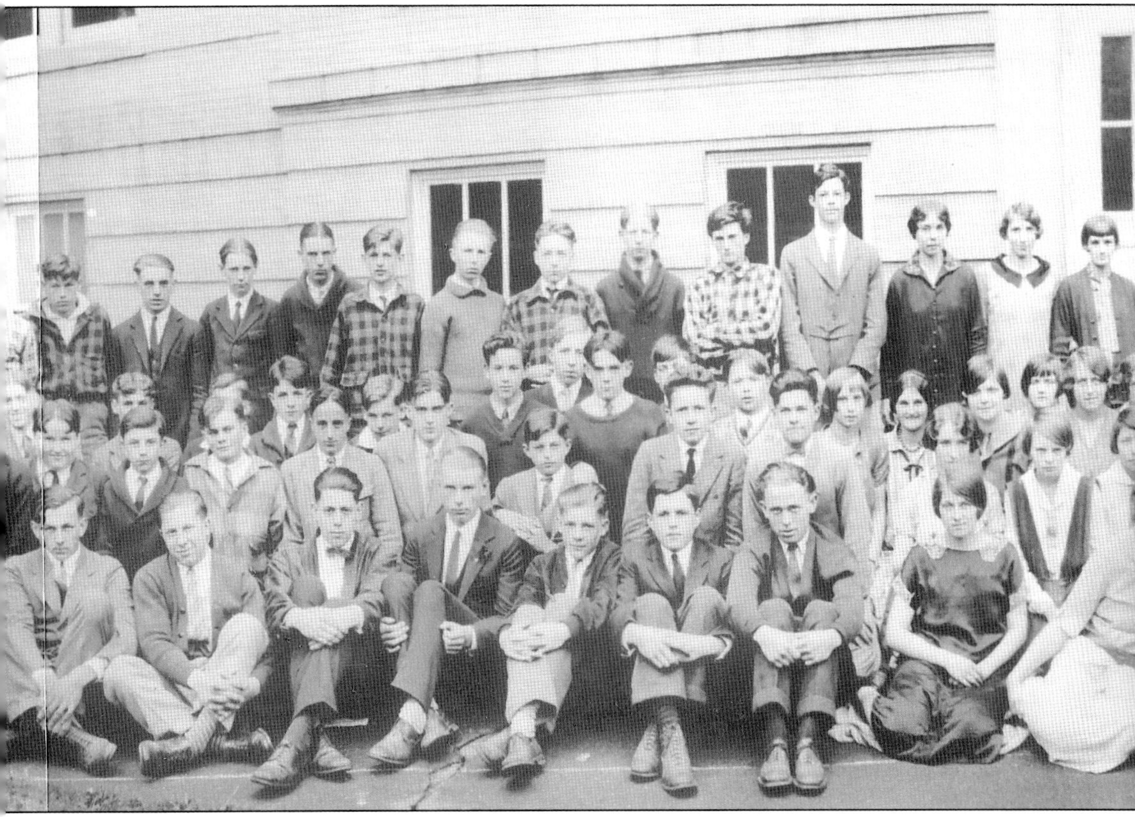

young men are shown above and most of the young women are pictured below.

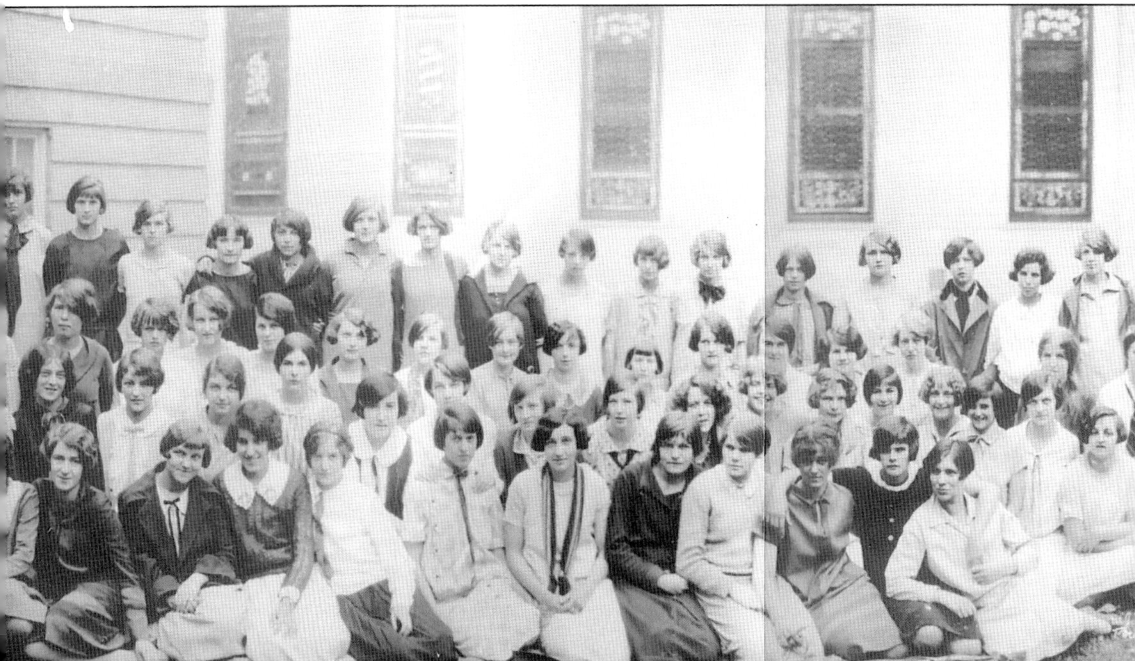

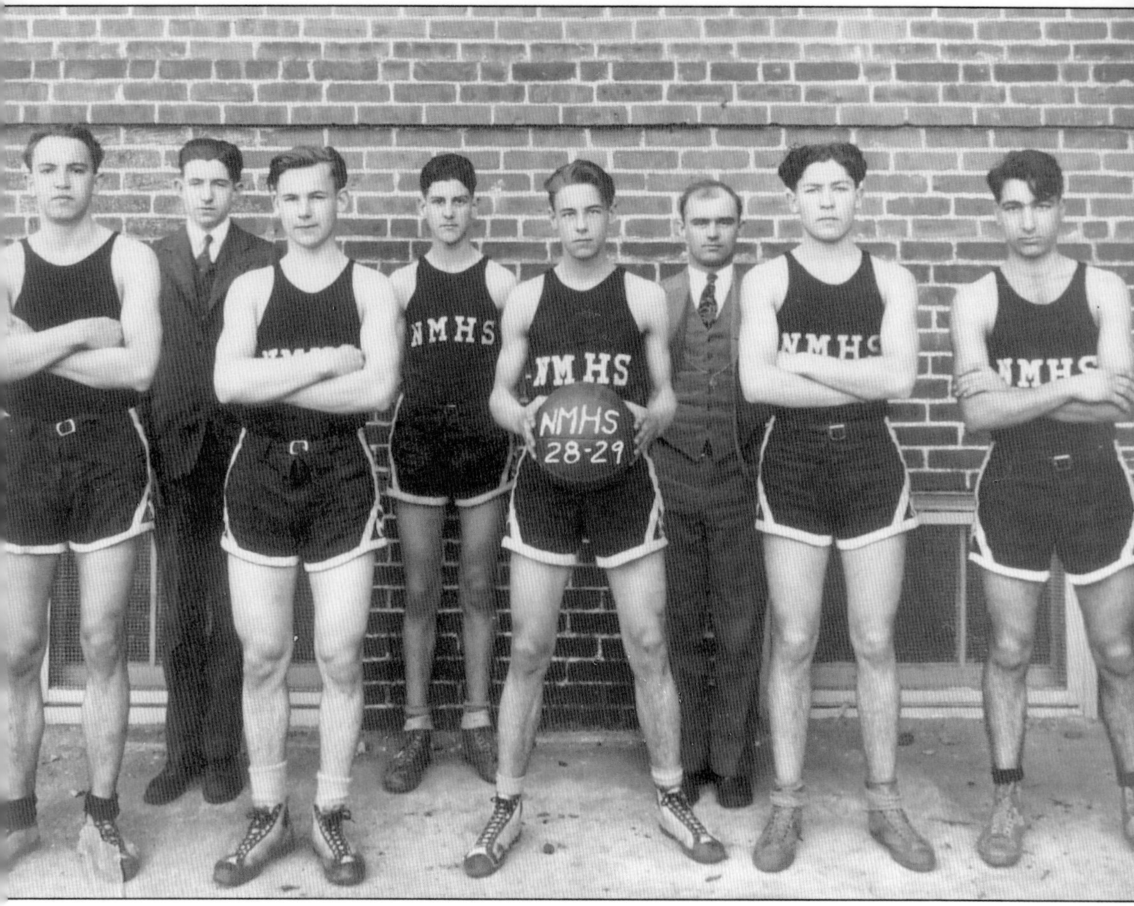

This is the New Milford High School basketball team of 1928–1929. Larry Lillis stands in the back row at the left. The team played hard and won many games. Notice the players' sneakers.

Three

THE HEACOCKS

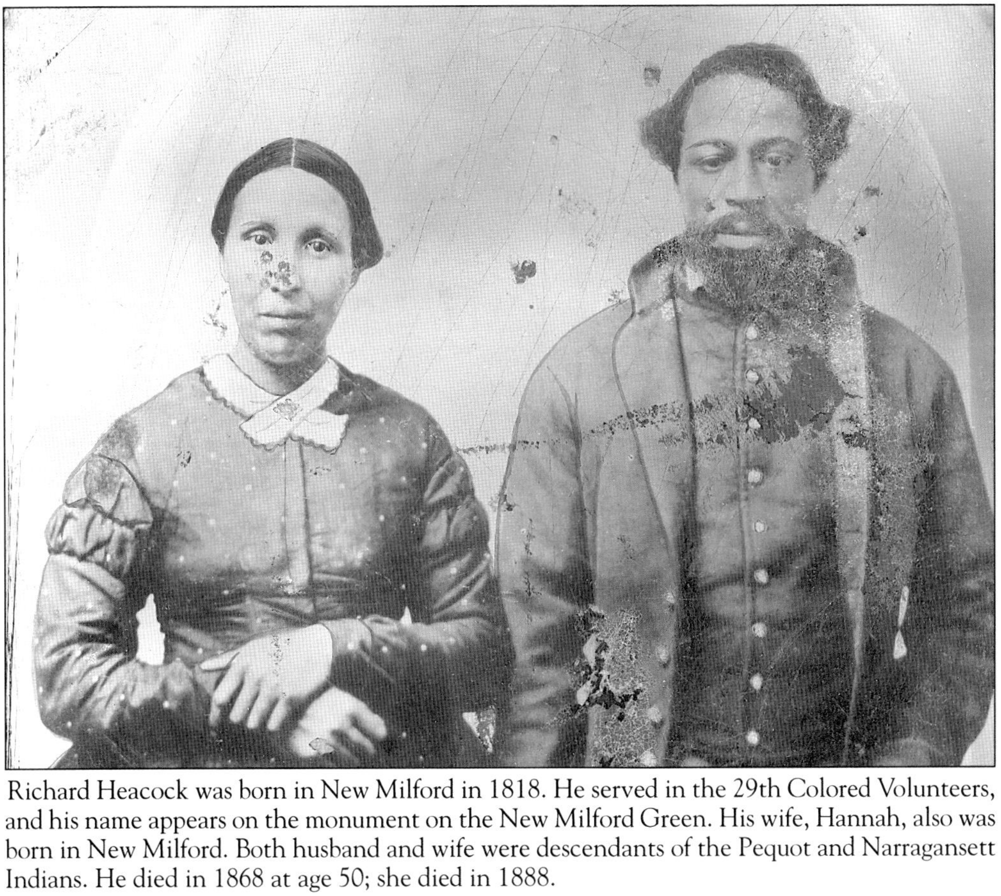

Richard Heacock was born in New Milford in 1818. He served in the 29th Colored Volunteers, and his name appears on the monument on the New Milford Green. His wife, Hannah, also was born in New Milford. Both husband and wife were descendants of the Pequot and Narragansett Indians. He died in 1868 at age 50; she died in 1888.

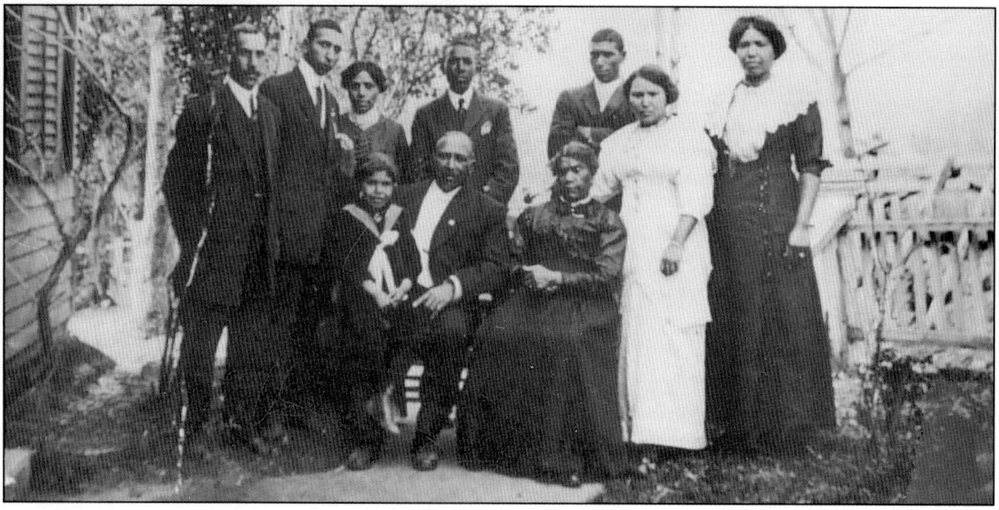

Rev. Stephen Heacock served as recording secretary of the Colored People's Temperance Union of New Milford. He and his family are pictured in 1912 in front of the homestead on Old State Road. They are, from left to right, the following: (front row) Reverend Heacock, son Stewart Heacock, and wife, Mary Gregory Heacock; (back row) Charles Freeman, Roland Heacock, Martha Benson, Granville Heacock, Steve Heacock, Mabel Heacock, and Sue Freeman.

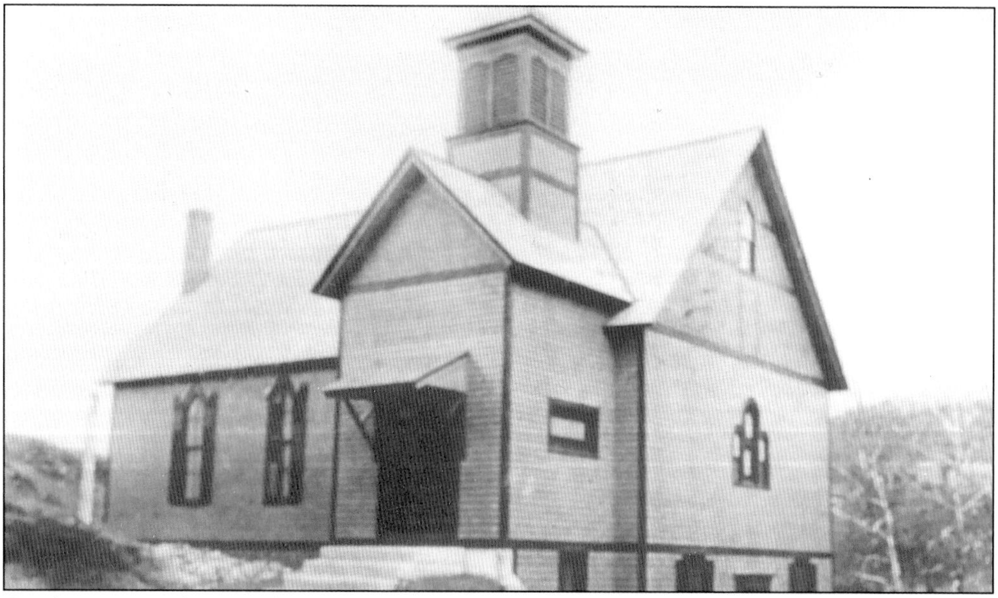

Stephen Heacock was publicly ordained to the ministry by the speaker and associates of the Ministers' Board of Conference on November 11, 1897, at the New Milford Town Hall. He became pastor of the Advent Christian Church of New Milford, organized on February 20, 1900, with 22 members. The church building pictured was erected on Brookside Avenue in 1901. Its bell was a gift from a Mr. Shonio, who presented it in memory of the tragic incidents of the Old French and Indian War. The bell was christened "Sansaman" in honor of the first Christian missionary of New England killed by King Philip of the Wampanoags in 1675. The bell was donated to the New Milford Historical Society by the Heacock family as part of the history of New Milford.

The Rev. Dr. Roland T. Heacock was the son of Rev. Stephen Heacock and Mary Gregory Heacock. Born in New Milford on December 30, 1893, he graduated from Howard University in 1921 and from Yale Divinity School in 1924. He received his master's degree in sacred theology in 1926 and a doctor of divinity degree from American International College. He married Lucille LaCour and had three children: Donald, Lucille, and Joan. In 1959, Heacock became one of the first black ministers to serve an all-white congregation when he assumed the pastorate of Staffordville Congregational Church in Stafford Springs. His children grew up to become Dr. Donald Heacock, Lucille Heacock Layton, and Joan Heacock Ghebreeschel. The pastor died in 1972.

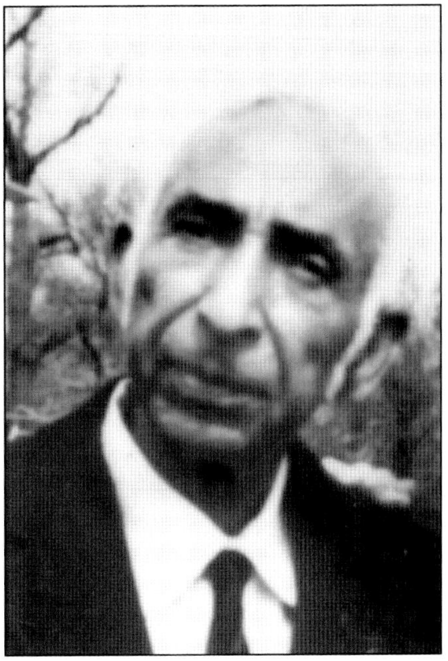

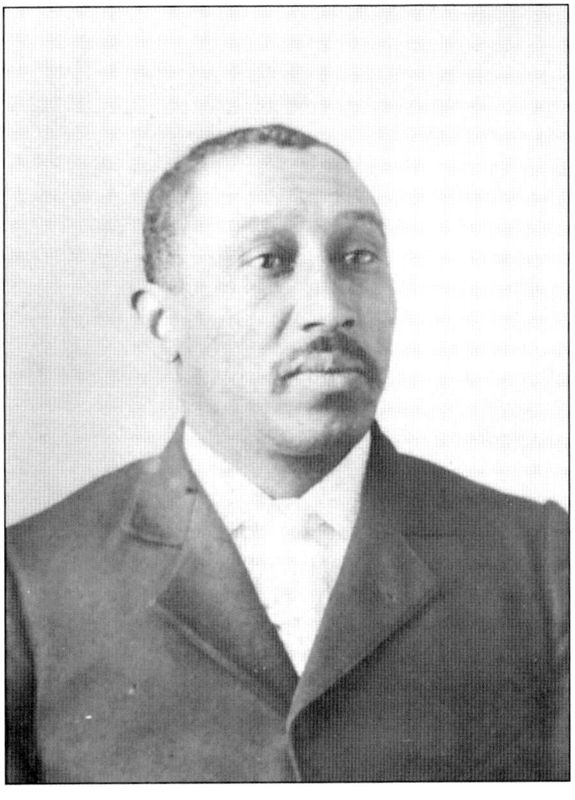

Tilman Heacock was born in New Milford. He went into the dry cleaning and the wood business. He also built homes and painted pictures, which were displayed in his home.

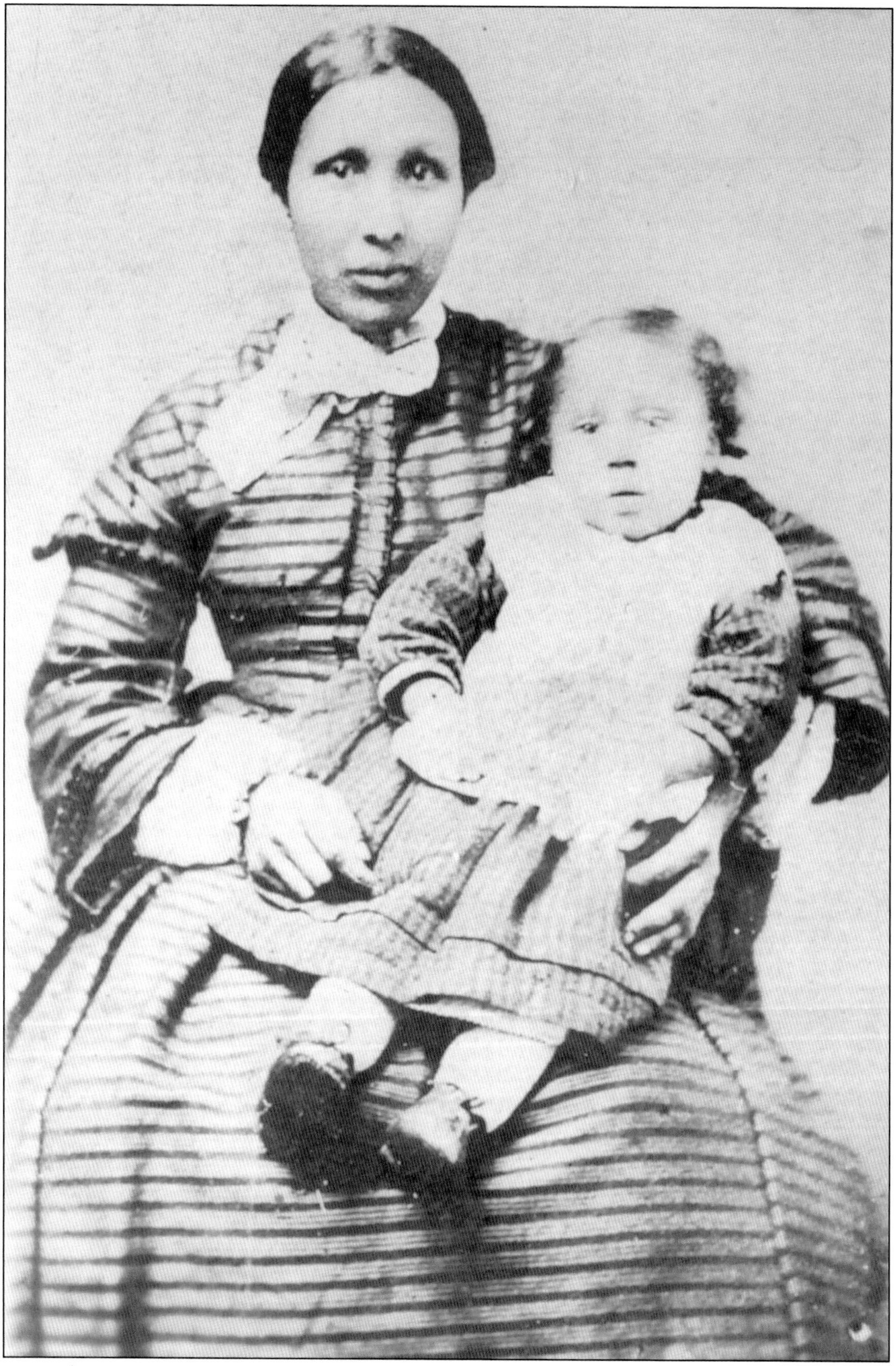

Hannah Heacock, wife of Richard Heacock, holds her son Tilman, who is just one year old.

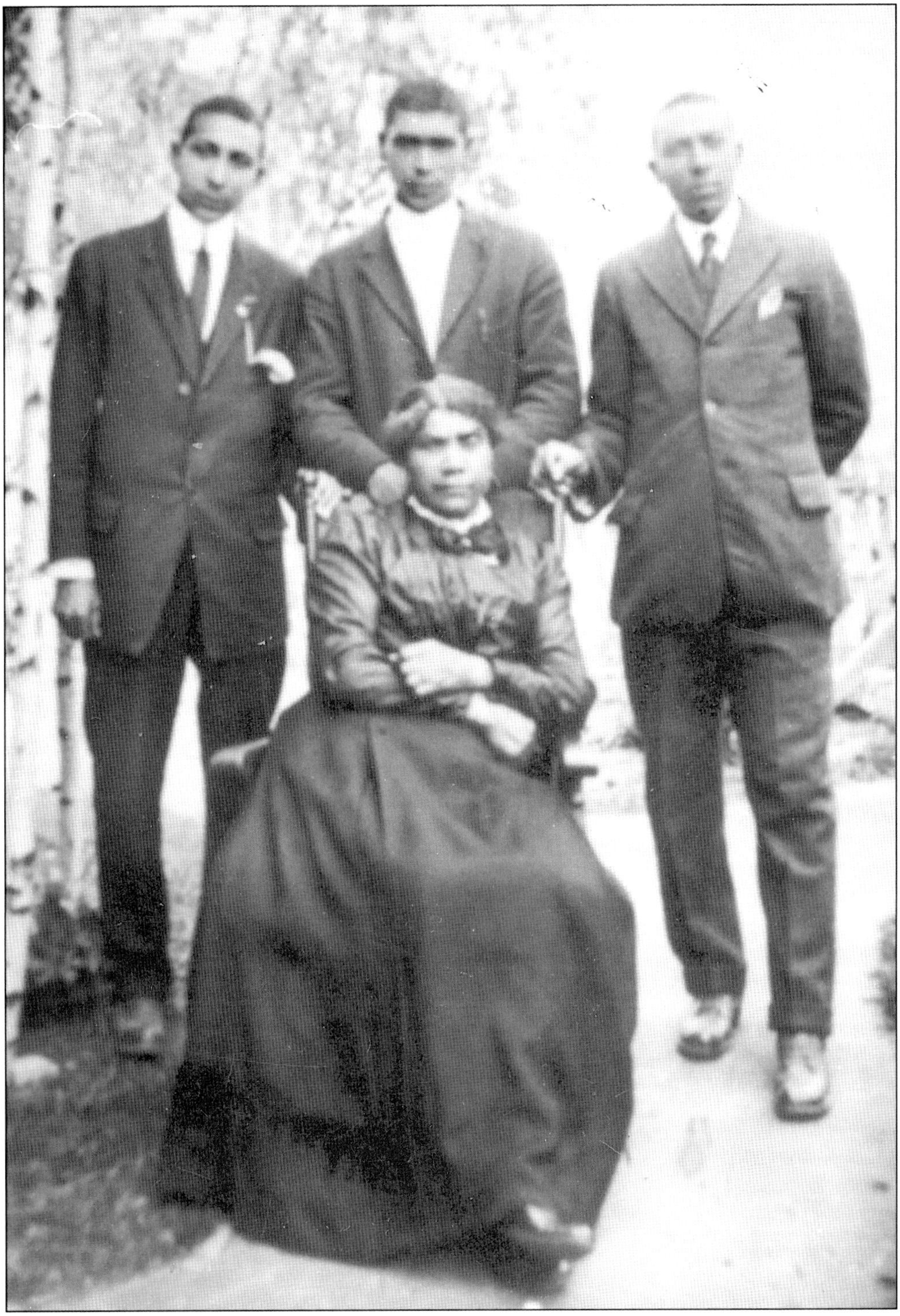

Mary Gregory Heacock, wife of Stephen Heacock, sits with her sons around her. The sons are, from left to right, Roland, Steve, and Granville Heacock. The photograph was taken in the yard of the Heacock Homestead on Old State Road in 1912.

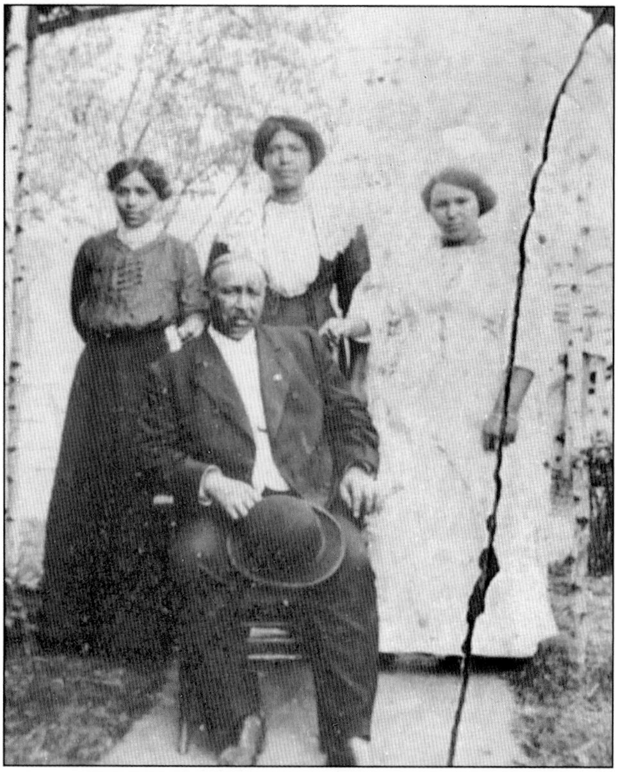

Rev. Stephen Heacock sits with his three daughters in 1912. The daughters are, from left to right, Martha Heacock Benson, Susie Heacock Freeman, and Mabel Galena Heacock.

Three couples stand outside the Granville Heacock home on Elm Street Extension. They are, from left to right, Net and Tilman Heacock, Ett and Granville Heacock, and the Rices from New Britain.

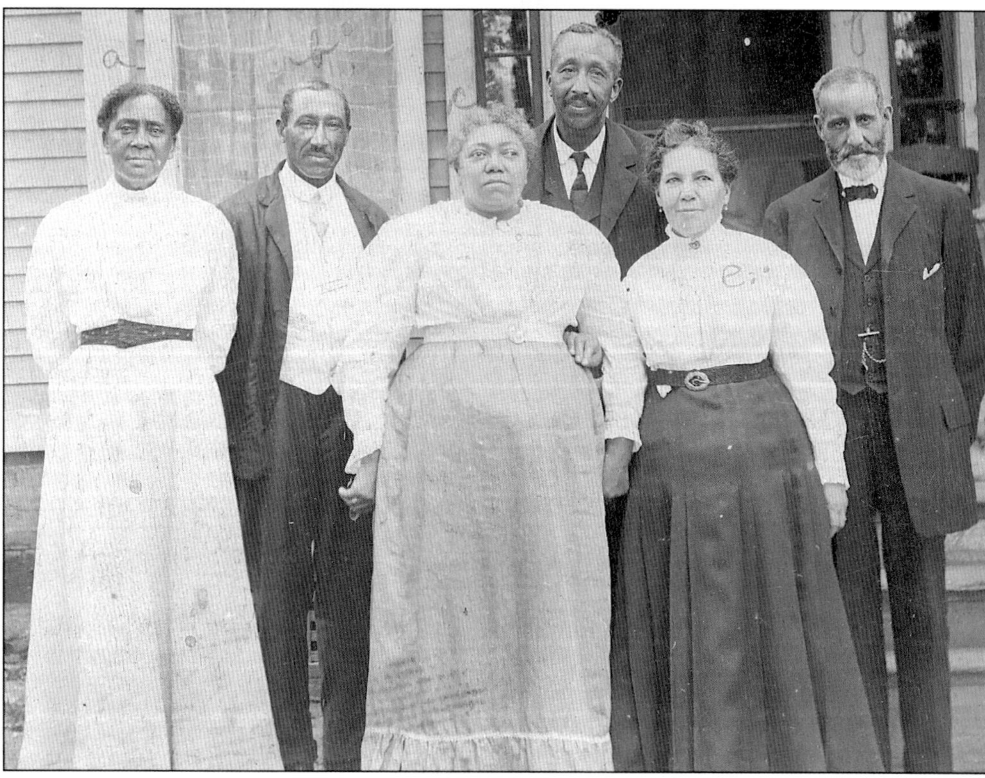

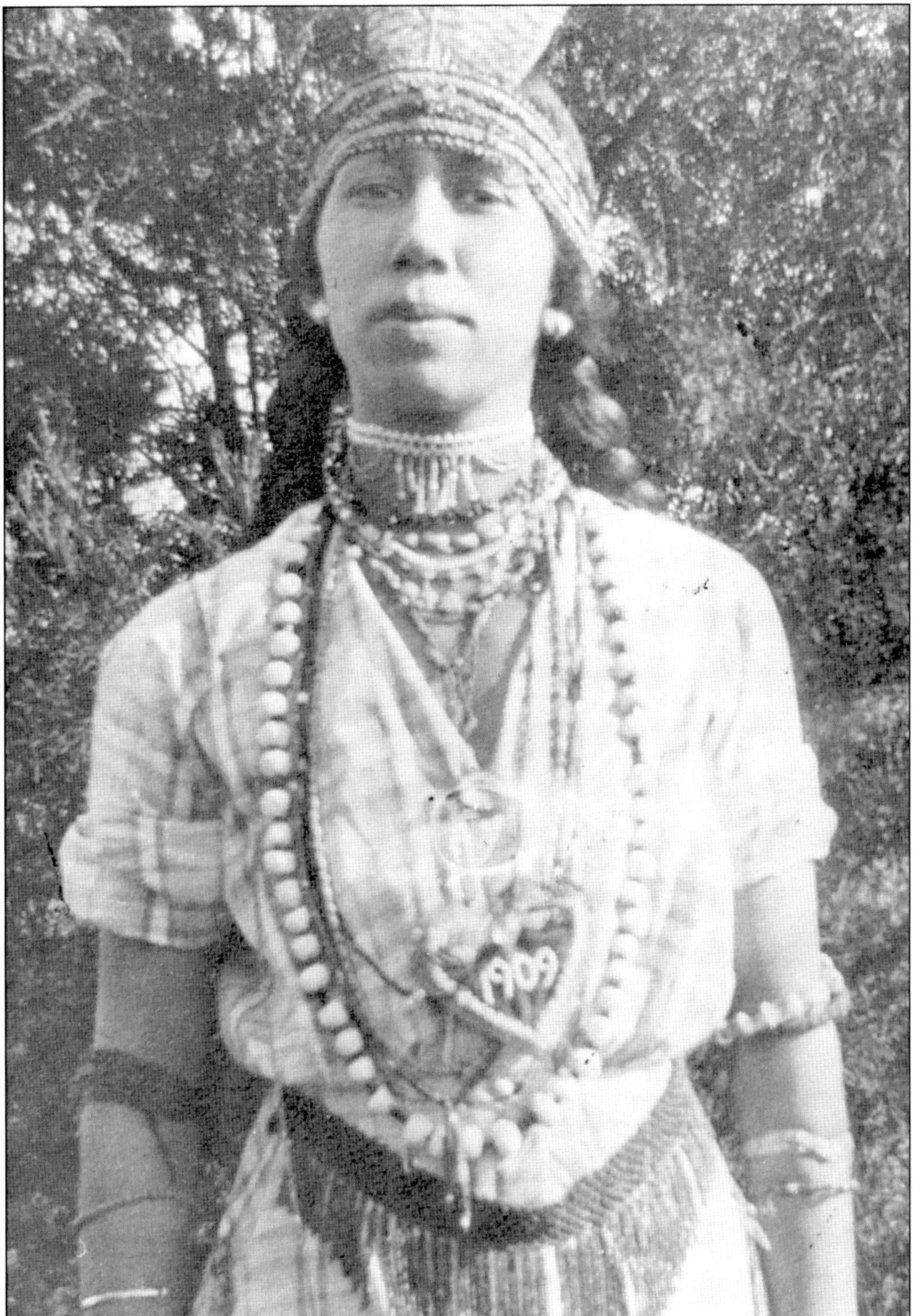

Alvira Heacock Killingsworth was the daughter of Alfred and Elizabeth Benson Heacock. Born in New Milford on March 29, 1894, she was a descendant of the Pequot and the Scaticook Indians and spoke the language of the tribes. She attended New Milford schools.

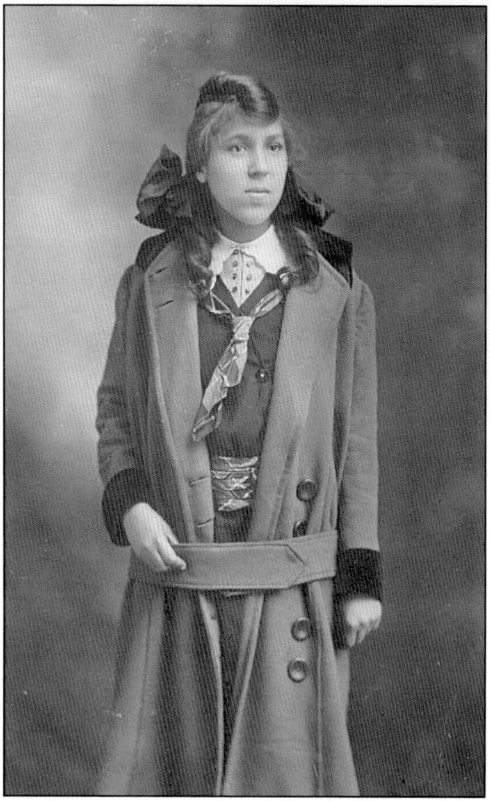

Mildred Heacock was the daughter of Alfred and Elizabeth Benson Heacock. Born in New Milford, she attended New Milford schools. She was one of the first blacks to graduate from Bellevue Hospital School of Nursing in New York City. Because of her light skin color, she was in the white class.

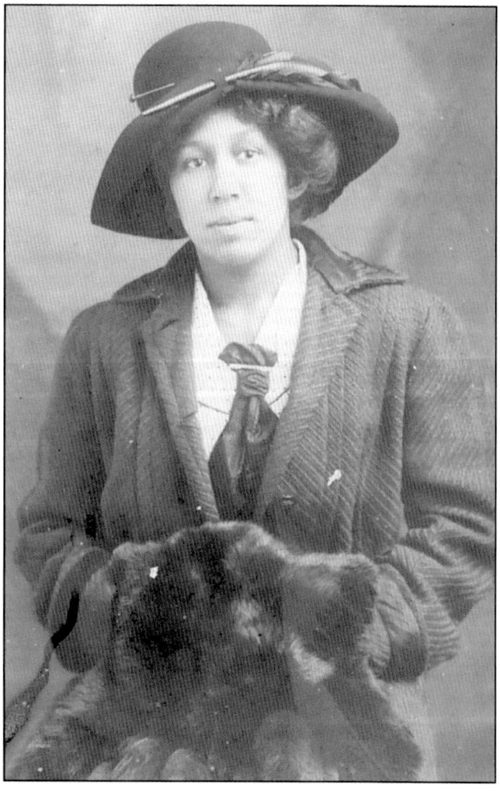

Alvira Heacock Killingsworth, the daughter of Alfred and Elizabeth Benson Heacock, is pictured here in 1913 at the age of 21 before she left for California. She lived to be 105 years old, dying in 1997.

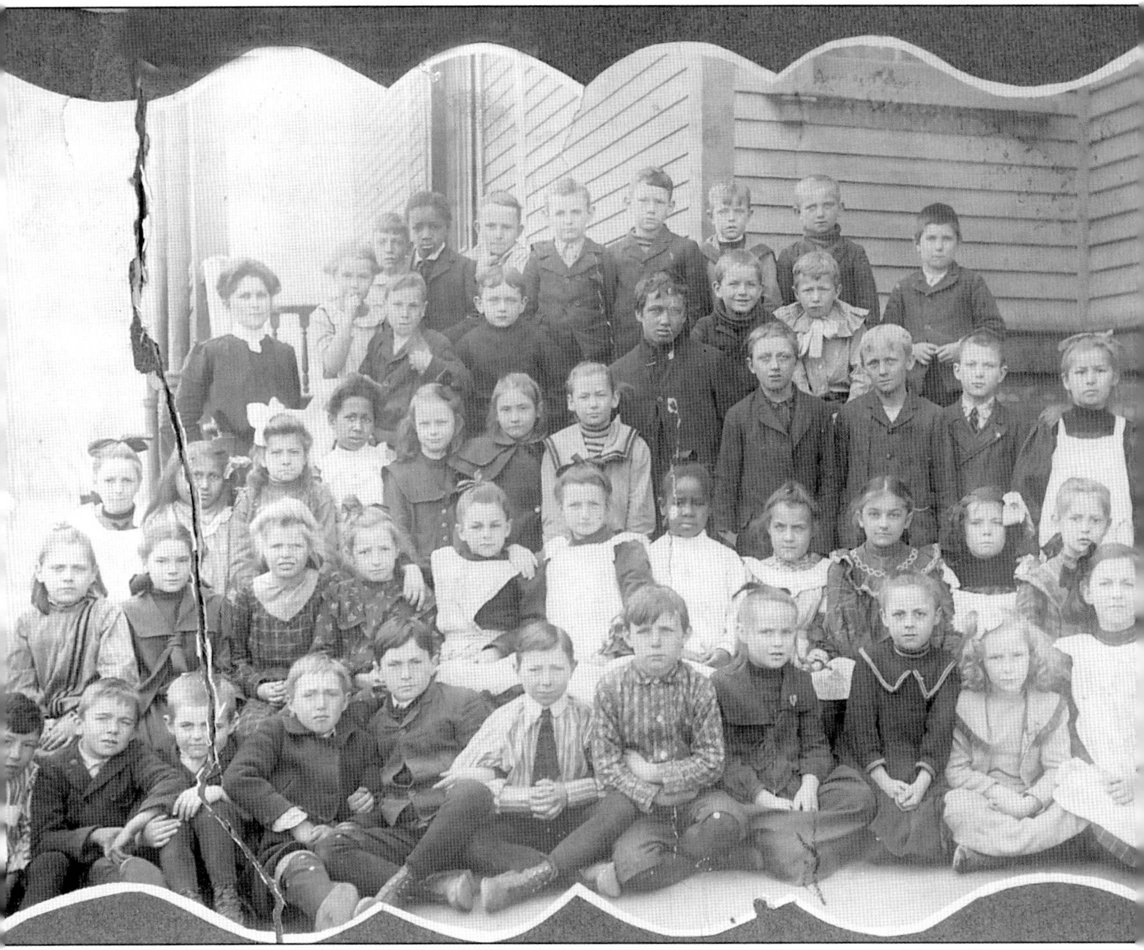

This photograph of a New Milford class was taken approximately 100 years ago. Alvira Heacock Killingsworth is in the third row, fourth from the left. Others pictured include Julia Cogswell, Otto Curry, and Kathleen Buffett.

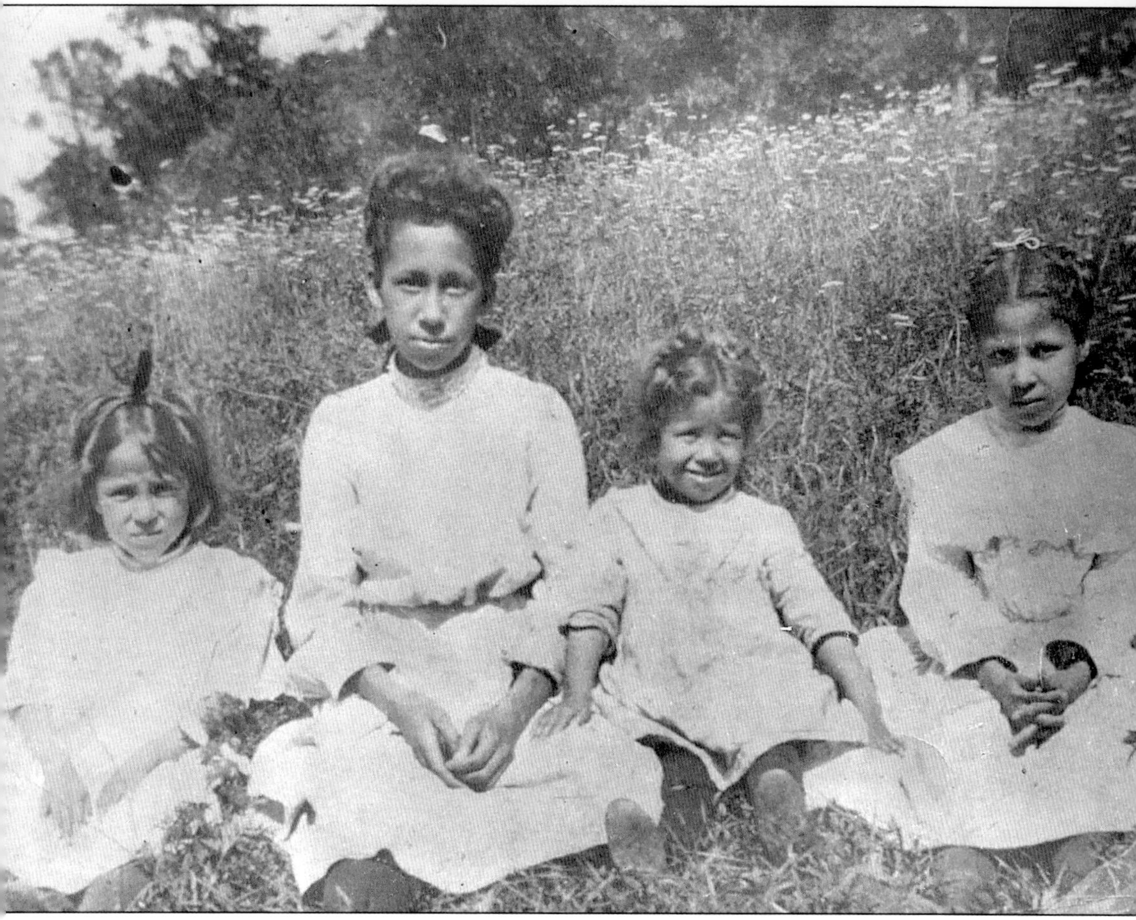

These sisters are the children of Alfred and Elizabeth Benson Heacock. Pictured in 1901, they are sitting in a field of wildflowers at the Sherman home of their maternal grandfather, Minot Benson. They are, from left to right, Cora, Alvira, Ethel, and Mildred Heacock.

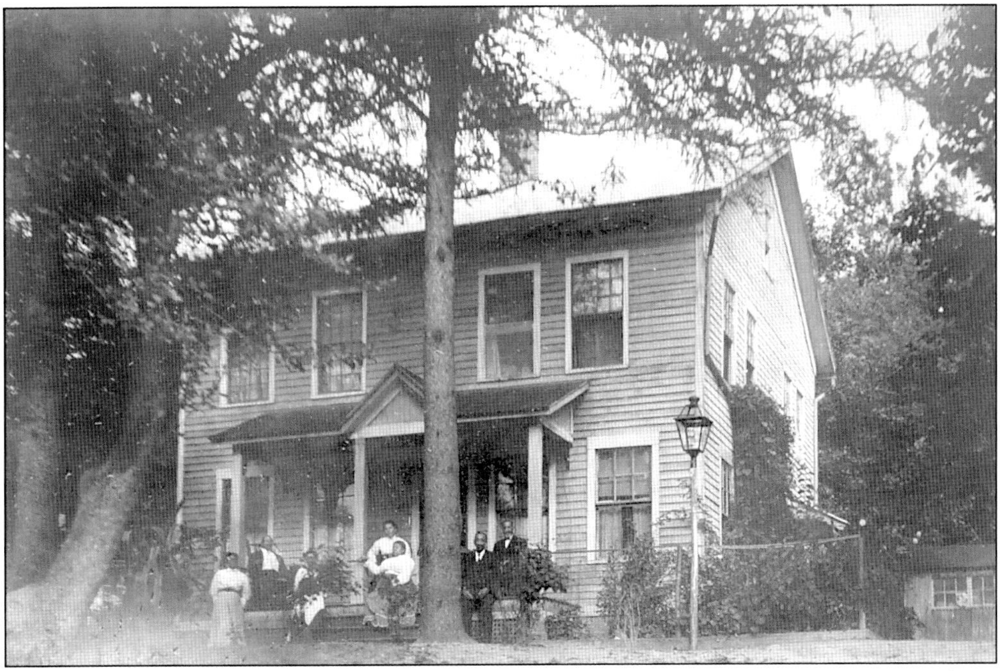

Outside Granville Heacock's house on Elm Street Extension are seven friends. Among those pictured with Granville and Ett Heacock in the late 1800s are Net and Tilman Heacock and the Rices of New Britain.

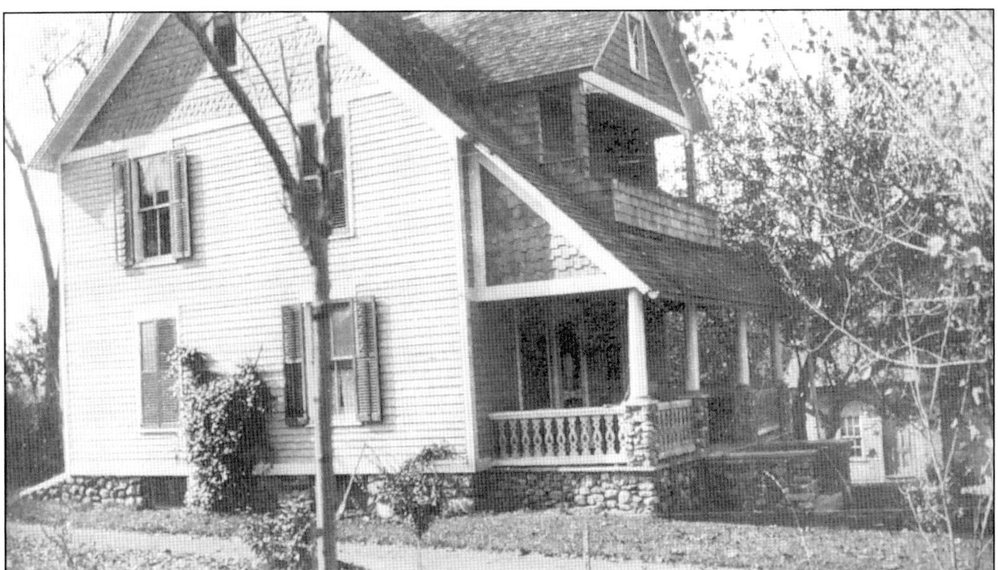

This house on Elm Street Extension is the home of William Alfred Heacock Jr.

Sally Benson was the sister of Elizabeth Benson Heacock. This photograph was taken in 1904.

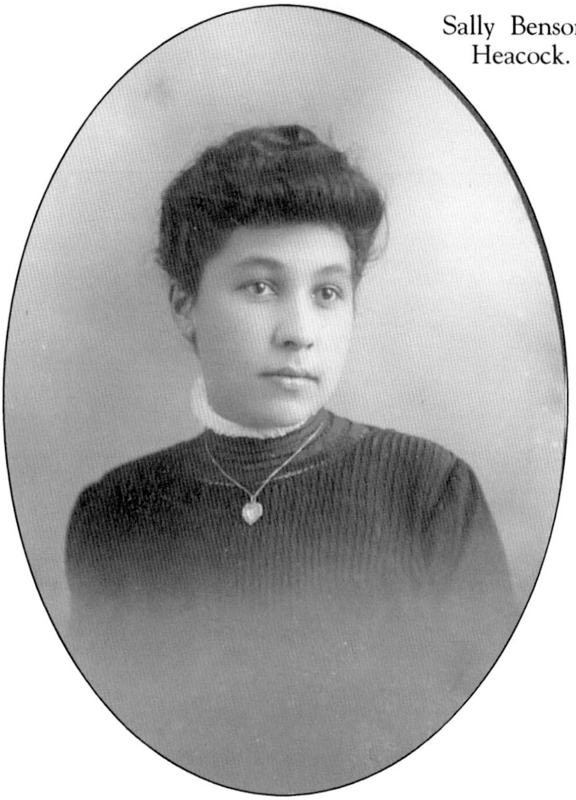

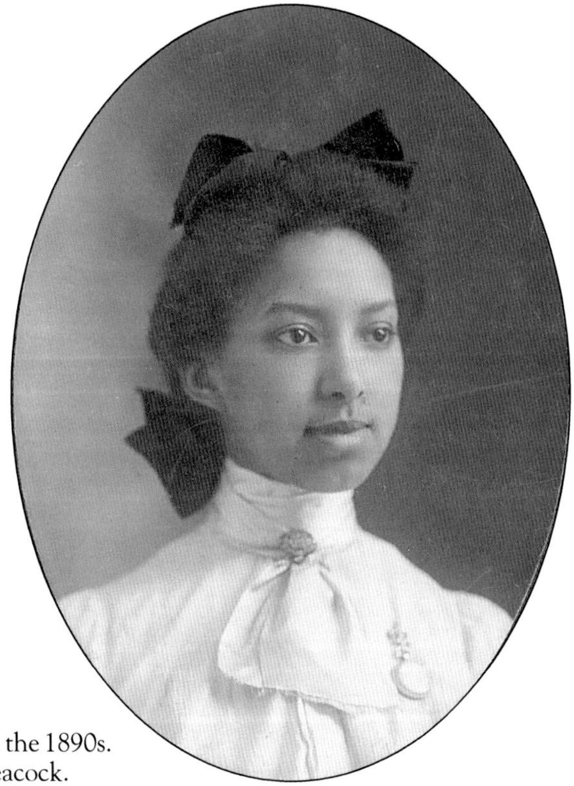

Nellie Brooks was born in New Milford c. the 1890s. She was the second wife of Granville Heacock.

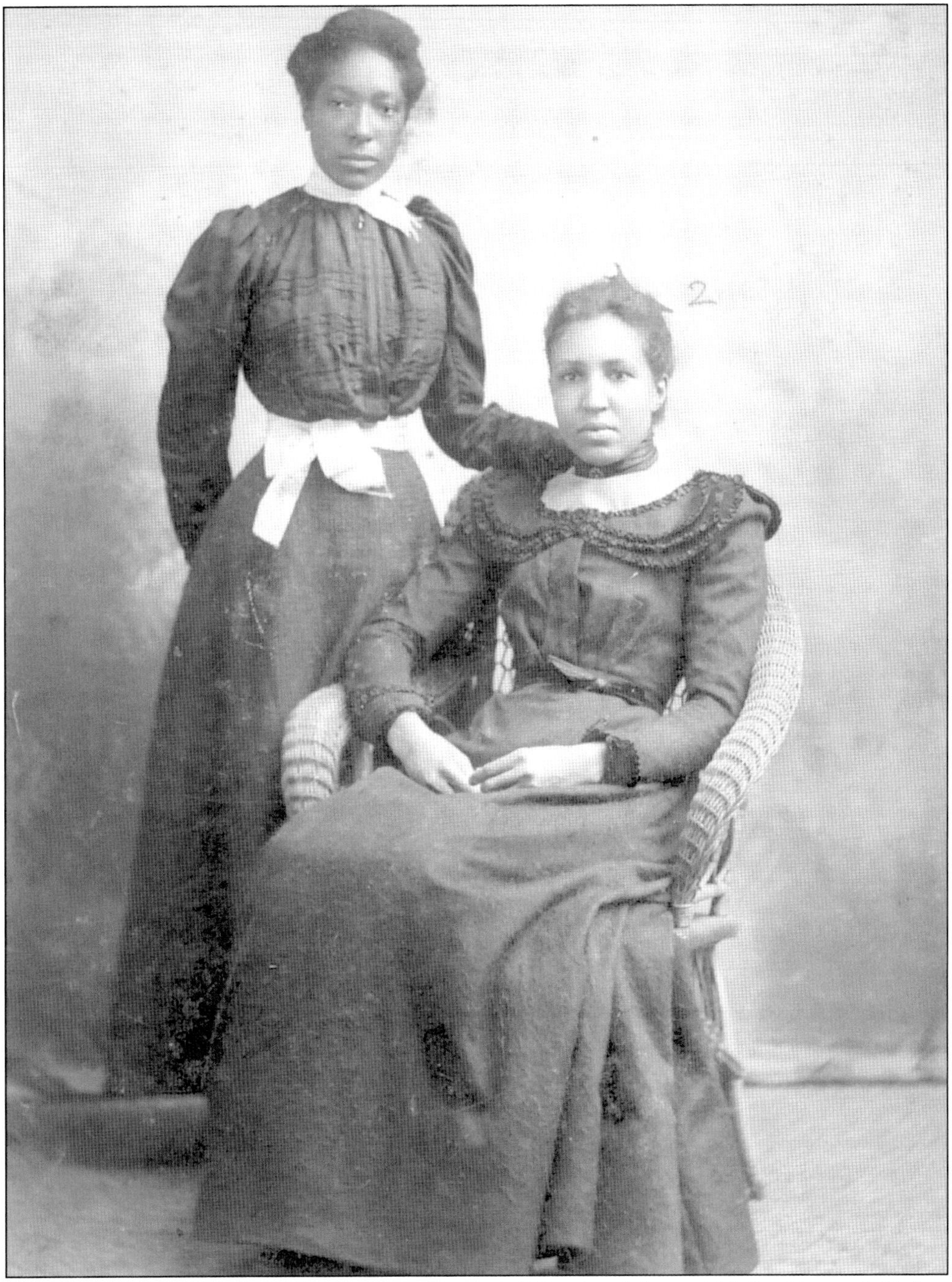

Pictured *c.* the late 1800s are Elizabeth Heacock Wheeler, left, and Nellie Heacock Bailey. Elizabeth Heacock married Walter Wheeler of New Milford. She had two sons, Walter and Arthur Wheeler. Both sons served in the Spanish-American War. Arthur Wheeler was lost in the war. Walter Wheeler was a Buffalo soldier and served as a special scout with Theodore Roosevelt's Rough Riders. He returned to New Milford and later moved to California. Nellie Heacock was born in New Milford. She married Mr. Bailey, and the couple lived in New Milford.

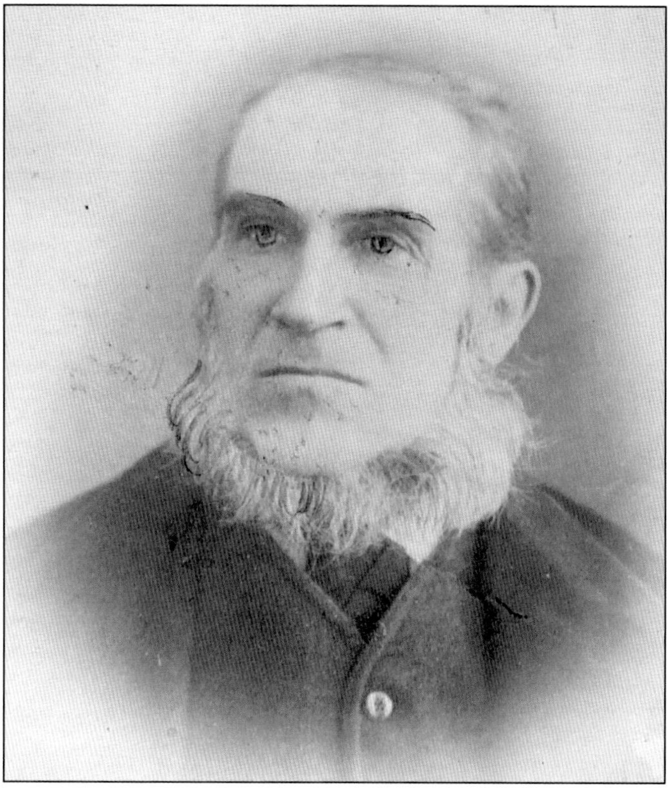

Minot Benson was the father of Elizabeth Benson Heacock. He was an English settler who moved to Sherman. He married an Indian woman.

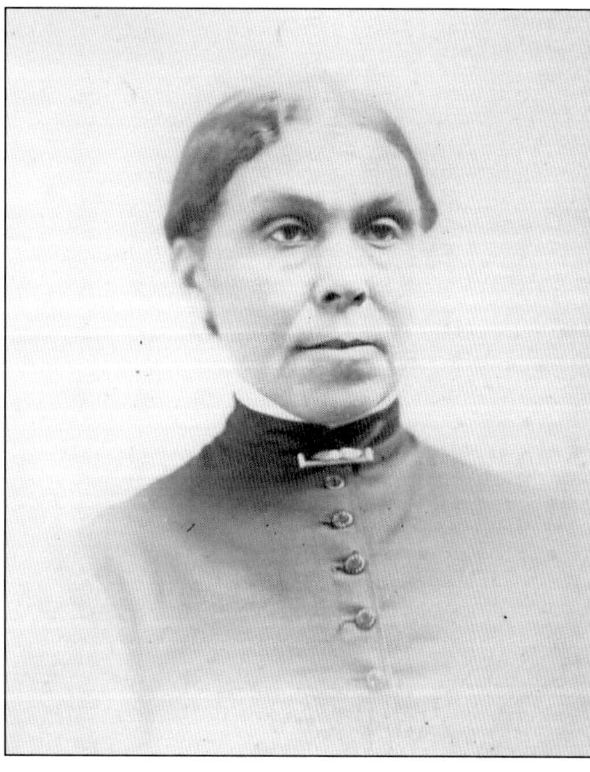

Mrs. Minot Benson was the mother of Elizabeth Benson Heacock. She was born in New Milford and was a descendant of the Pequot, Narragansett, and Scaticook tribes.

Star Benson was the brother of Elizabeth Benson Heacock.

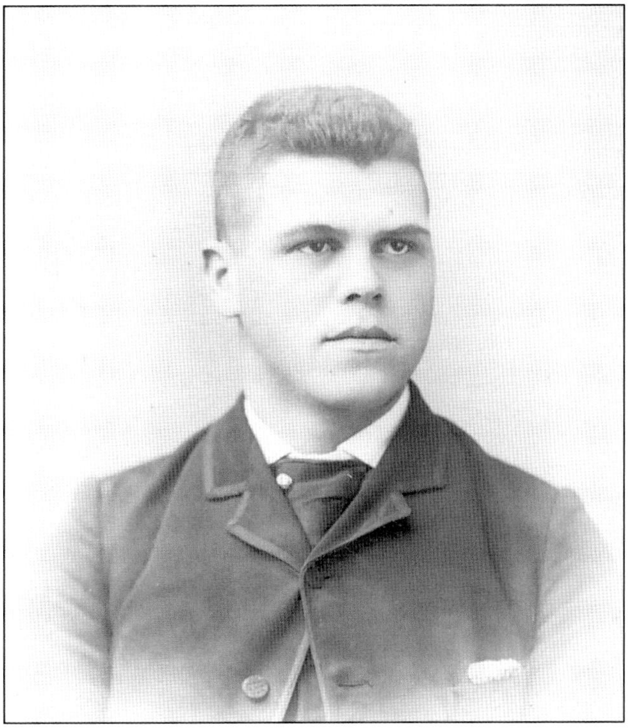

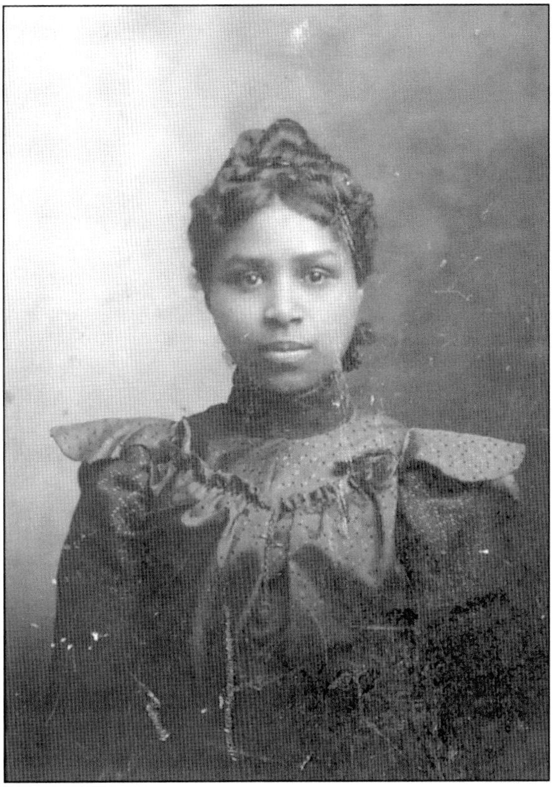

Martha Heacock Benson was the eldest daughter of Rev. Stephen Heacock and Mary Heacock. Born *c.* 1877, she is pictured here in the 1890s. She made a living crocheting tablecloths for people in New Milford. She died in July 1969 at the age of 92.

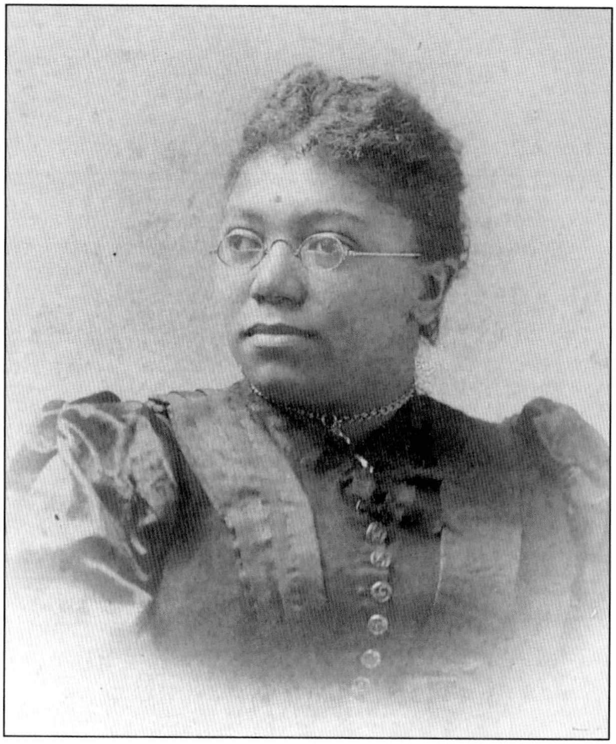

Ett Heacock was the wife of Granville Heacock. She was very fashionable and wore the latest style clothing. This photograph was taken in the 1890s.

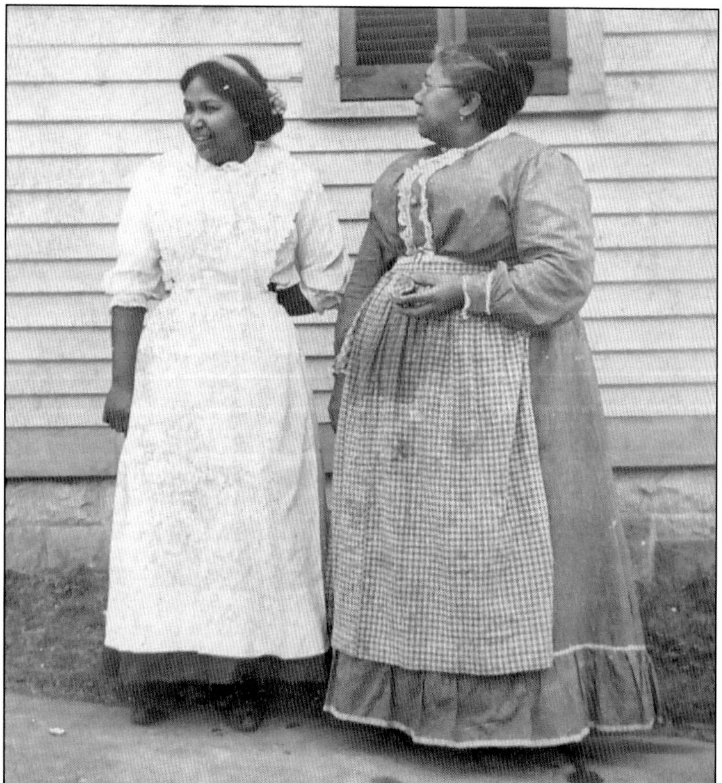

Pictured in the 1890s are Mabel Galena Heacock, left, and her aunt Ett Heacock. Mabel Heacock was the daughter of Rev. Stephen Heacock and Mary Heacock. She was born in New Milford on March 25, 1889. She enjoyed cooking and had a winning personality.

Four

HOMES, CHURCHES, AND HOSPITALS

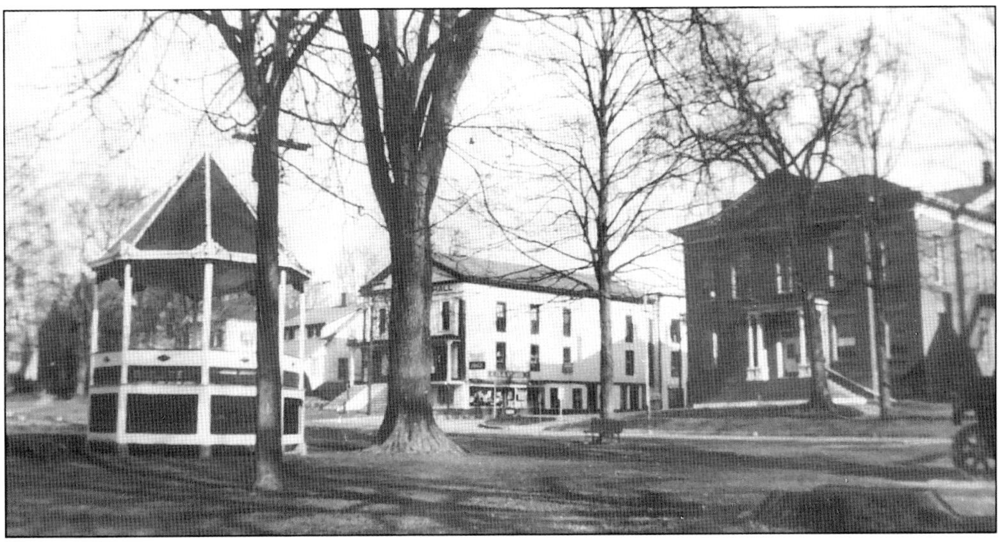

New Milford's bandstand was built in 1896. It was originally placed farther north on the town green. It survived the fire of 1902. The bandstand housed a barbershop until Bank and Railroad Streets could be rebuilt. On November 27, 1852, the Town appointed a committee of five to choose a site for the new town hall. Two proposals were required. C.S. Roberts was chosen as architect and the New Milford Town Hall was built in 1875 at a cost of $26,000 on what was formerly the site of the Roger Sherman Home. From 1837 to 1882, the building that became the Village Hardware Store served as the third home of St. John's Episcopal Church. When the church moved to its present home in 1882, the building was remodeled and the steeple was removed. It became a hard goods store, which also sold wood wagons and farm supplies. The present owners are Tom and Barbara Leahy. The store is in the process of becoming an antique mall.

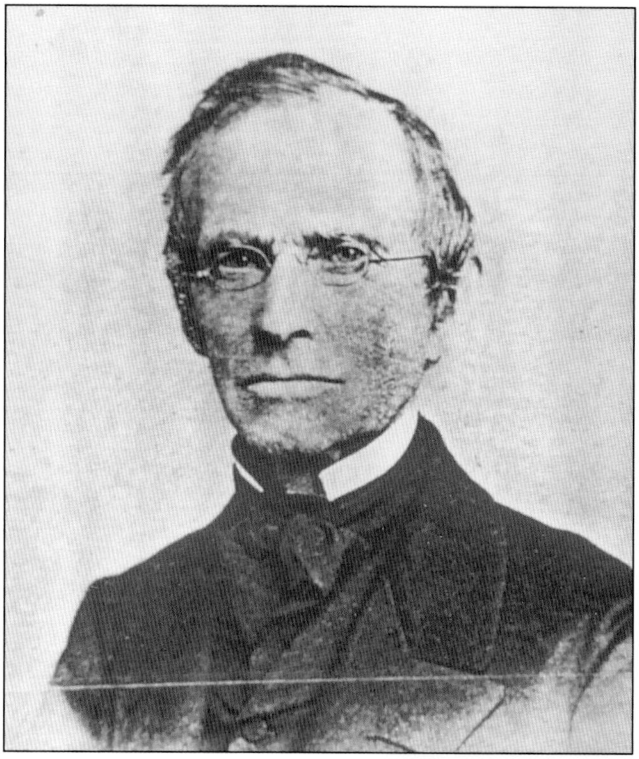

Levi Sydney Knapp was a shoemaker by trade. This photograph was taken in 1870.

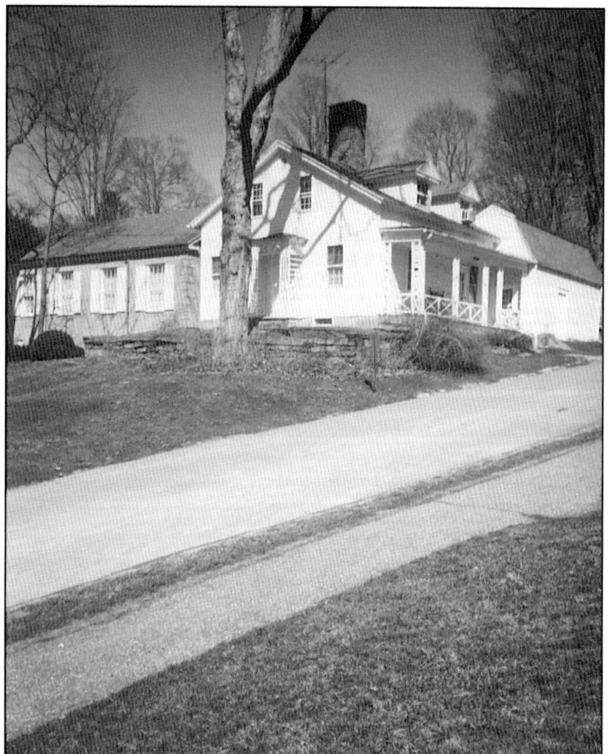

Daniel Burritt built this house *c.* 1770. In 1838, the house became the home of the Knapp family. The Knapps moved to New Milford from Stratford. Mary Clissold Knapp, the last living member of the family, gave the home to the New Milford Historical Society with the provision that the home be restored.

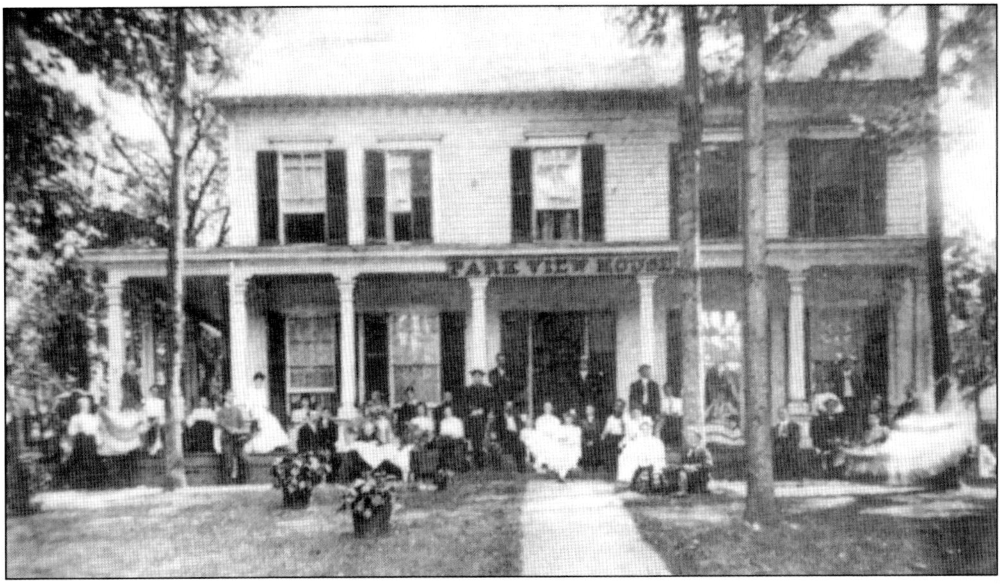

This photograph of the Park View House on Bridge Street dates from *c.* 1900. Ithnar and Bessie Canfield built the house in 1823 for their son Royal S. Canfield and his wife. In 1871, Merritt Beach purchased the house and, over the next 40 years, leased it and operated it as a boardinghouse—first as the Wheaton House and then as the Park View House. In 1910, C.M. Beach remodeled the house as a Greek Revival-style residence. The house is now the Lillis Funeral Home.

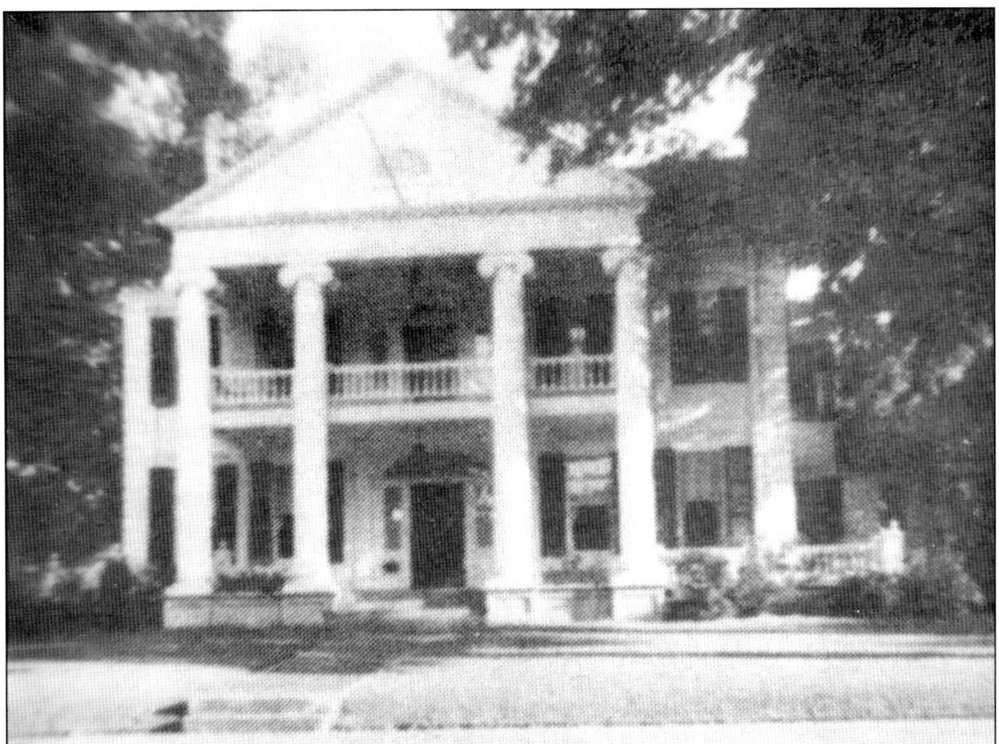

This photograph shows the Lillis Funeral Home.

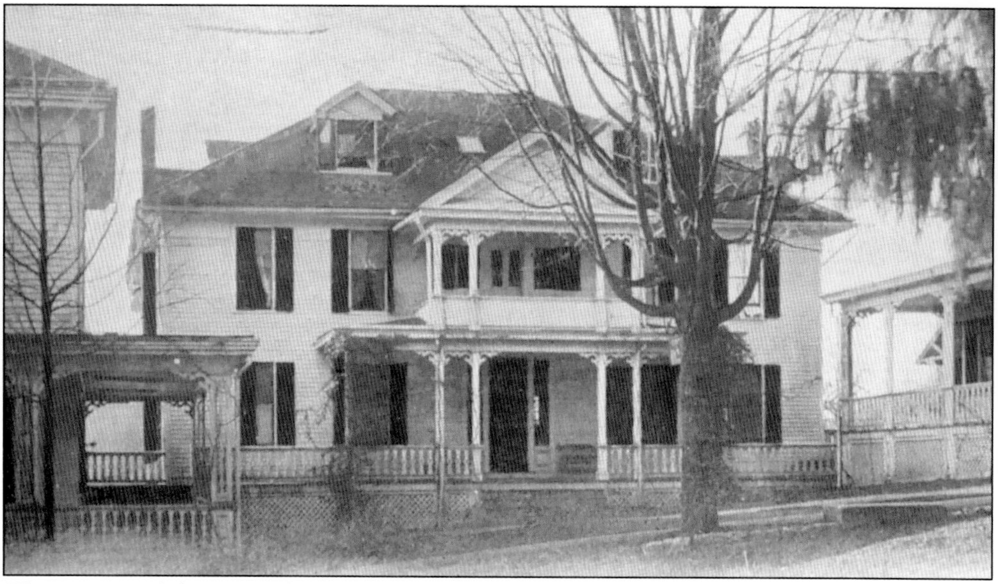

This picture of the Wayside Inn was taken in 1905. The inn catered to many travelers who came into the area.

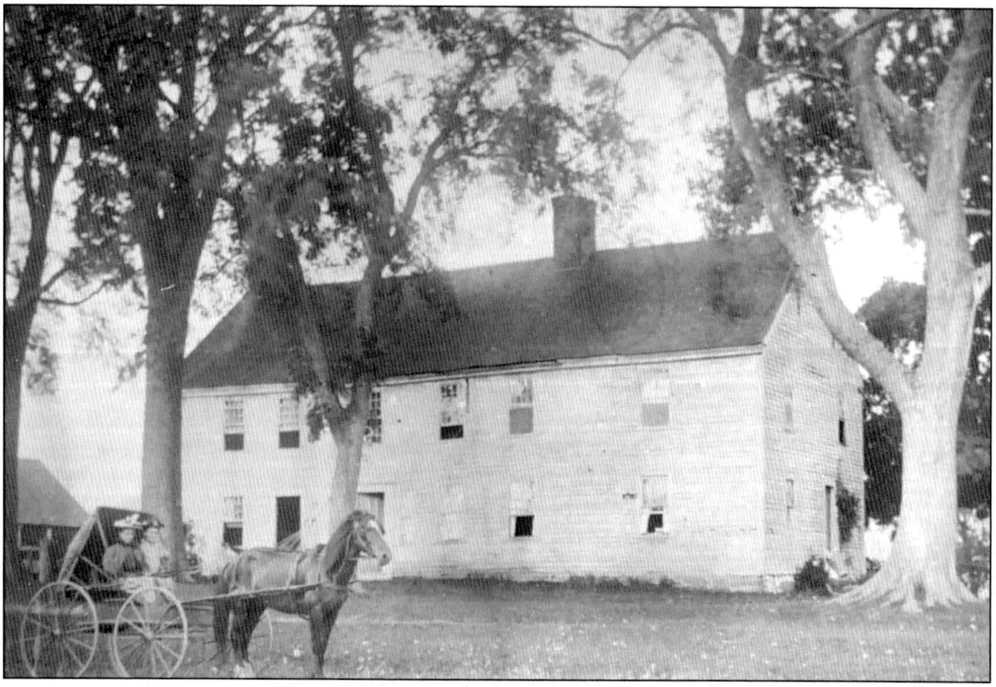

At the time this photograph was taken in 1898, the house shown was 100 years old. It was the home of Tommy Wells. Edwin Bostwick later purchased it. The two women in the carriage are Anne and Mary Doty Bostwick.

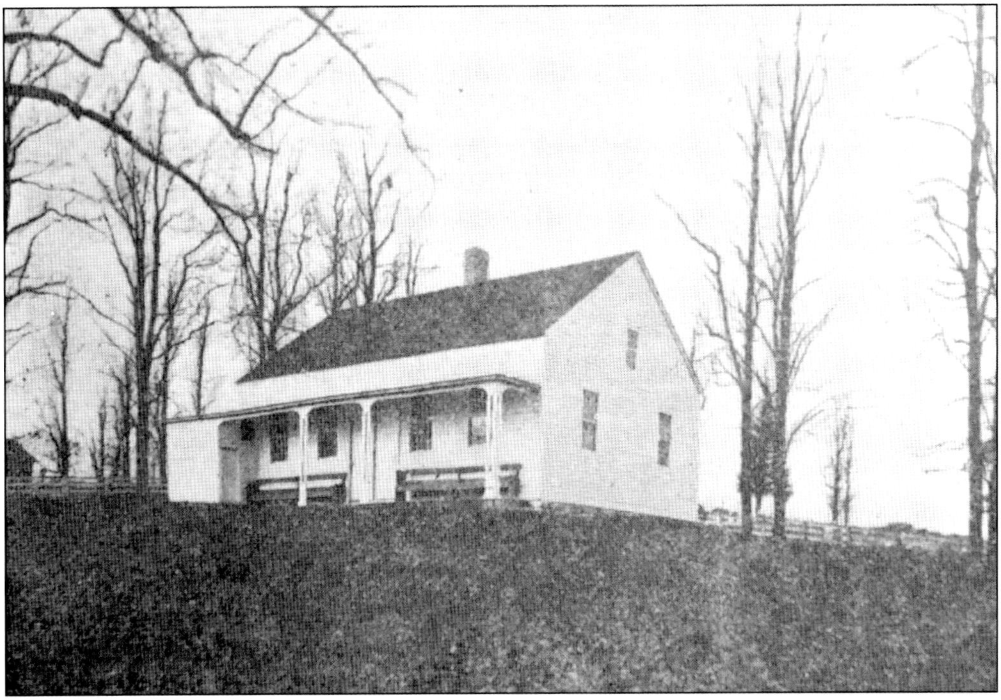

In 1788, Nicholas Wanzer deeded land to the Quakers. It is the same land on which the Quaker Meeting House still stands, complete with the adjoining burying grounds. The old Quaker Meeting House was removed to the site from the Pickett district.

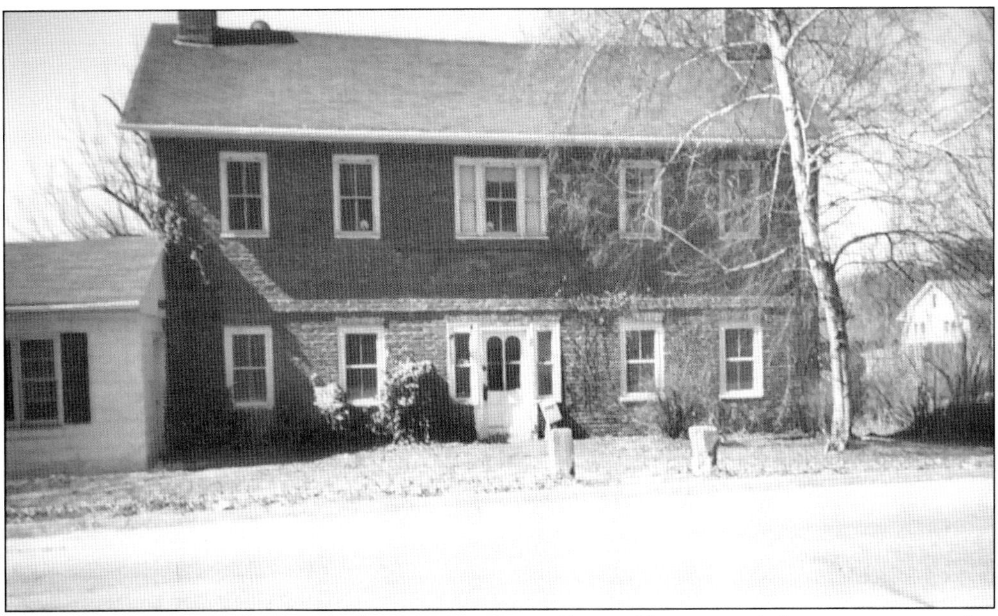

Elisha Bostwick built the Bostwick House on Grove Street. He acquired the property upon his return from the Revolutionary War. The house was completed in 1782. Bostwick served as the town clerk for 55 years; he also was a justice of the peace, a land surveyor, and a colonel in the state militia. In the mid-1800s, the Bostwick House was a station on the Underground Railroad.

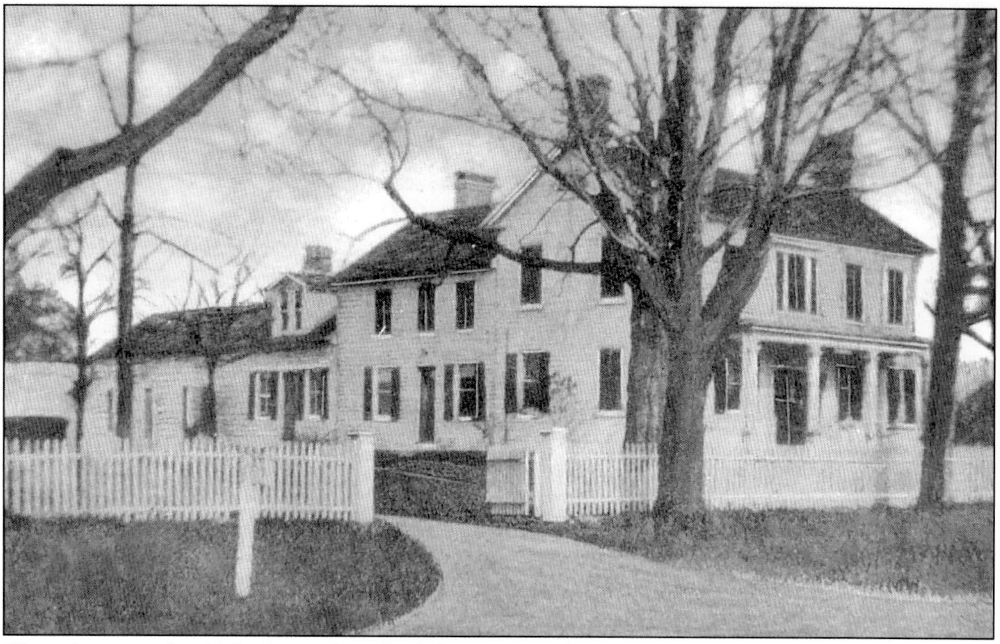

This photograph of Maplewood on Park Lane was taken in 1905. Maplewood was an inn for travelers. It later became the Bostwick Homestead.

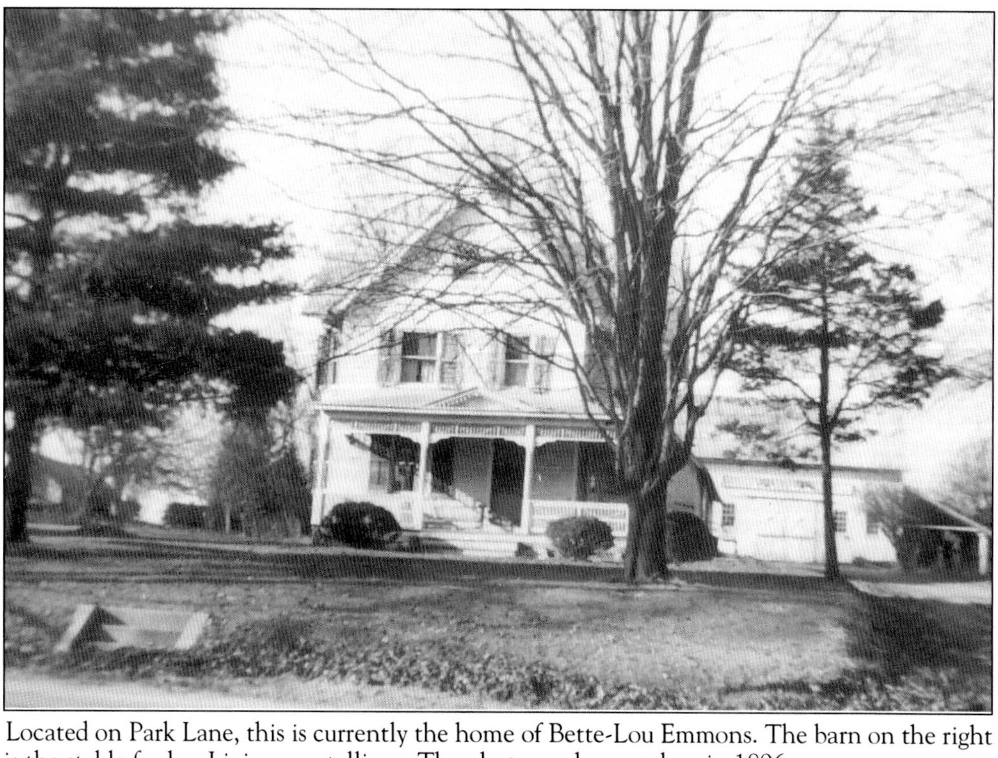

Located on Park Lane, this is currently the home of Bette-Lou Emmons. The barn on the right is the stable for her Lipizzaner stallions. The photograph was taken in 1896.

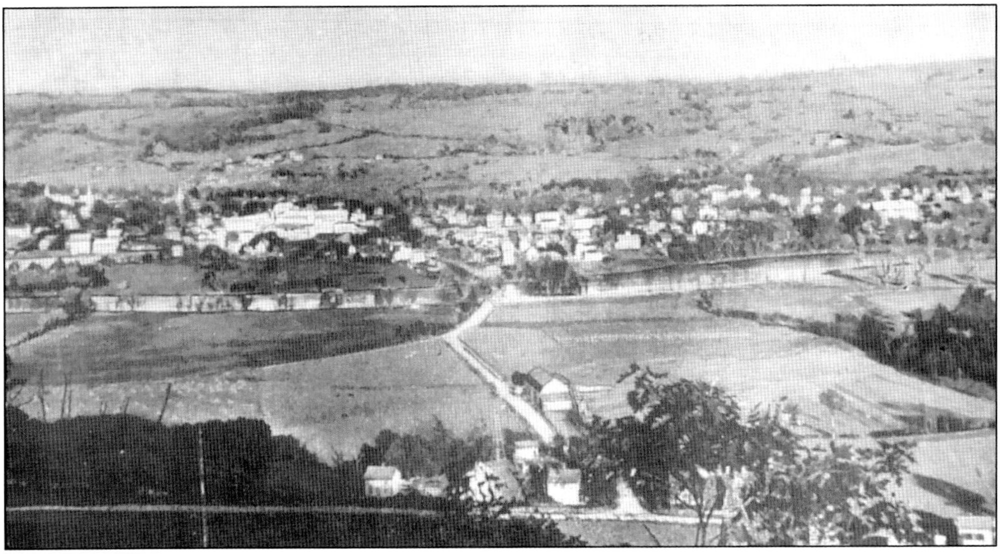

This bird's-eye view of New Milford was taken looking toward the Kimberly-Clark Corporation, which for the past 40 years has been the town's largest employer and taxpayer.

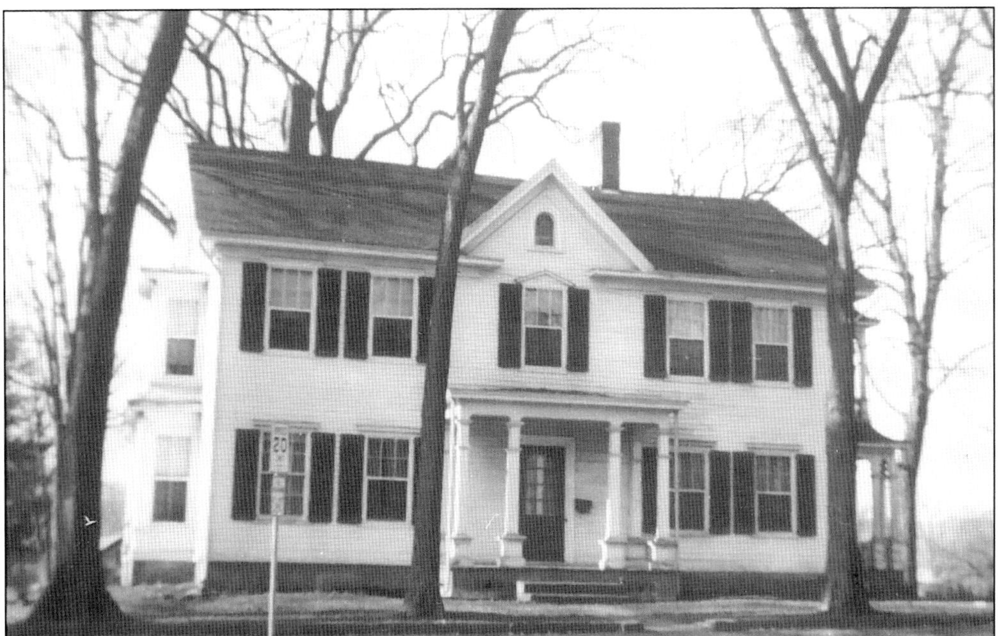

Originally, this house on Main Street belonged to Solomon Edgar Bostwick. Bostwick built the house *c.* 1905.

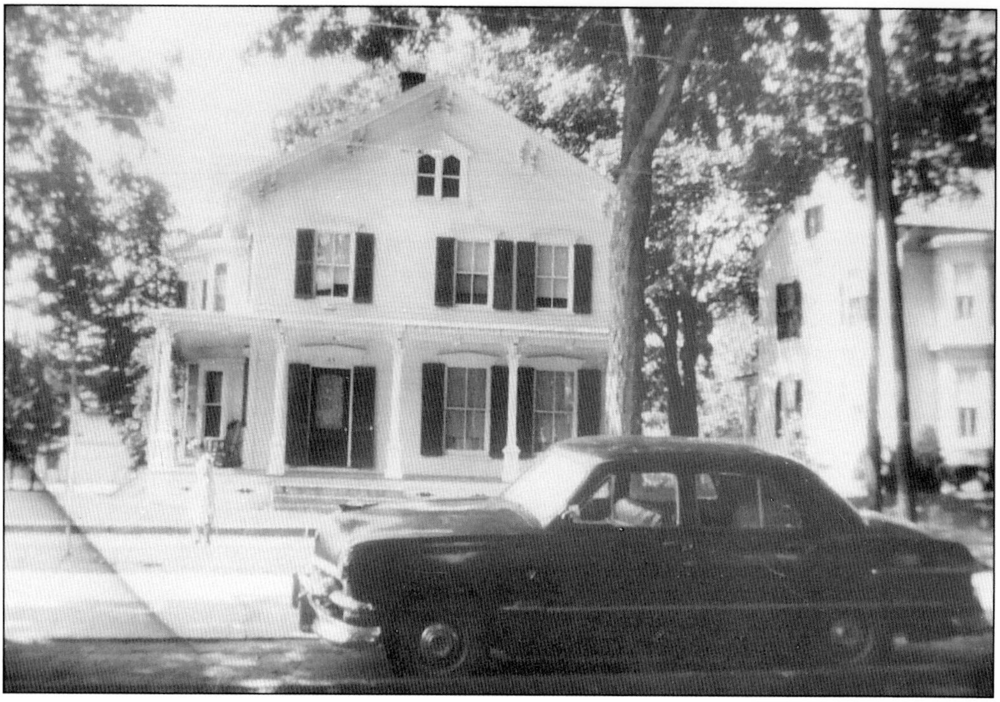

These two photographs are of house that was once owned by Walter Bostwick and later owned by the Nettleton family. The view above shows the front entrance of the house. The side view, below, was taken just before the house was torn down in 1959.

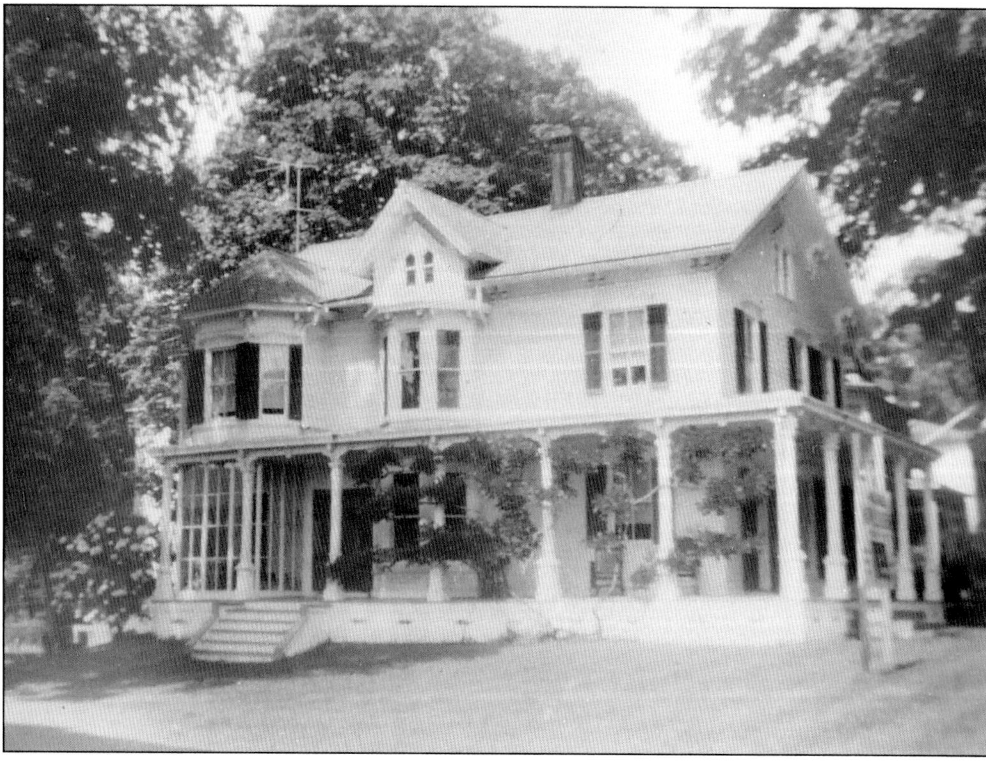

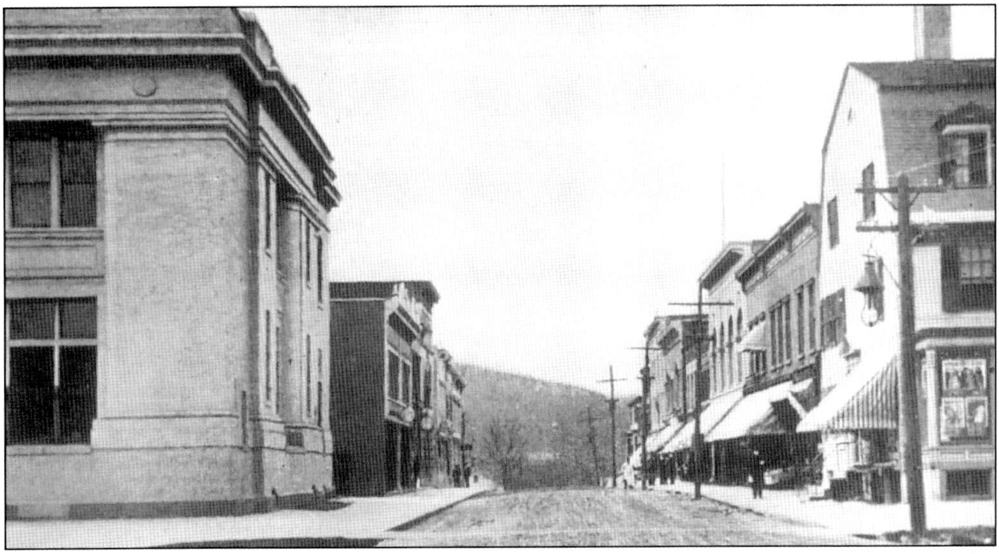

This 1910 picture shows Bank Street, looking west. The Slone Pharmacy is to the right on the corner. Notice the streetlights.

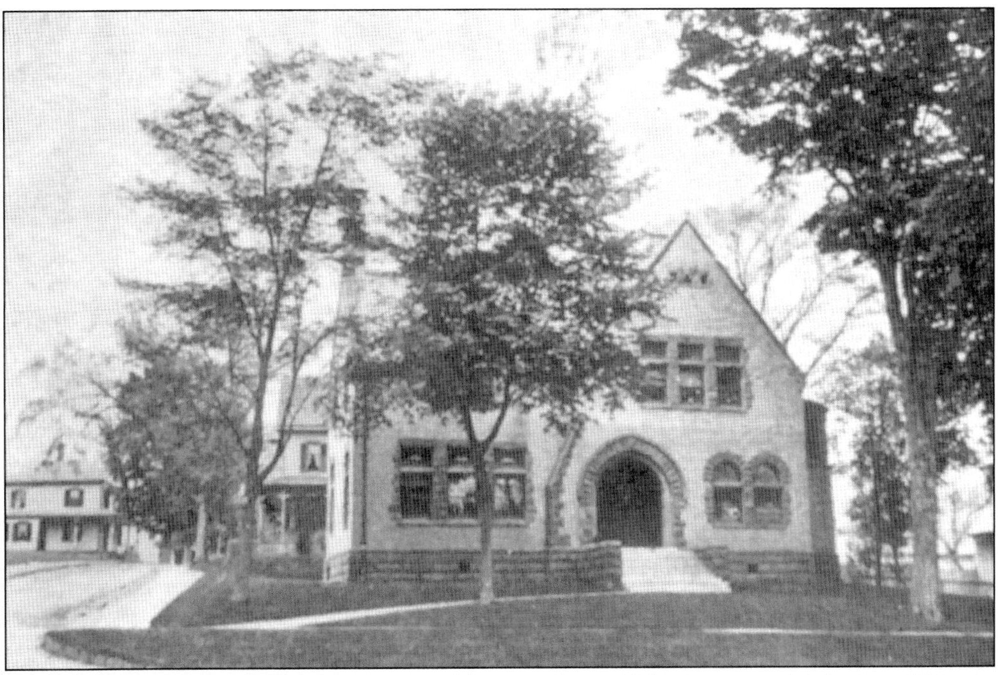

This is the present town library. The first library in New Milford was established in 1796. At that time, the collection of more than 355 volumes was housed in private homes. Later, the New Milford Library Association opened a library in the town hall. Later still, Egbert Marsh donated land and the association built the first public library. The Egbert Marsh Memorial Library, the small building on the left, was used until the library outgrew it. The building then became the home of Col. William J. Starr.

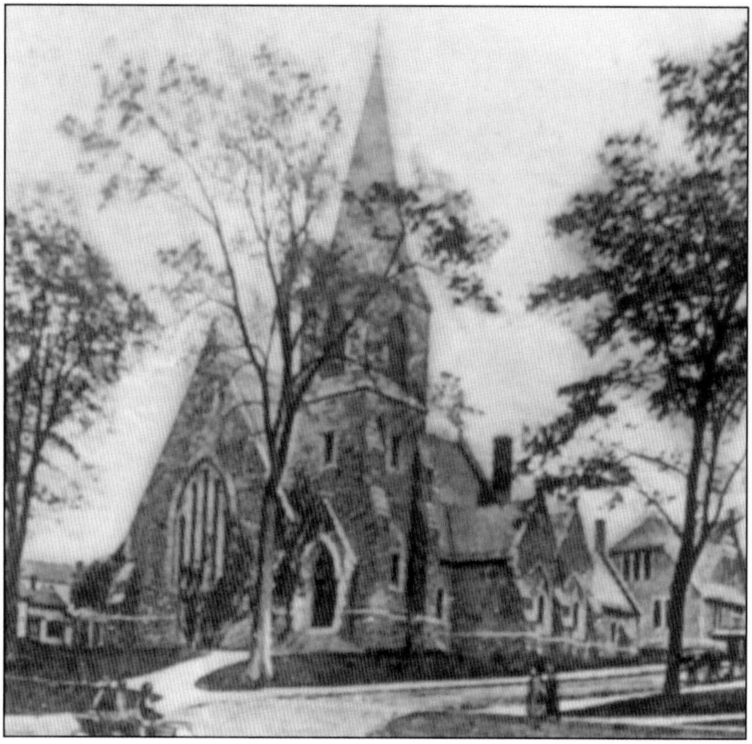

St. John's Episcopal Church was built in 1882. Gothic in style, the church was constructed of native stone and granite. The parish house was completed in 1959.

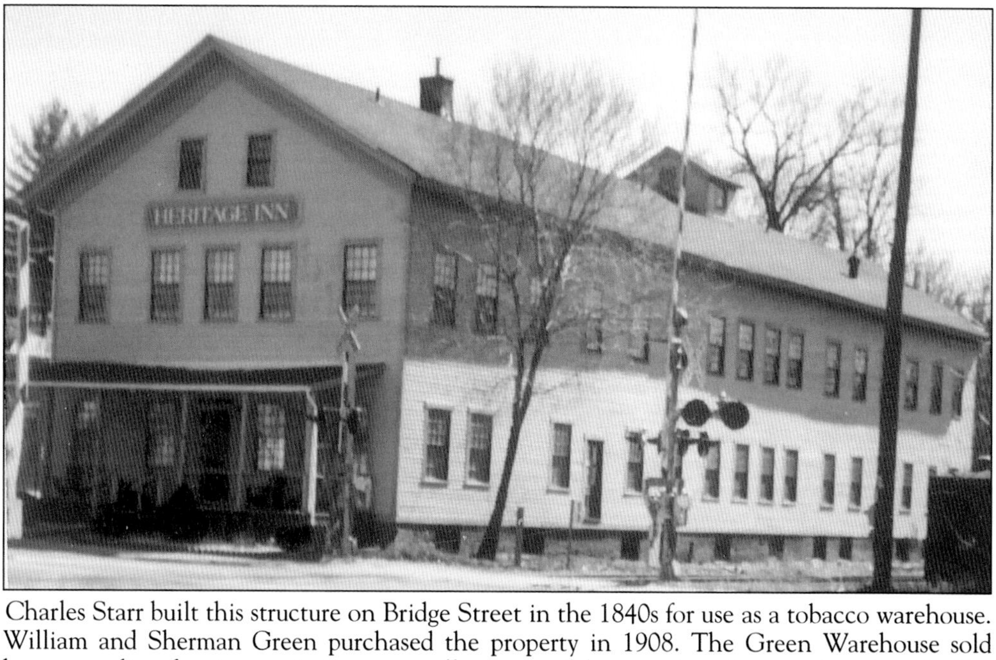

Charles Starr built this structure on Bridge Street in the 1840s for use as a tobacco warehouse. William and Sherman Green purchased the property in 1908. The Green Warehouse sold house supplies, farming equipment, as well as general lawn and garden needs and coal. The porch of the building was always graced with a white horse—a landmark. At the present time, the building is the Heritage Inn of Litchfield County.

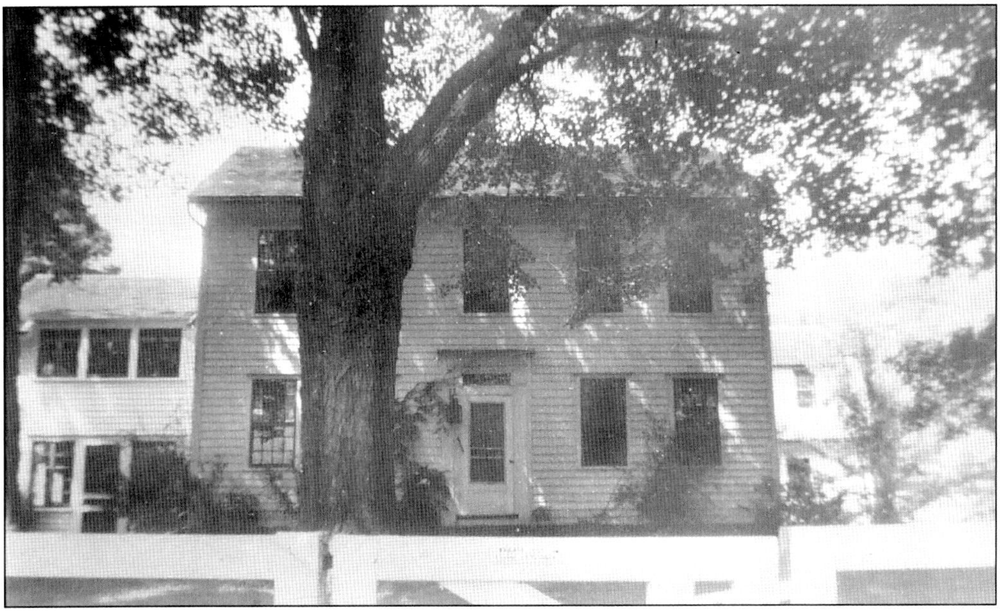

This house in Merryall was the homestead of Epenatus Platt, who is is buried in the upper Merryall Cemetery. The photograph was taken in the late 1800s.

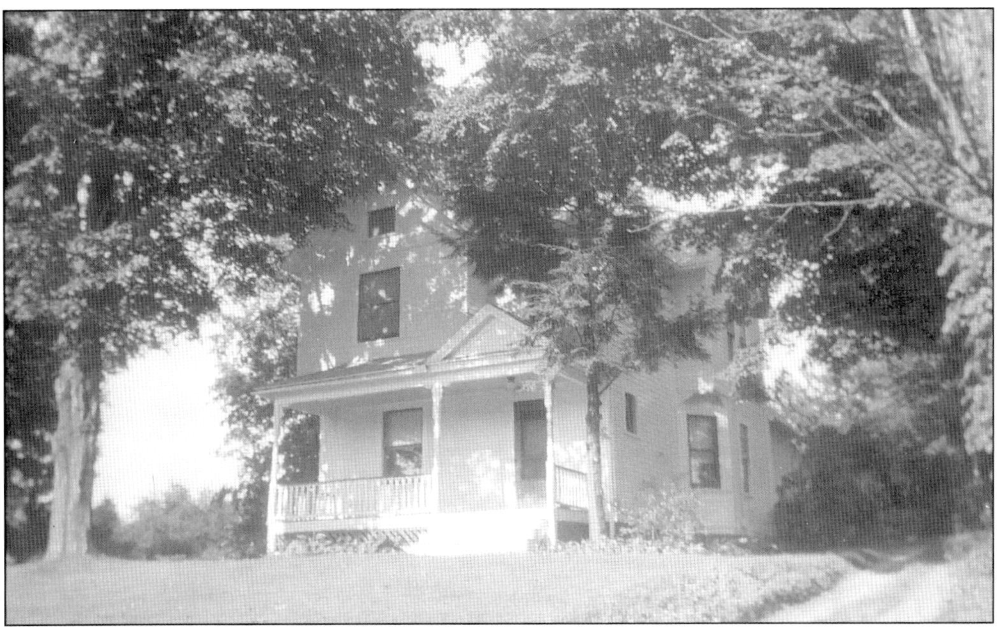

The Berry Homestead was located at 49 Park Lane Road (Route 202), on the corner of Park Lane West. It was sold to Bette-Lou Emmons in 1967 and then to Jack Gulliver in 1971. Later, it was destroyed by fire.

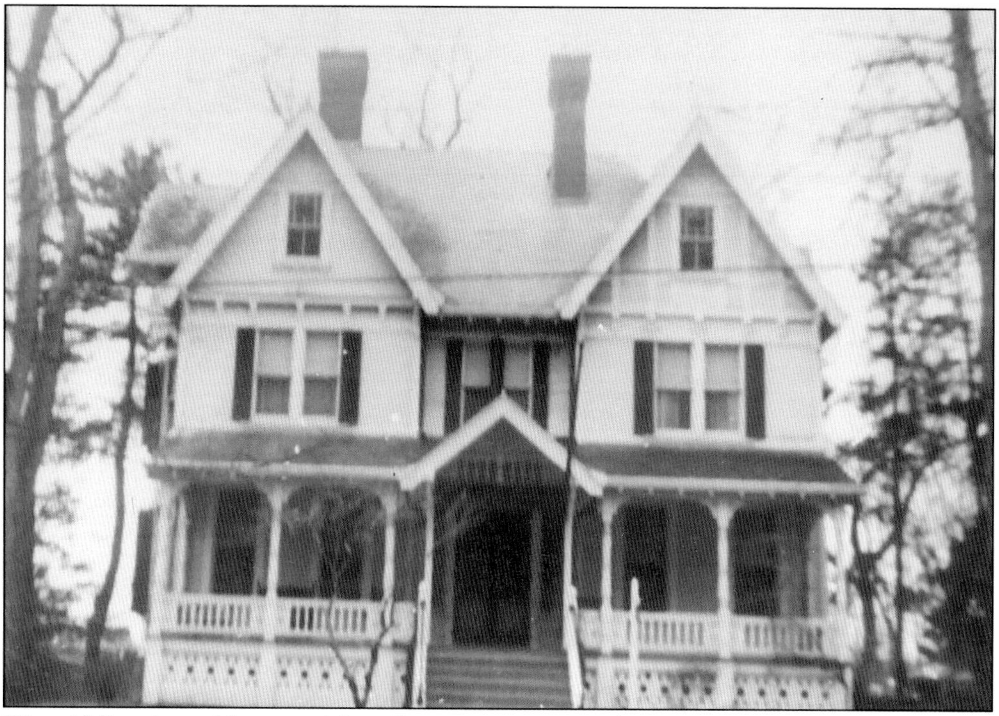

The old Boardman Home on Main Street was given to the New Milford Historical Society. This photograph was taken in 1959. The house was torn down in 1965 to make way for further land development.

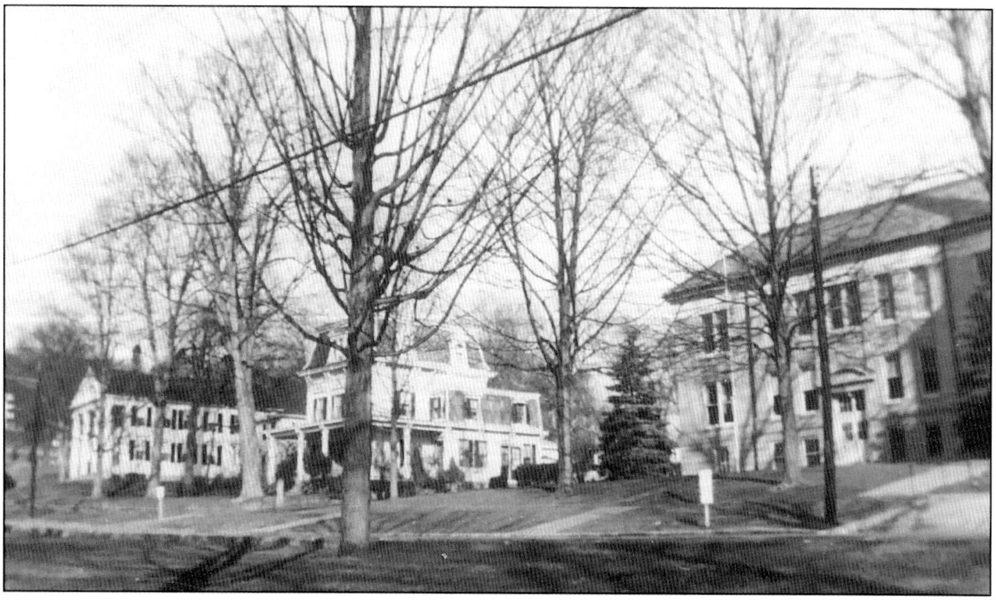

This photograph shows the upper east side of the green. The brick building is the first high school in New Milford. The second building is the Hine House, built *c.* 1843, which is now the private home and offices of attorneys John and Suzanne Powers. The third house belonged to Dr. George Taylor and had an unclear history. It is currently the private law office of Moots, Pellegrini, Spillane, & Mannion.

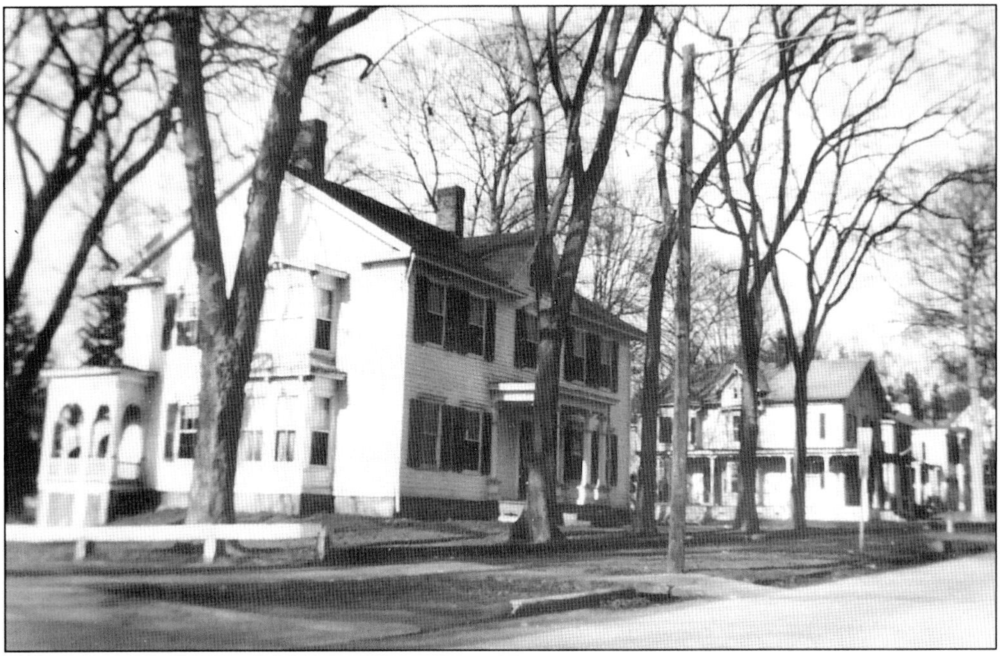

This is the south view of Solomon Edgar Bostwick's house. The house to the right is the home of Walter Bostwick.

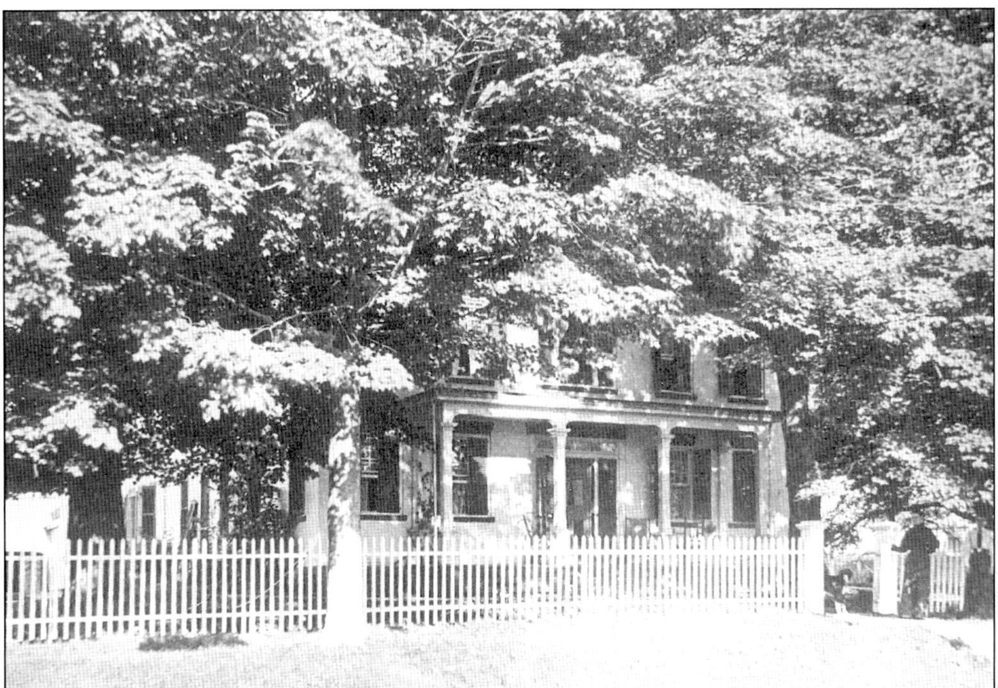

The Bostwick Homestead graces this land. The two women entering the gate are Mary Doty Bostwick and her daughter.

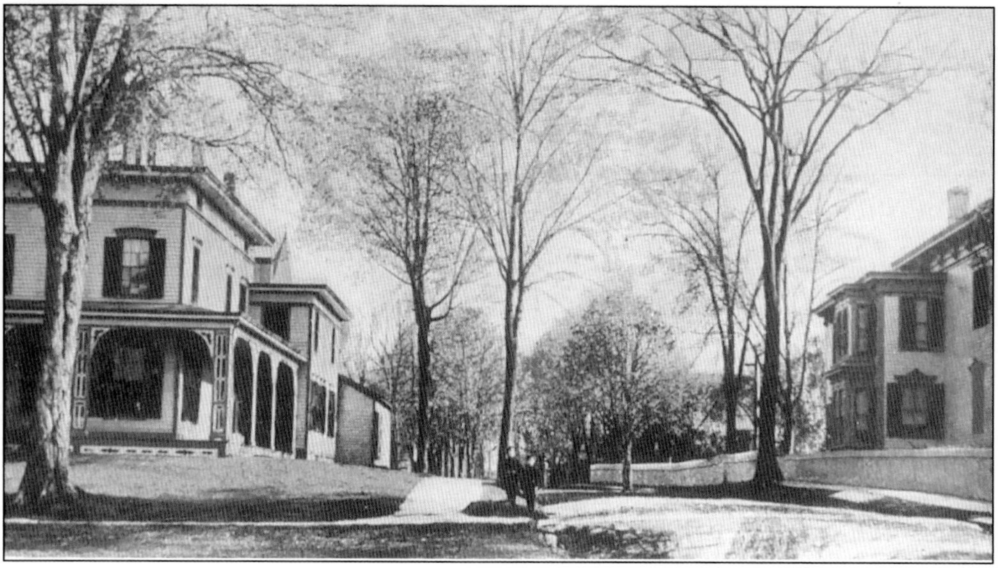

This 1908 photograph shows South Main Street. The Webster Bank currently owns the house on the left. The house on the right was torn down, and the Fleet Bank building now occupies that site.

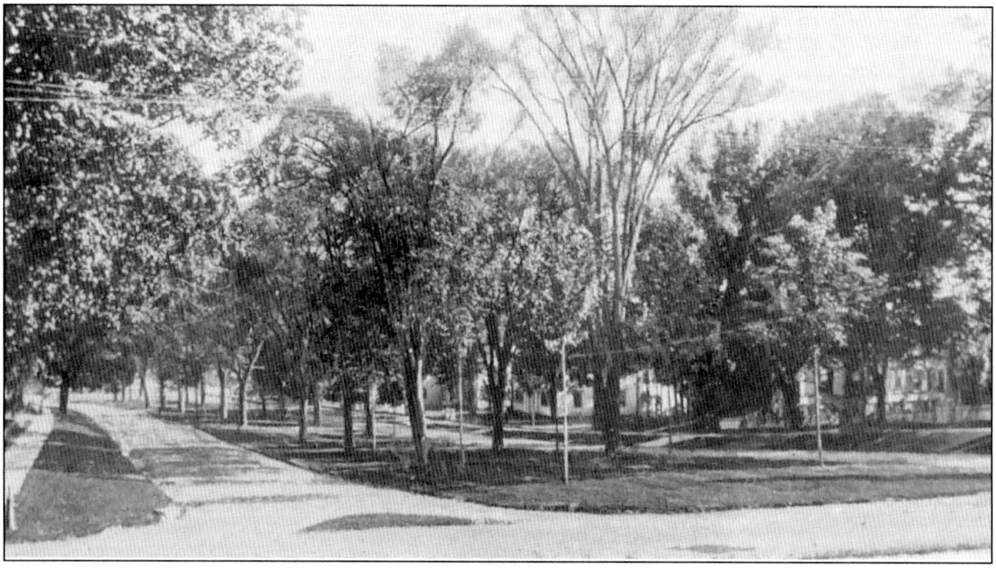

This photograph of Main Street was taken looking south in 1908. The New Milford Green is still one of the loveliest greens in the country.

Rev. Noah Porter, D.D., L.L.D, served as pastor of the New Milford Congregational Church from 1836 to 1843. In later years, he became the president of Yale College, a position that he held from 1871 to 1886.

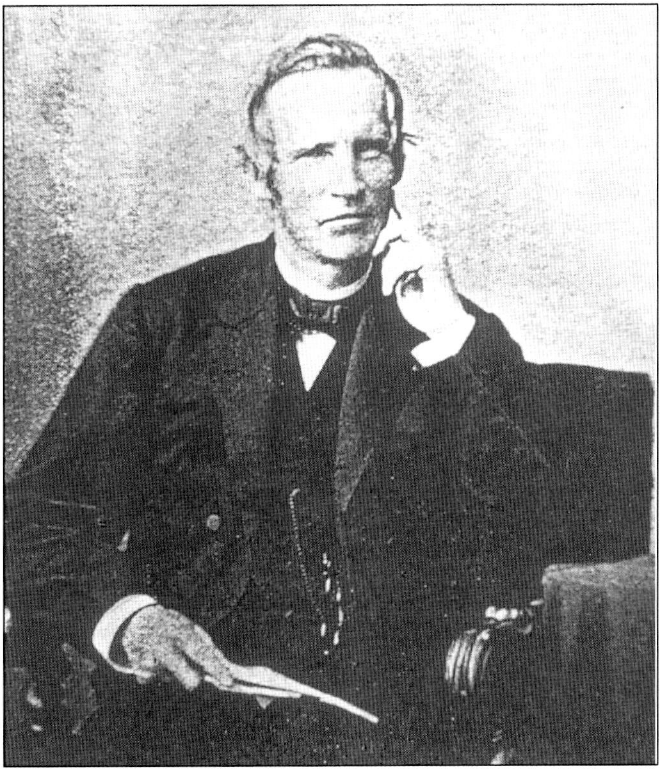

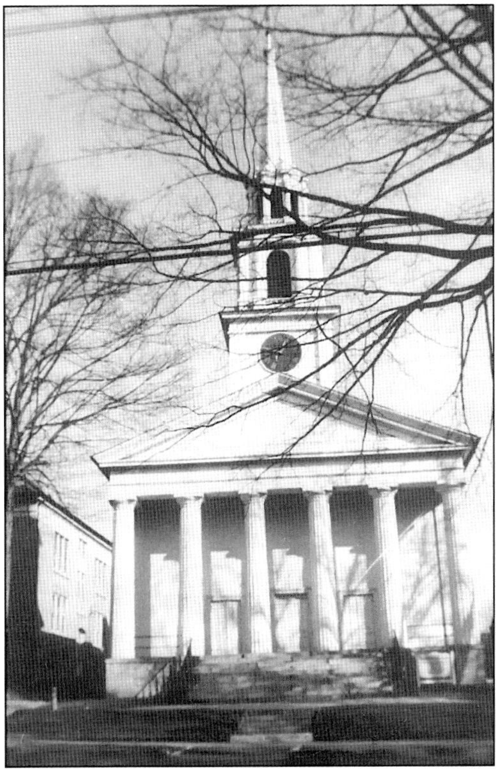

The Congregational church was organized on November 21, 1716, with 13 members. The first church was built between 1718 and 1719 and was opened in 1720. Drums called people to worship. A second church was built in 1754. Pictured is the present Federal-style First Congregational Church, which was built in 1833. The steeple of the church contains a 1905 Seth Thomas Clock made in Thomaston. The Jones Bell Company manufactured the steeple bell in 1880.

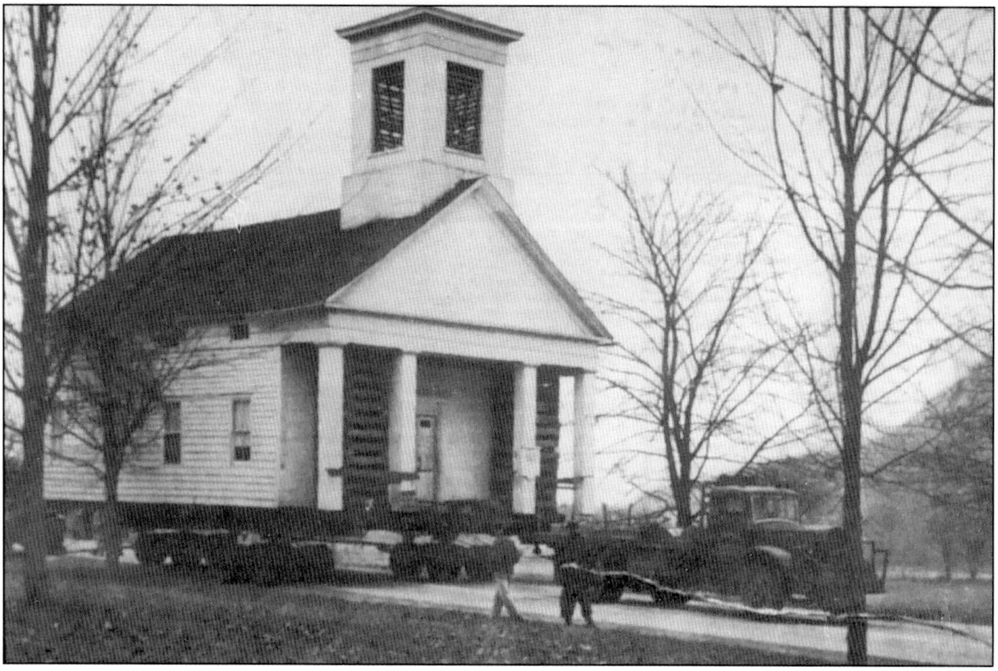

In the 1960s, the Old Northville Church was moved from its original site next to the post office down the road to a new location. The original building, the center of community life for many years, still stands; however, a new church was built at 9 Little Bear Hill.

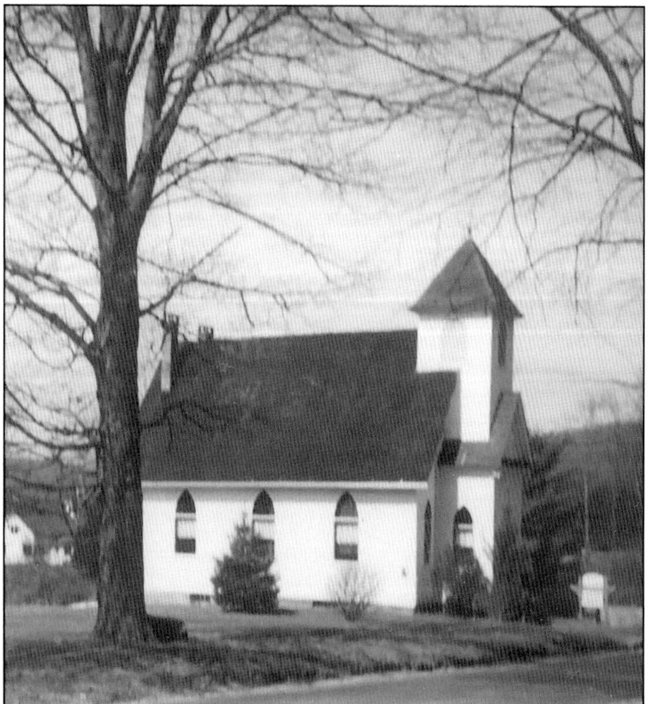

The Merryall Chapel, built December 18, 1890, is one of the oldest churches in the area. It still stands on this country road in Merryall.

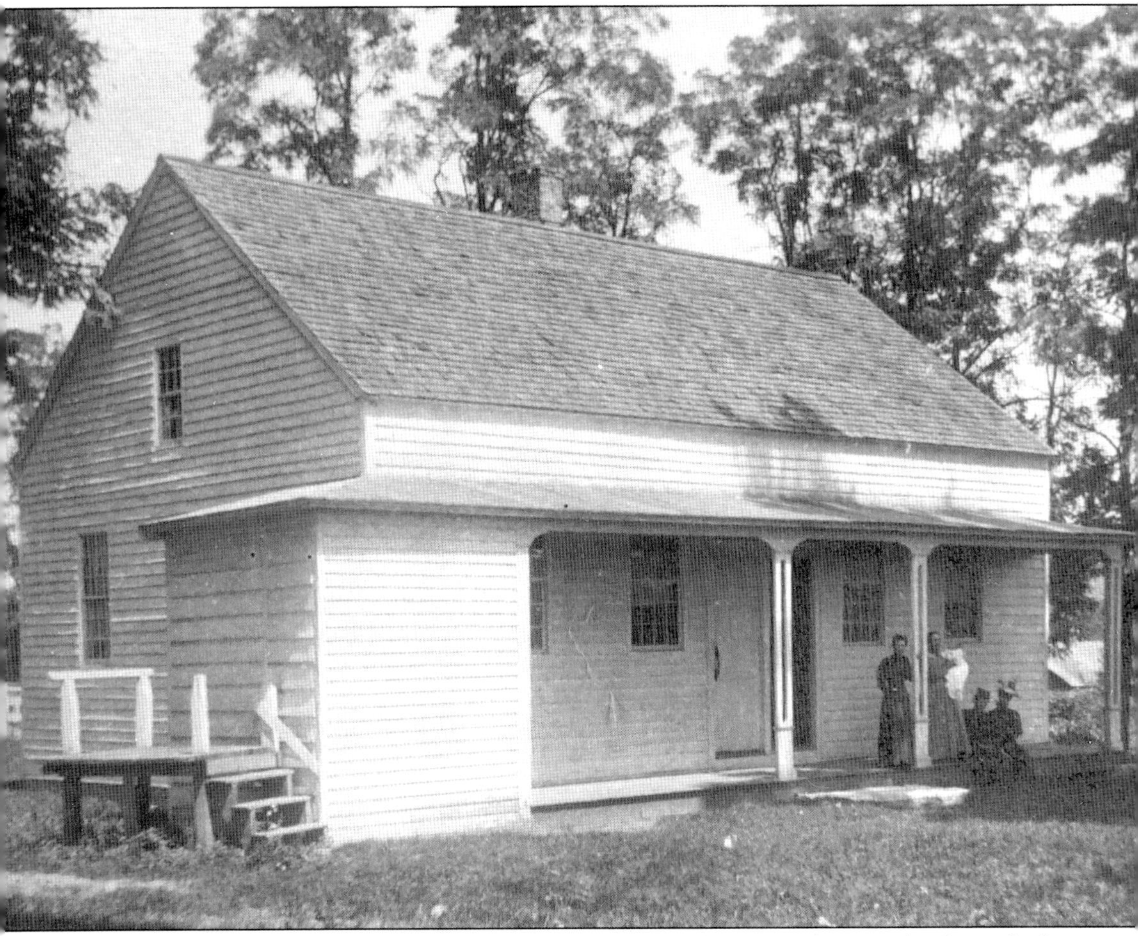

In the early 1700s, Nicolas Wanzer deeded land to the Quakers. It is the same land on which the old Quaker Meeting House now stands, with the burial grounds adjoining. The old Quaker House was moved here from the Pickett district.

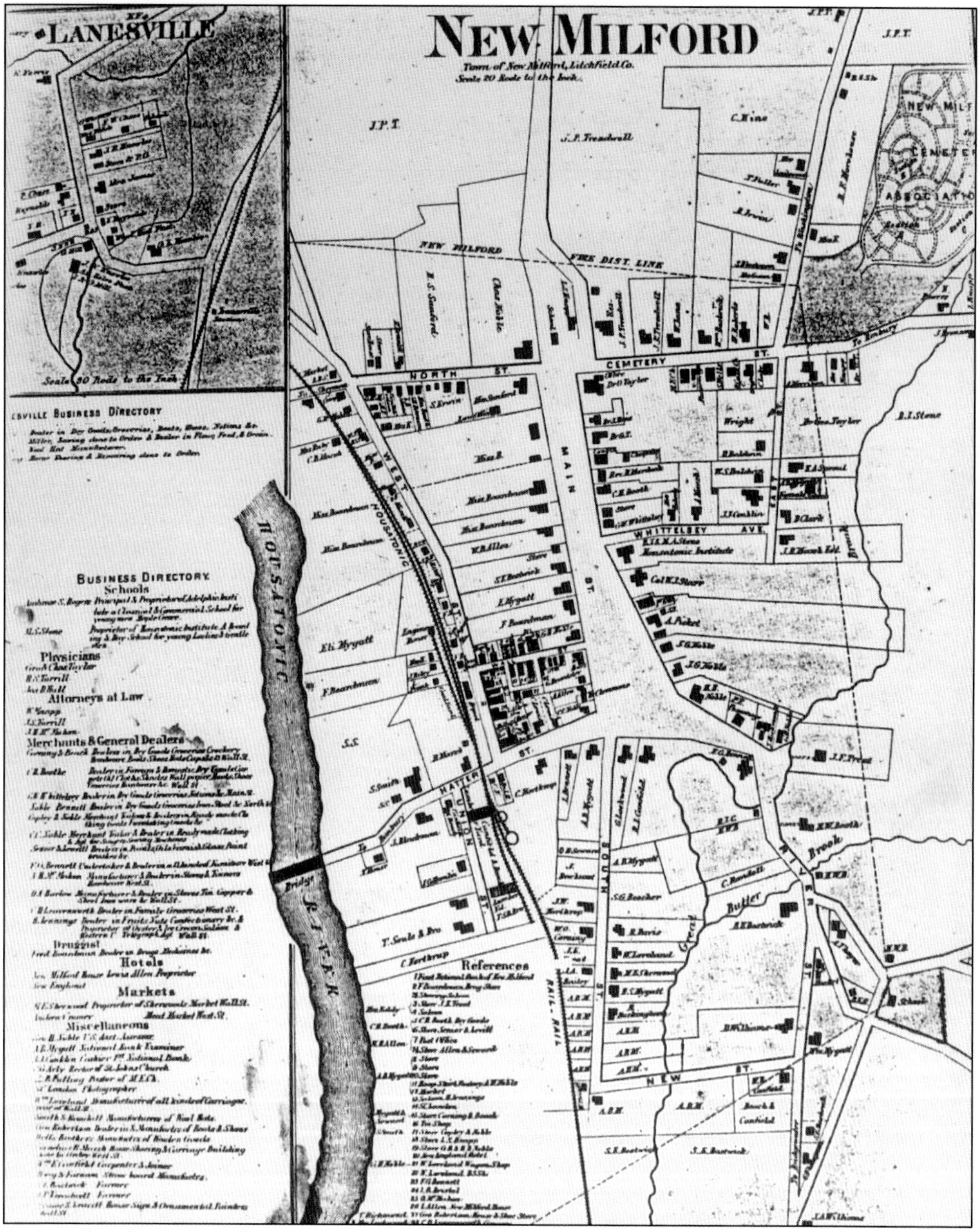

Pictured is the Lanesville area of New Milford, the location of the old Quaker Church.

Ada Ducksworth, who came to the United States from England, married Alfred C. Worley in the late 1800s.

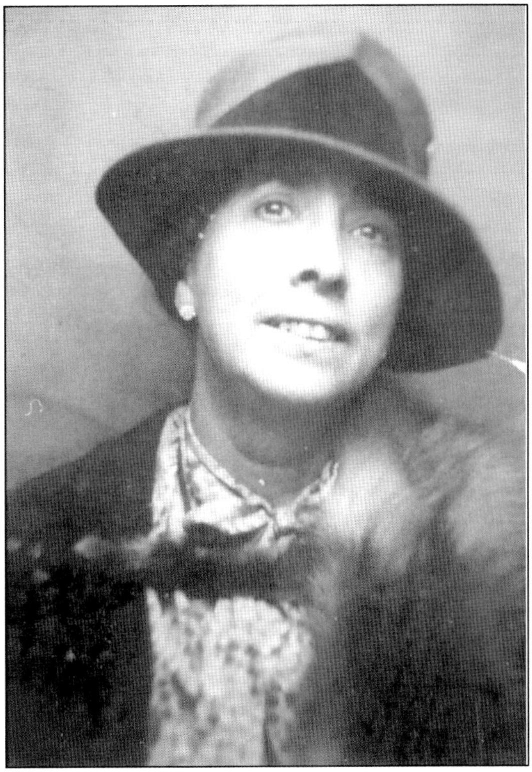

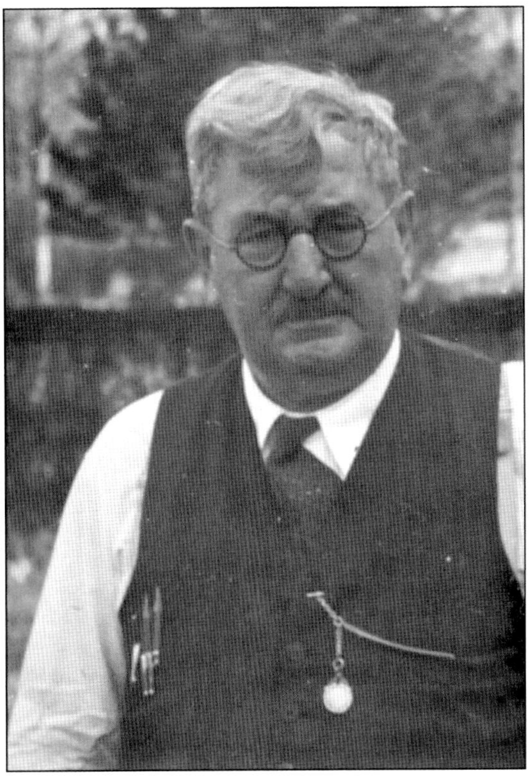

Alfred Worley, husband of Ada Ducksworth Worley, bought the *New Milford Gazette* and changed its name to the *New Milford Times*. The Worleys had four children: George, Harry, Philip, and Ethel. For 50 years, Harry "Sandy" Worley wrote the *Times* column "Sandy Sez."

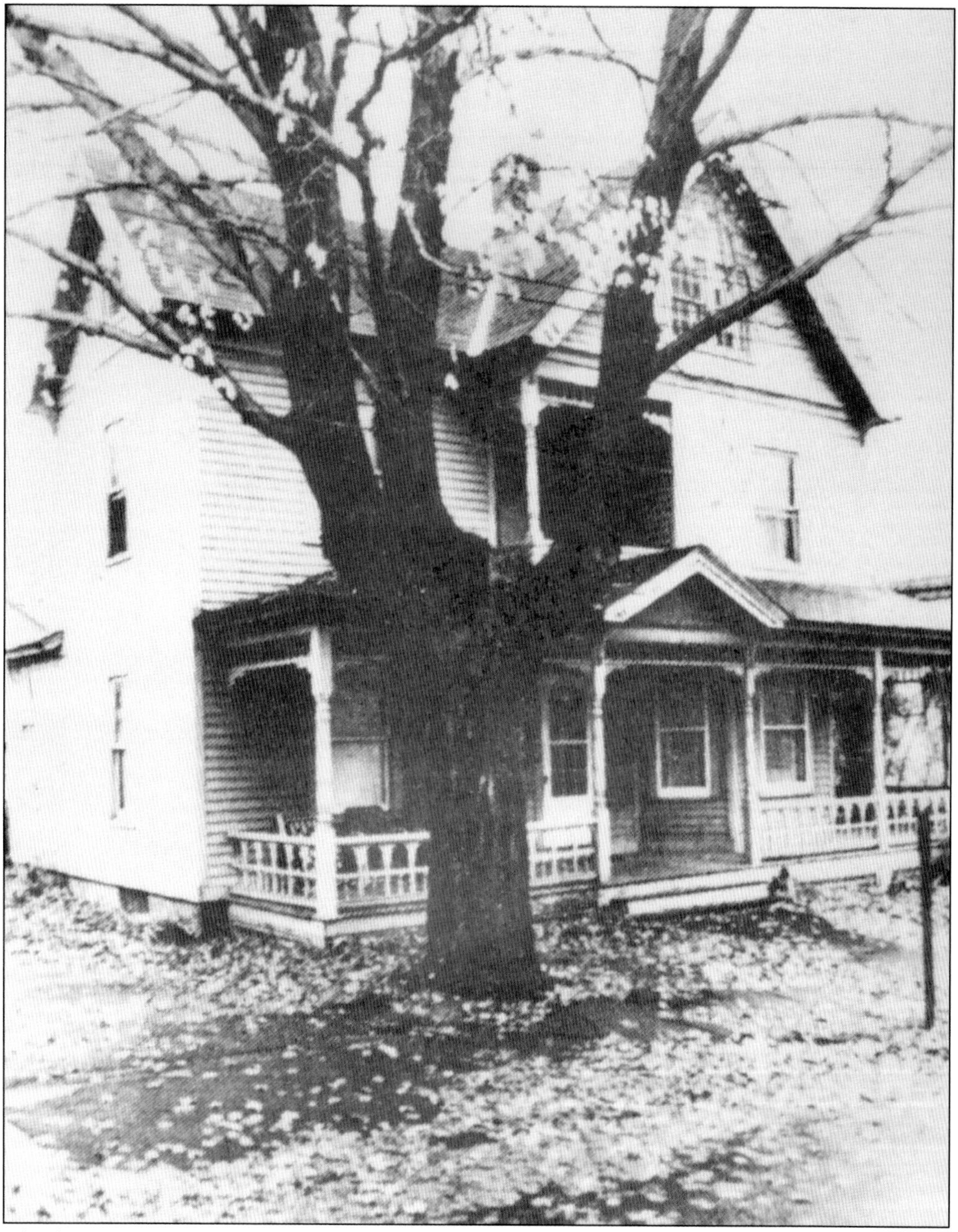

The first New Milford Hospital was on Whittlesey Avenue. It consisted of a 10-bed institution in a house that was owned by a Mrs. Robert P. Strong. When the hospital moved to larger quarters on Elm Street, Dr. Ruppert Day purchased the property on Whittlesey Avenue for his home and lived there for 46 years.

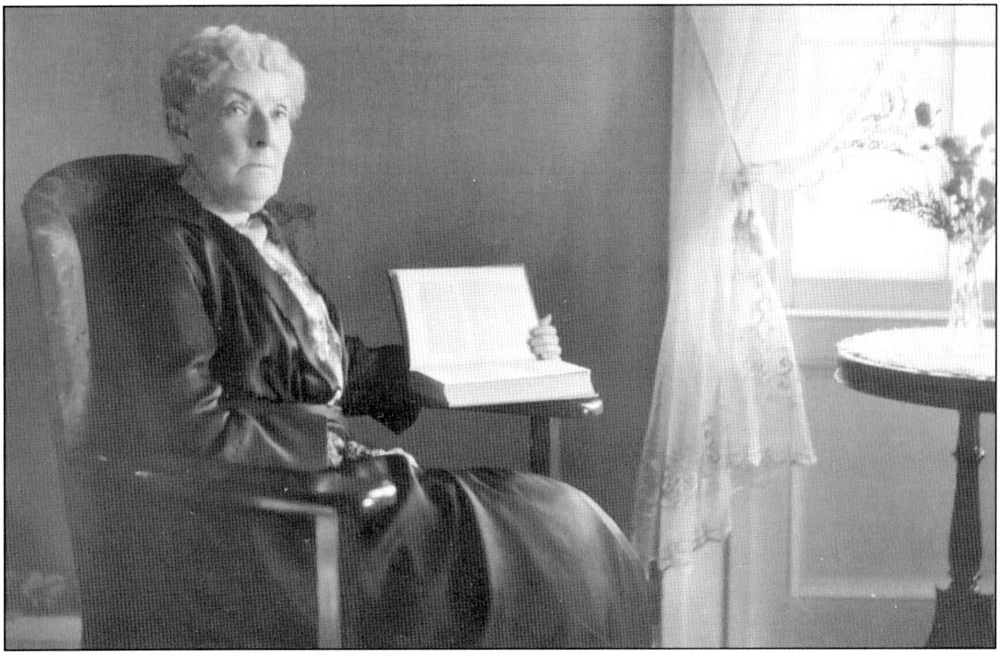

In 1924, Lile Bostwick donated her home on Elm Street to the New Milford Hospital. The hospital had the capacity to handle 24 patients.

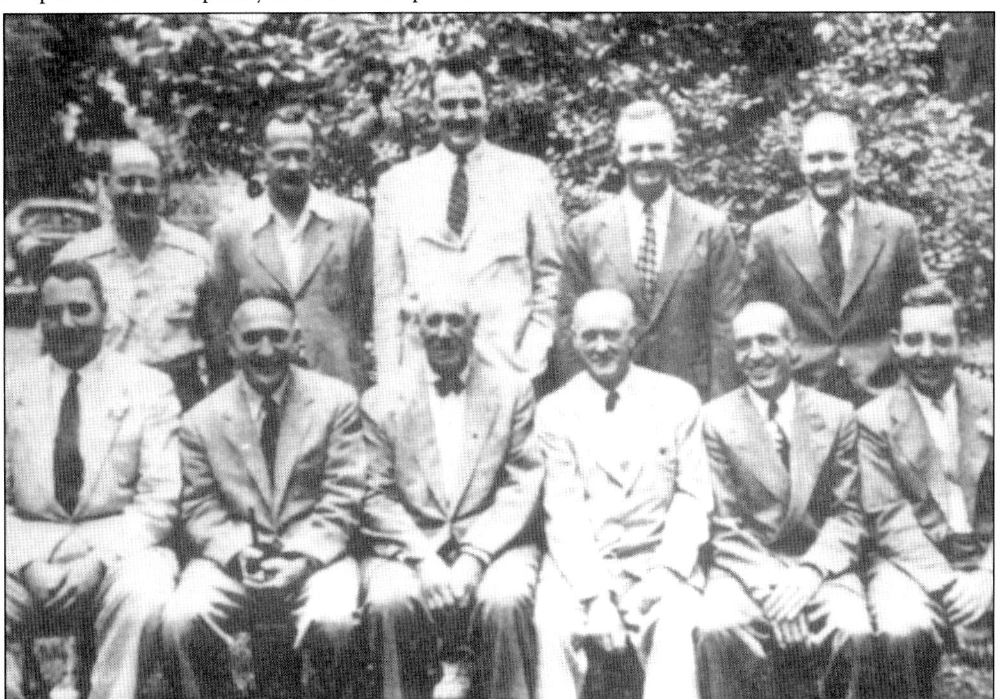

The medical staff of the New Milford Hospital included, from left to right, the following:(front row) Dr. C. George Lataif, Dr. ? Opper, Dr. Howard G. Stevens, Dr. Robert S. Day, Dr. Richard Ireland, and Dr. William Dobbs; (back row) Dr. Warren G. Koehler, Dr. John Simonds, Dr. ? Wolfe, Dr. Howard S. Morrow, and Dr. John Street.

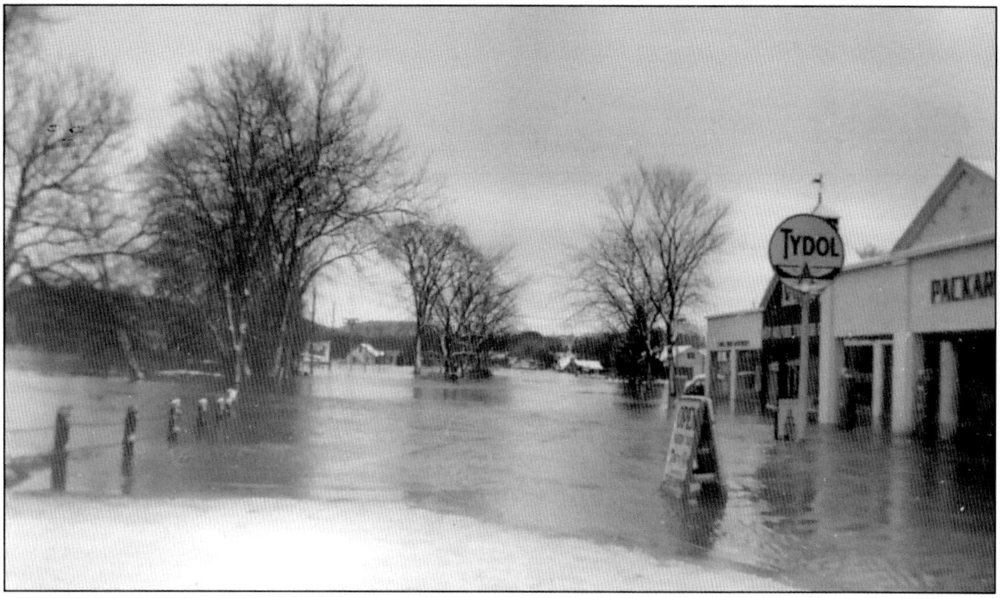

Looking south from the bridge along Route 7, this view shows the 1948 flood of the Housatonic River.

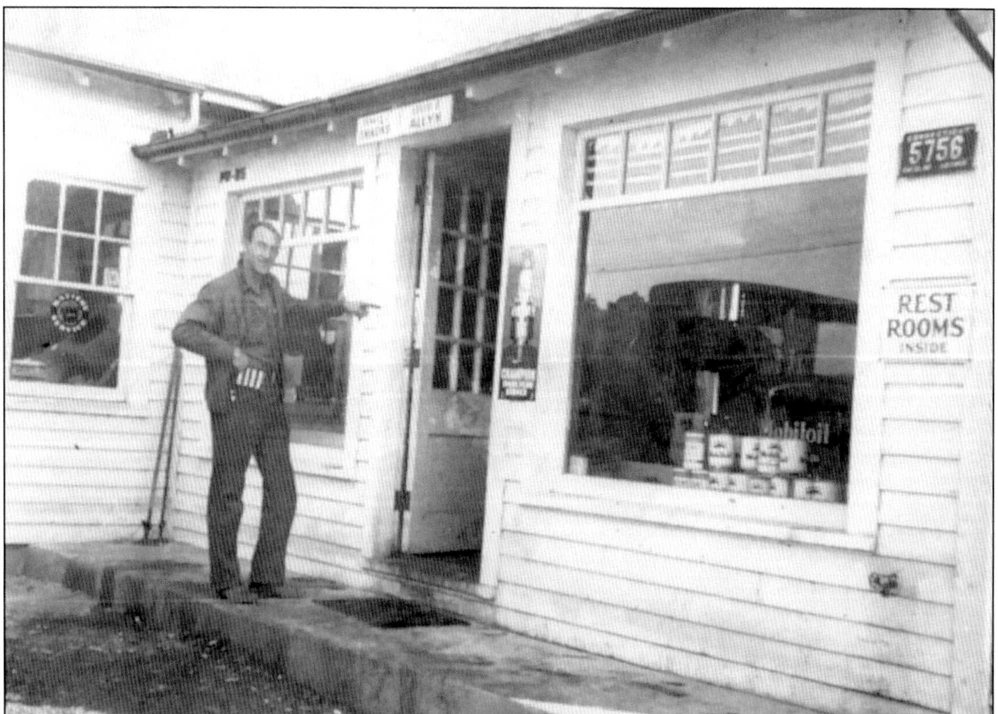

An earlier flood of the Housatonic River occurred in 1936. Don Emmons indicates the high-water mark outside the Socony gas station.

New Milford Hospital cofounder Mrs. Robert P. Strong not only helped establish the town's first hospital but also served as its first treasurer for 46 years. She retired on October 25, 1967.

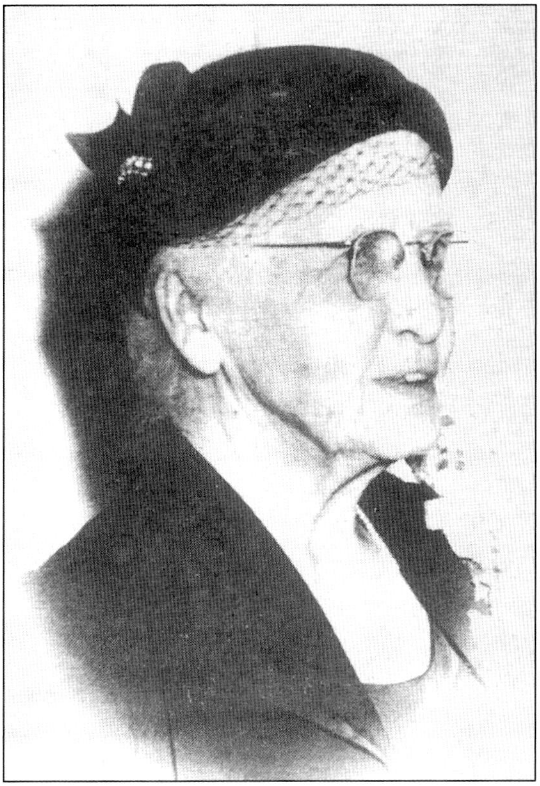

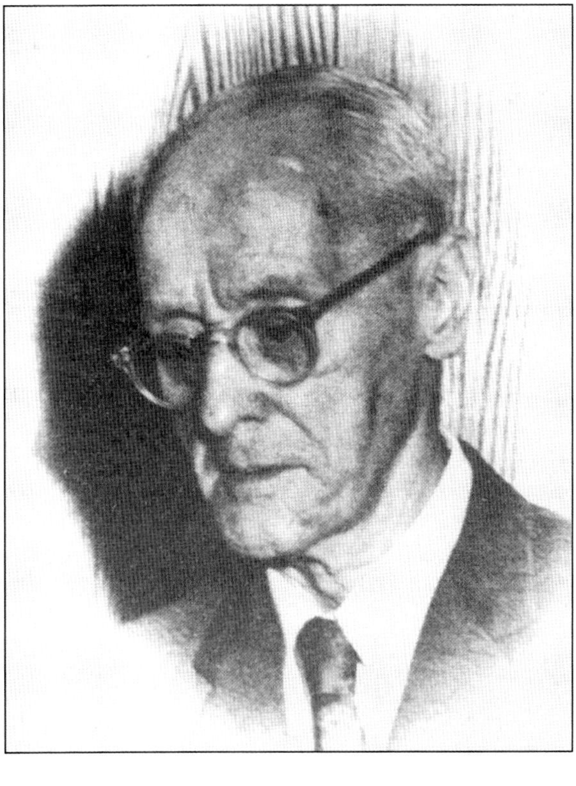

New Milford Hospital cofounder Robert S. Day, M.D., graduated from New York Medical College in 1906. After graduating he moved to Bridgewater, where he practiced for one year. In 1910, he came to New Milford and became the hospital's first surgeon.

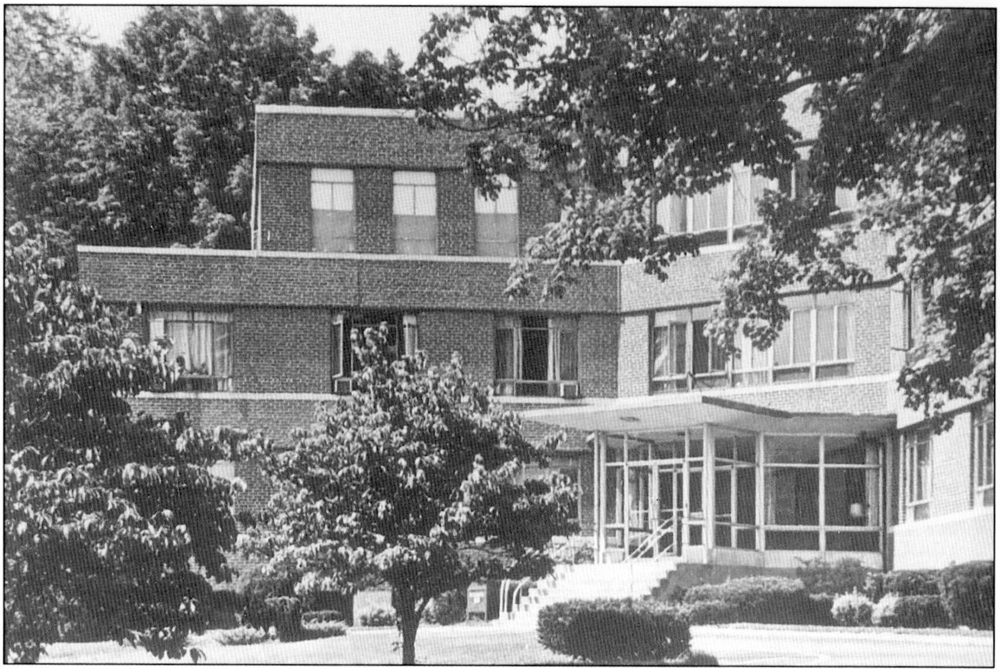

This photograph shows the present new New Milford Hospital, an affiliate of Columbia Presbyterian Medical Center. The hospital is located on 21 Elm Street Extension.

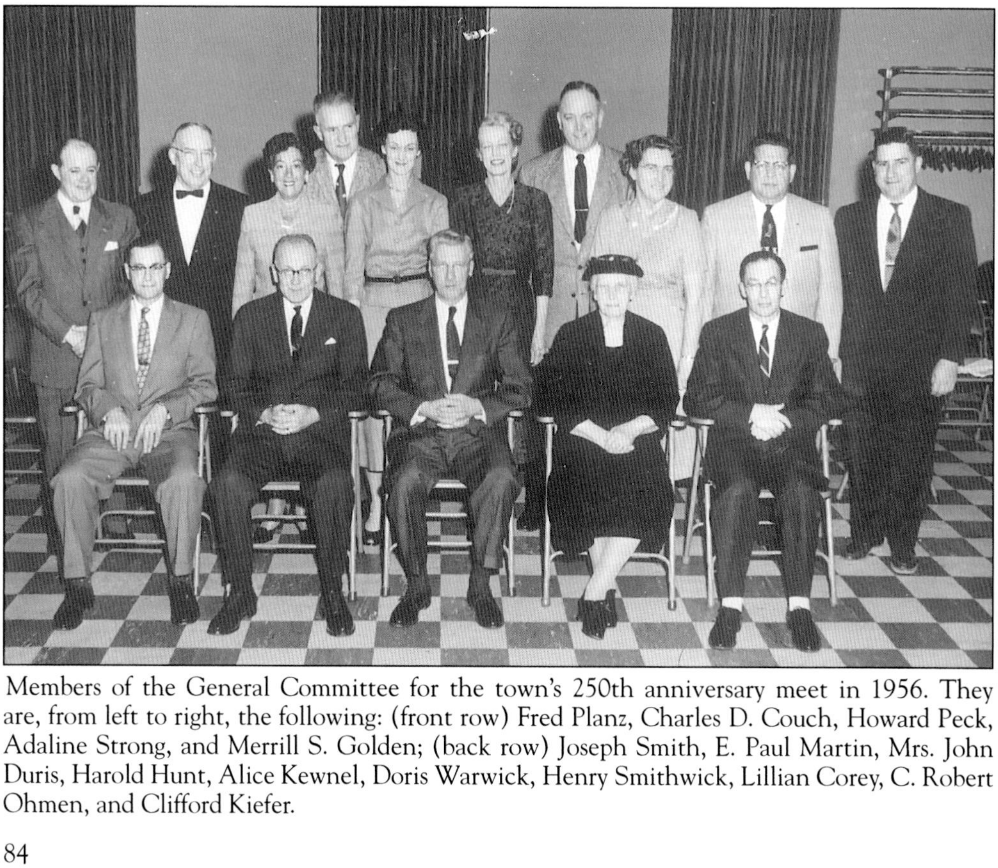

Members of the General Committee for the town's 250th anniversary meet in 1956. They are, from left to right, the following: (front row) Fred Planz, Charles D. Couch, Howard Peck, Adaline Strong, and Merrill S. Golden; (back row) Joseph Smith, E. Paul Martin, Mrs. John Duris, Harold Hunt, Alice Kewnel, Doris Warwick, Henry Smithwick, Lillian Corey, C. Robert Ohmen, and Clifford Kiefer.

Five

THE KING FAMILY

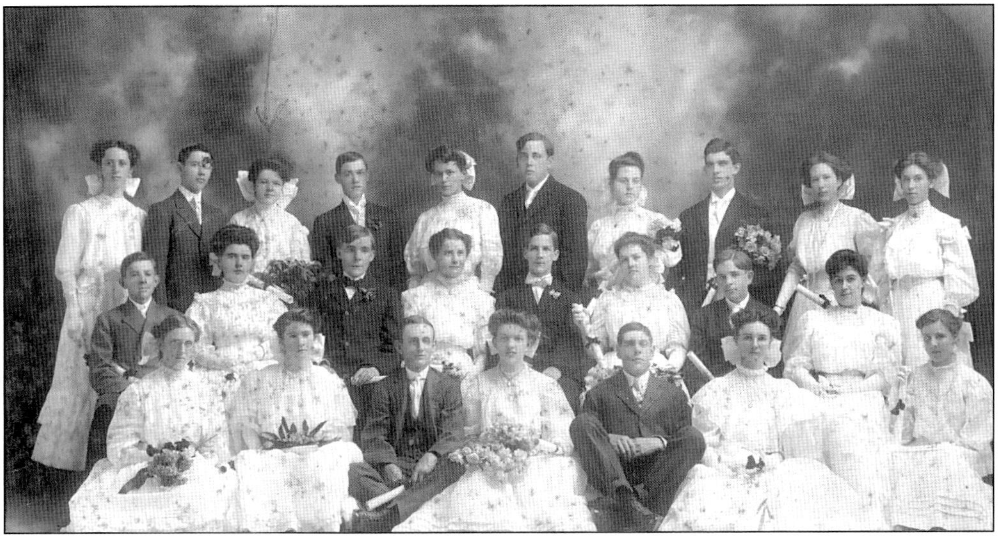

Taken during graduation exercises of the New Milford High School Class of 1907, this photograph shows Eugenia King, the only child of Dr. Frederick King and his wife, Sarah Bostwick King. Eugenia King is in the back row, third from the left. She was born on January 25, 1890, with a heart condition that resulted in her death at the age of 21 years.

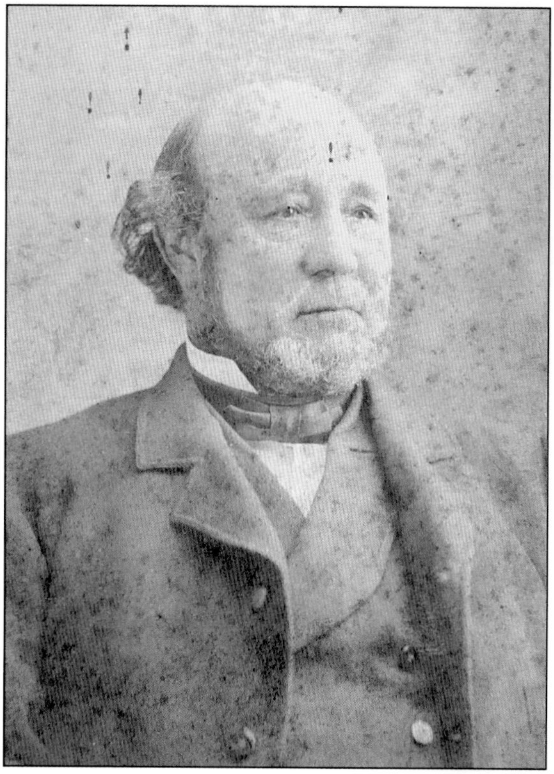

This is a mid-1800s photograph of the father of Dr. Frederick S. King.

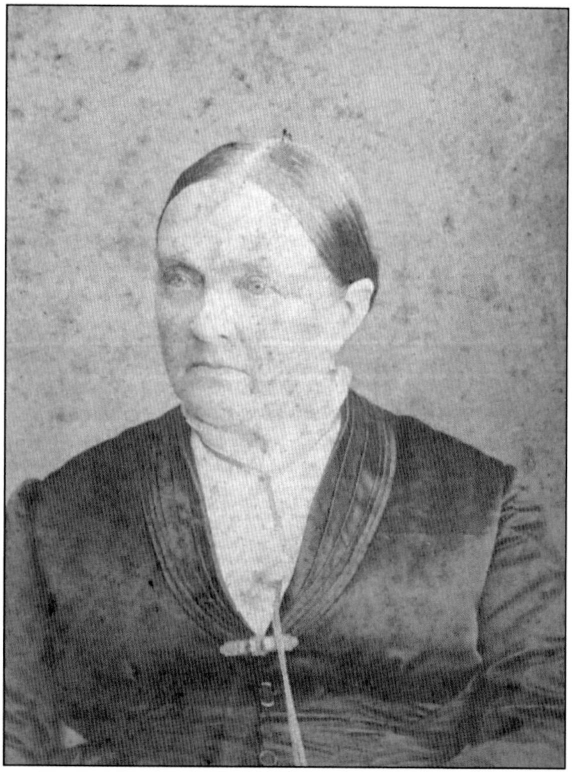

Pictured in the mid-1800s is the mother of Dr. Frederick S. King.

This 1895 photograph shows Eugenia King, age 5, with her father and mother, Dr. Frederick King and Sarah Bostwick King.

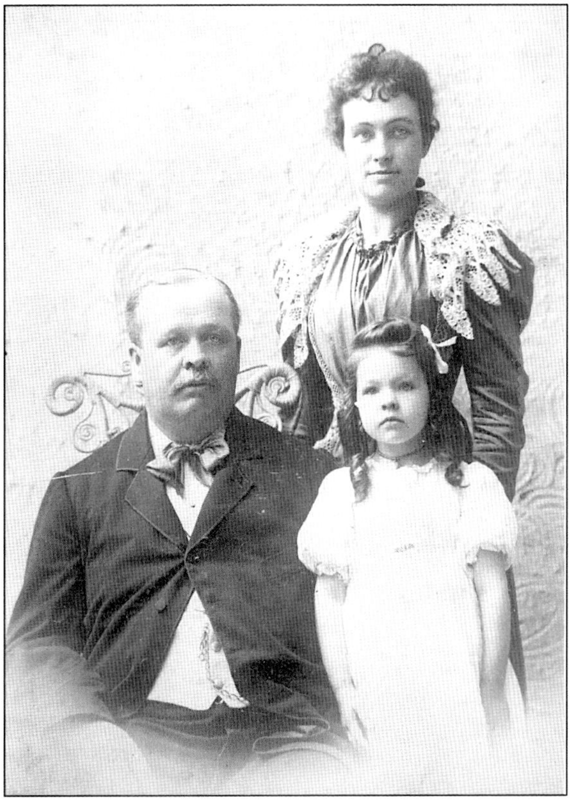

This picture was taken in Dr. Frederick King's medical office on Bridge Street in 1899. It shows Dr. Frederick King, his wife, Sarah Bostwick King, and their daughter, Eugenia King.

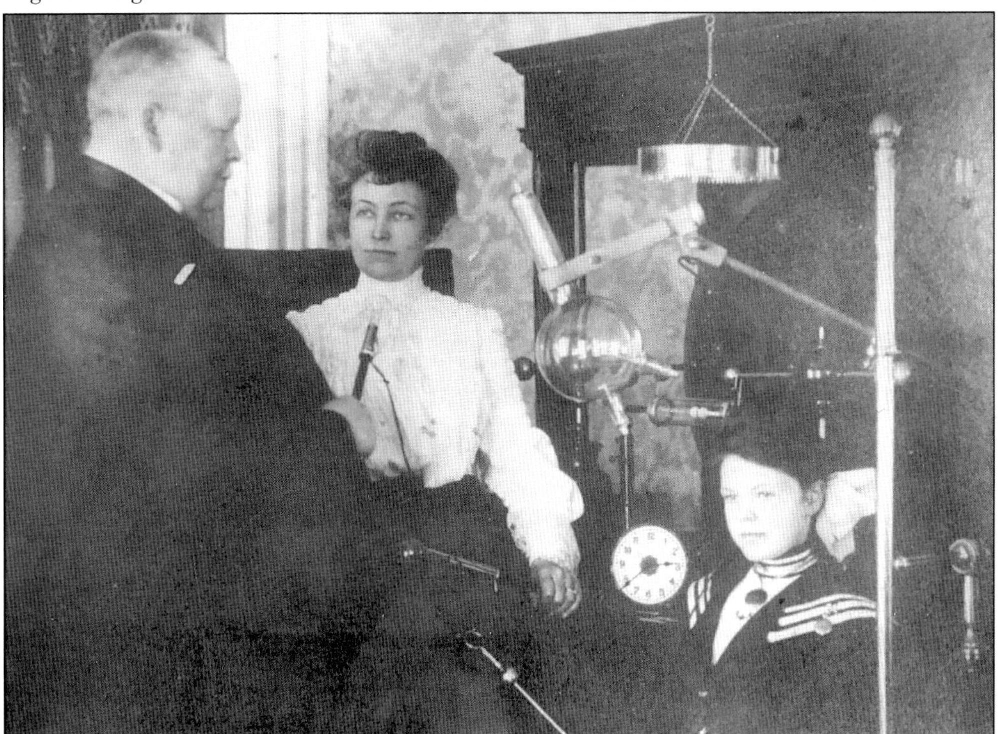

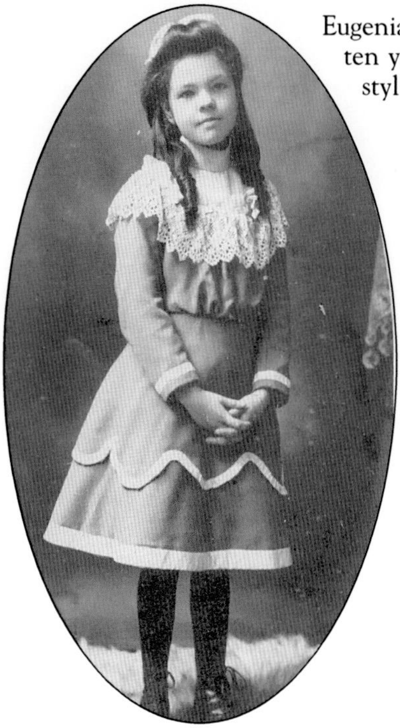

Eugenia King was born on September 17, 1891. She was about ten years of age when this photograph was taken. Notice her stylish dress.

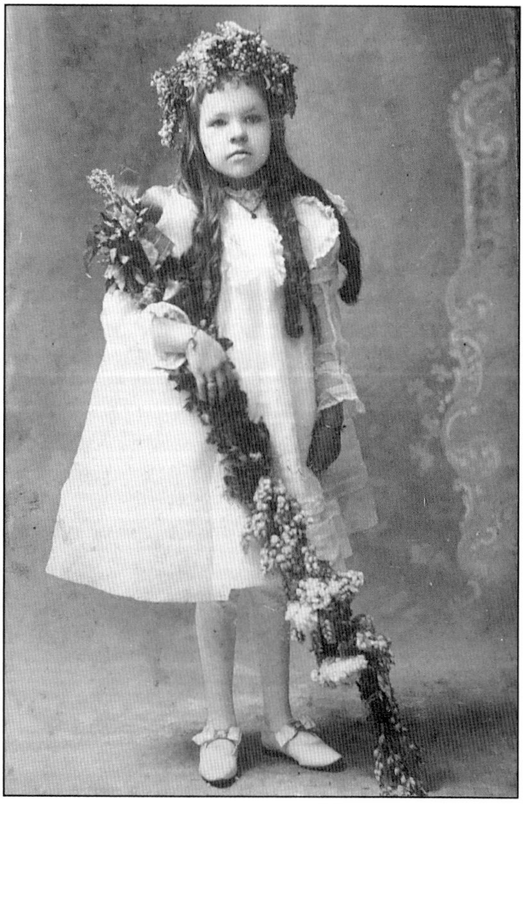

Eugenia King participated in a May Day celebration in New Milford when she was nine years old. The lovely dress, jewelry, and flowers suited her perfectly.

Pictured in 1912 is Eugenia King, the daughter of Dr. Frederick and Sarah King. Eugenia King died later that year, at age 21.

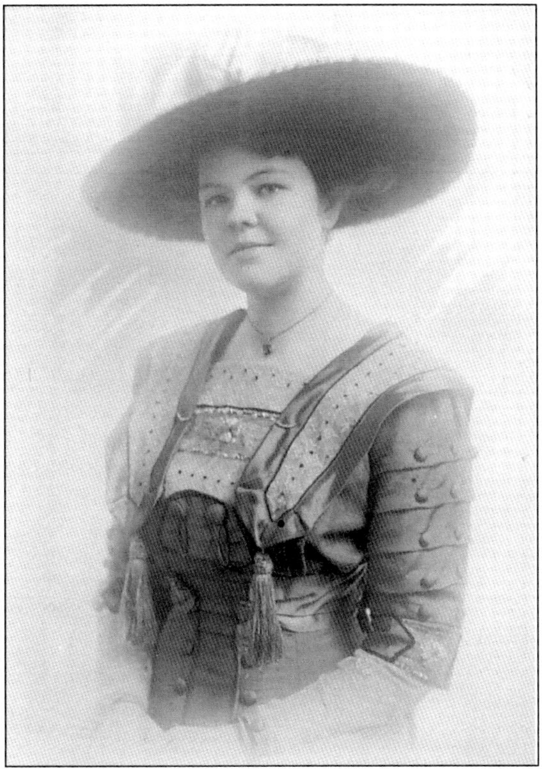

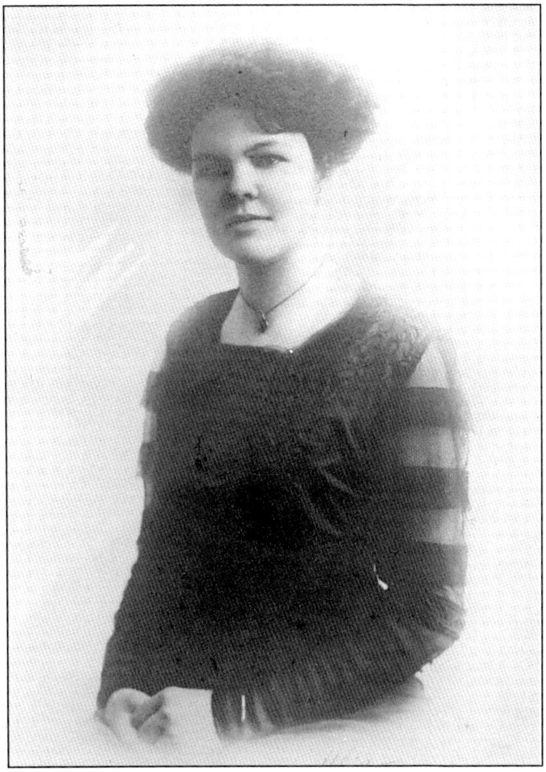

Dr. and Mrs. Frederick King gave the baptismal font at the New Milford Congregational Church in memory of their daughter, Eugenia King, shown at age 21.

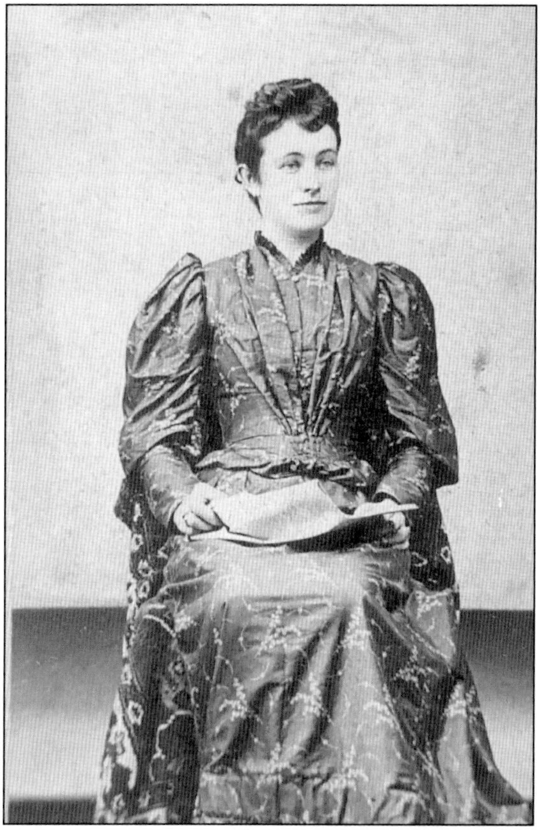

Sarah Bostwick King was born in New Milford. She married Dr. Frederick King in 1886 and gave birth to Eugenia King in 1890. A resident of Bridge Street, she died on April 5, 1937.

This picture of the King family was taken at the King home on Bridge Street in 1899. Eugenia King is standing on the flower box. Behind her are her father, Dr. Frederick King, and her mother, Sarah Bostwick King.

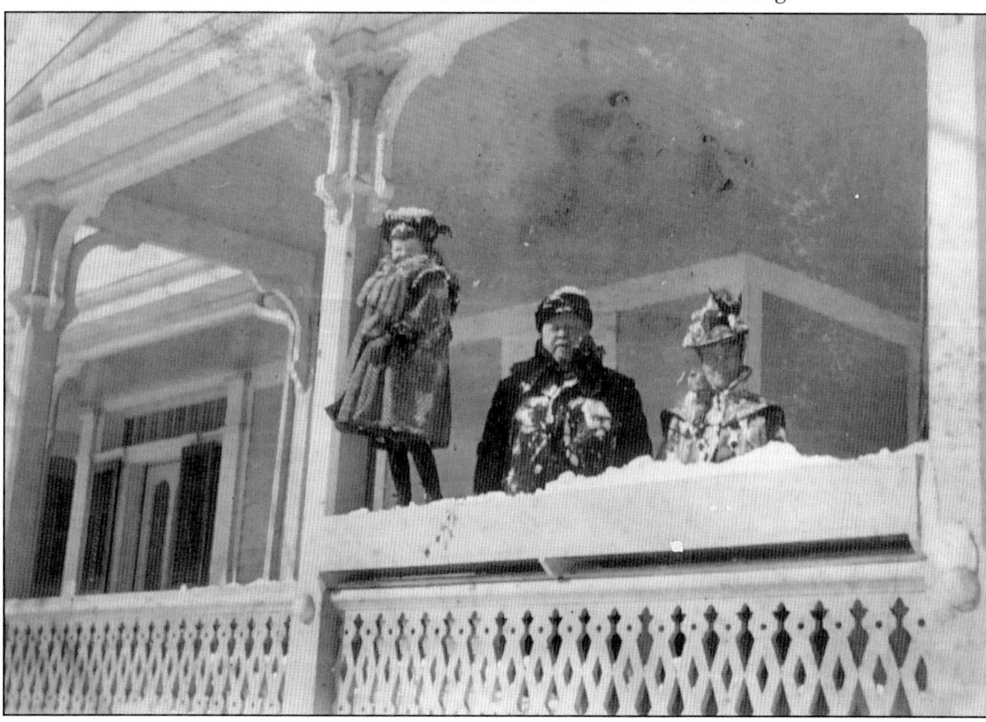

Six

FARMING

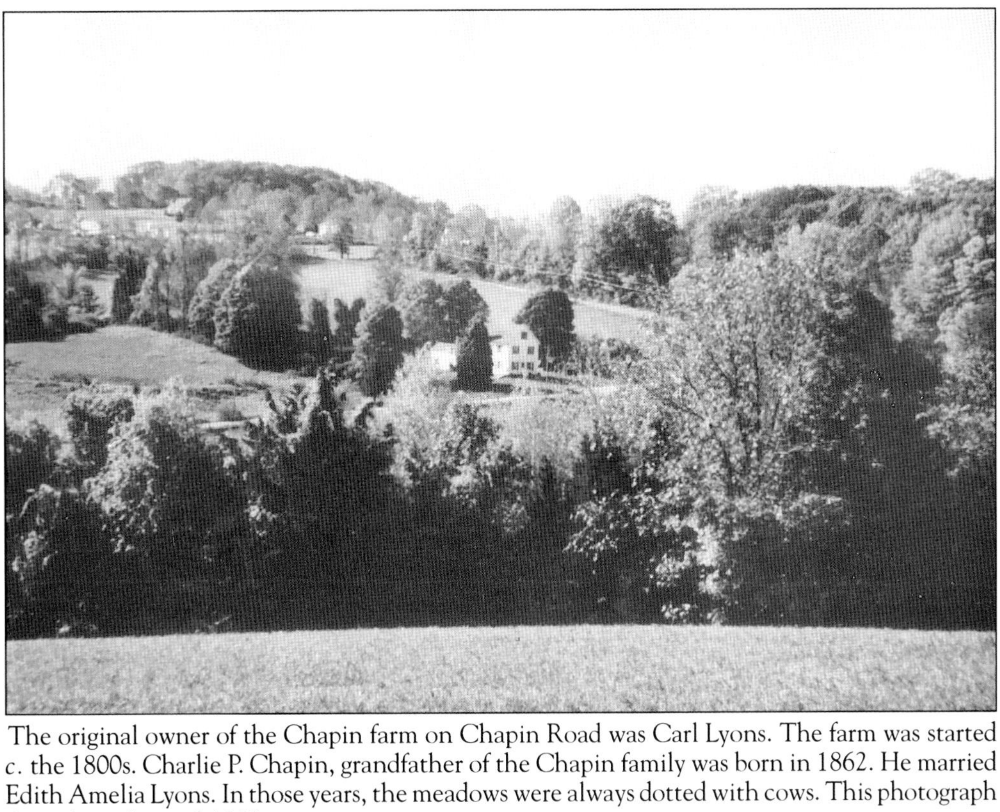

The original owner of the Chapin farm on Chapin Road was Carl Lyons. The farm was started *c.* the 1800s. Charlie P. Chapin, grandfather of the Chapin family was born in 1862. He married Edith Amelia Lyons. In those years, the meadows were always dotted with cows. This photograph dates from the mid-1800s.

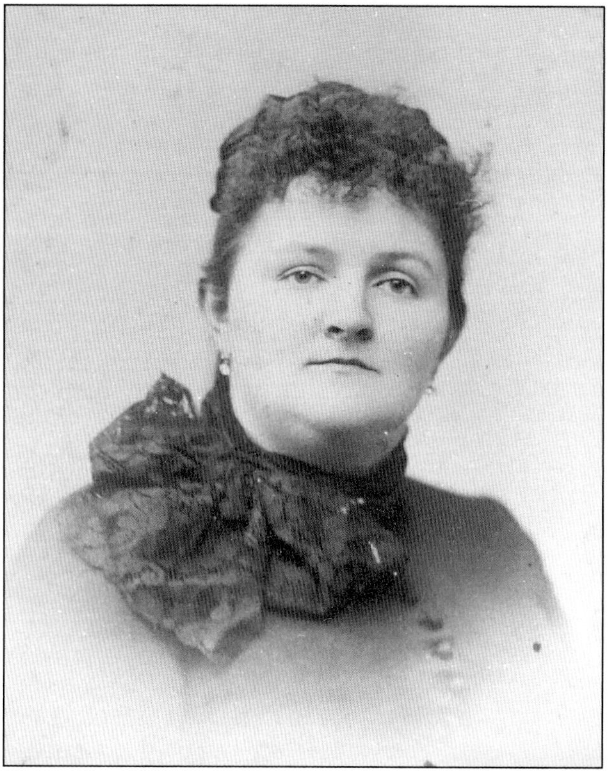

Sarah Morrisey Halpine was the grandmother of New Milford-born Betty Halpine and Stewart Francis Halpine, who became a town selectman.

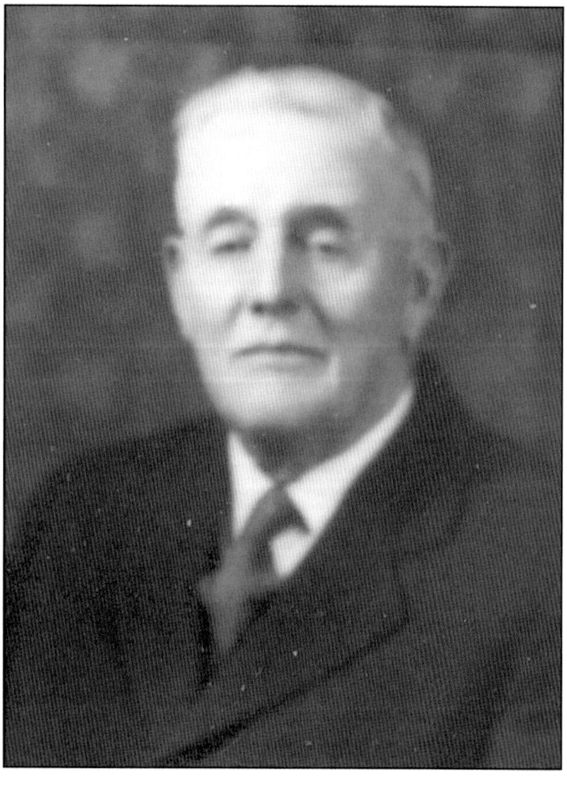

J. Stuart Halpine was the grandfather of Stewart Francis Halpine and Betty Halpine of New Milford. This photograph was taken of at Christmastime in 1932.

Stewart Halpine had the largest tobacco farm in the Housatonic Valley in the 1930s. He is shown with young Stewart Francis Halpine and Betty Halpine in the garden. The house behind them is the Honeymoon Cottage at the Homestead Inn in New Milford.

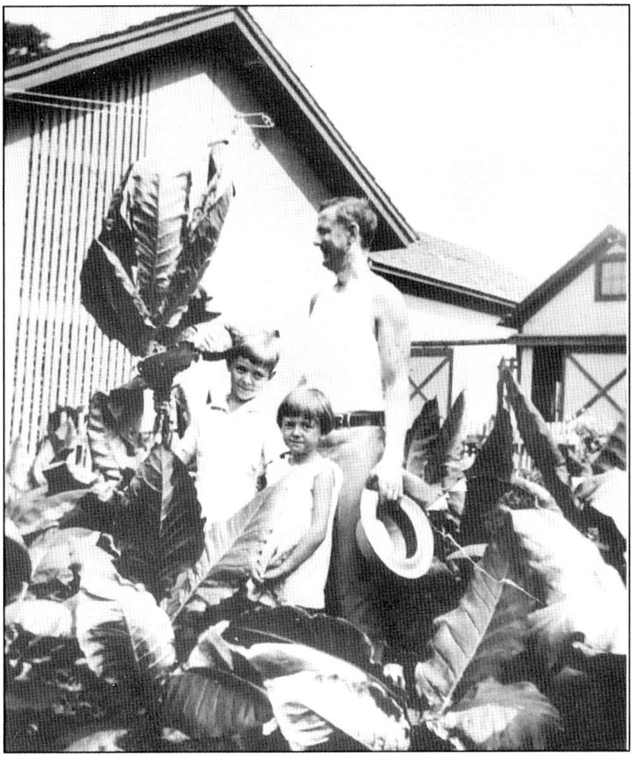

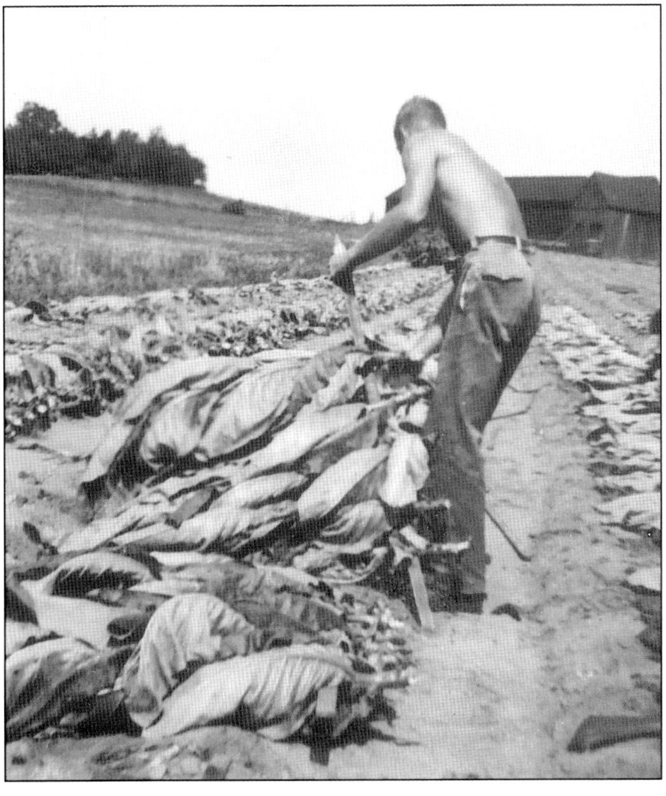

Stewart Halpine leans forward, stacking the tobacco at his farm. The farm was the largest grower and packer of tobacco in the Housatonic Valley.

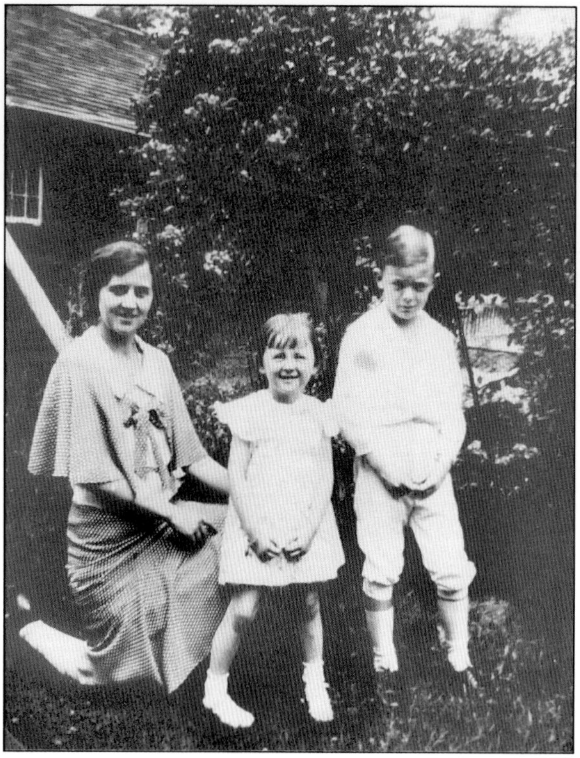

Alice Dickenson Halpine, left, wife of Steward Halpine, poses with her children Stewart Francis and Betty Halpine.

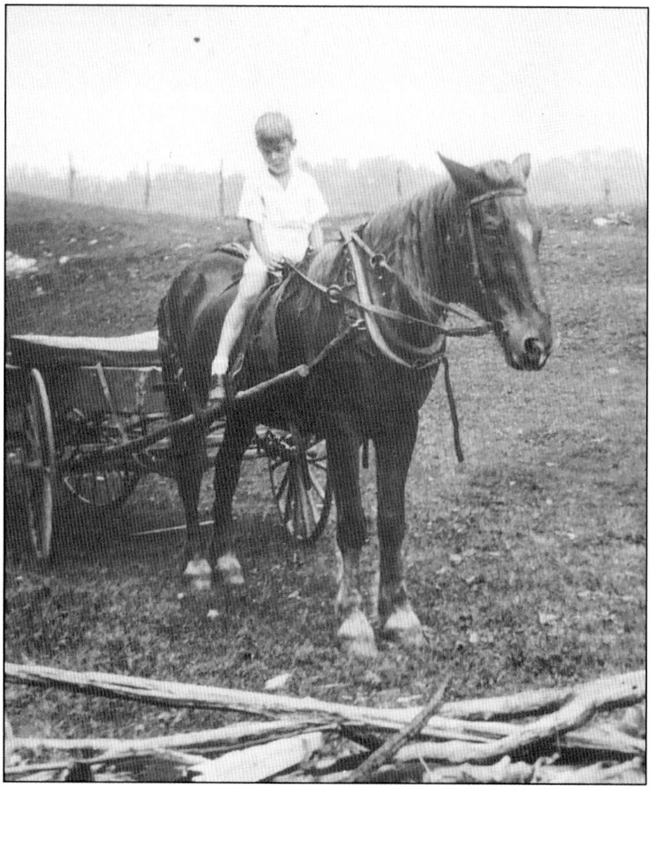

Young Stewart Francis Halpine sits astride the horse Pop Eyes, pulling the farm cart. This photograph was taken in 1932.

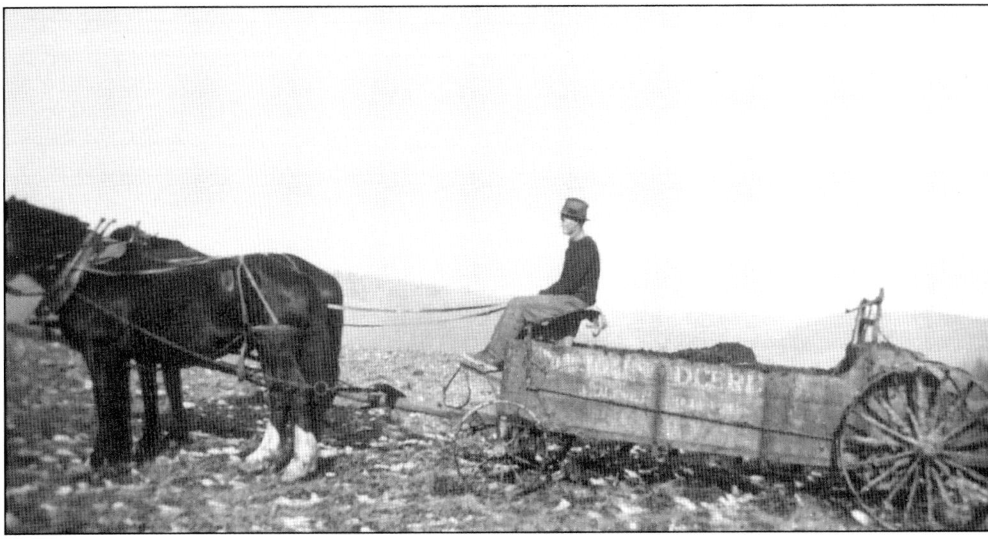

Phillip Hipp uses the manure spreader at the Hipp farm on Route 109 *c.* 1940.

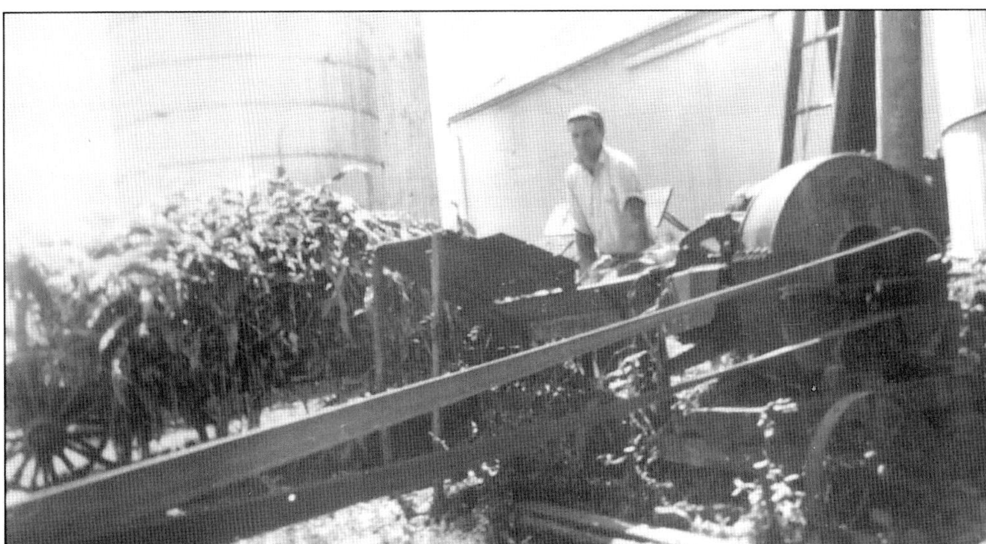

At the Hipp farm on Route 109, Bill Hipp uses a machine that automatically pushes corn into the silo to store for fodder. This photograph was taken in the 1950s.

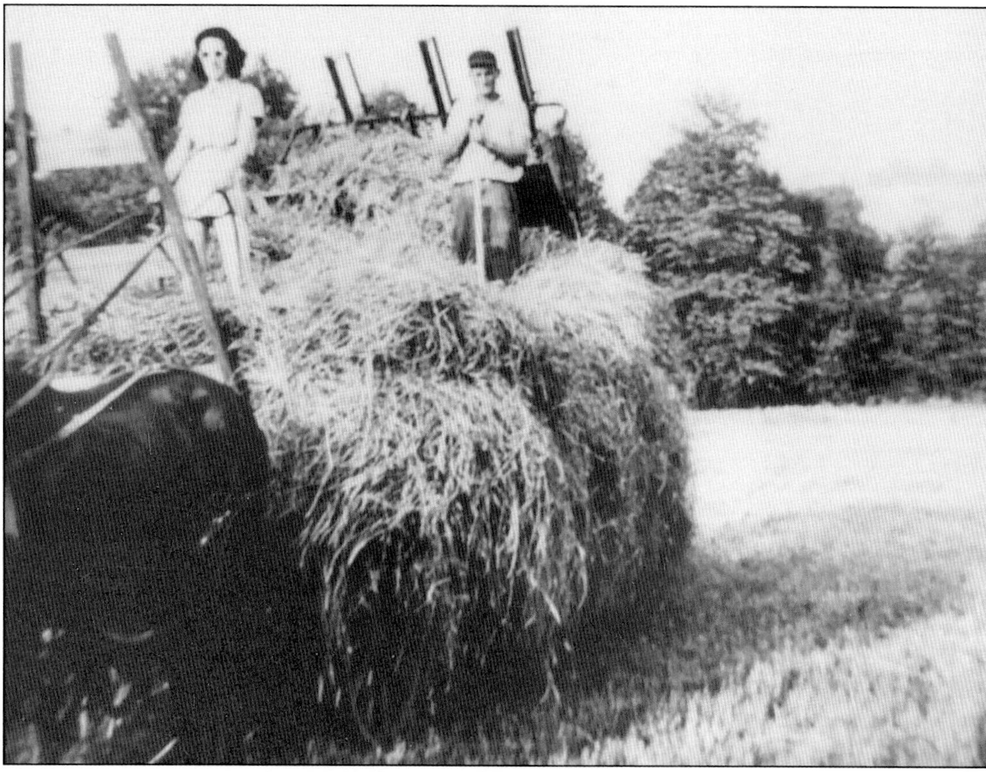

Phillip Hipp and Elizabeth Hipp gather up the hay at the Hipp farm in the 1930s.

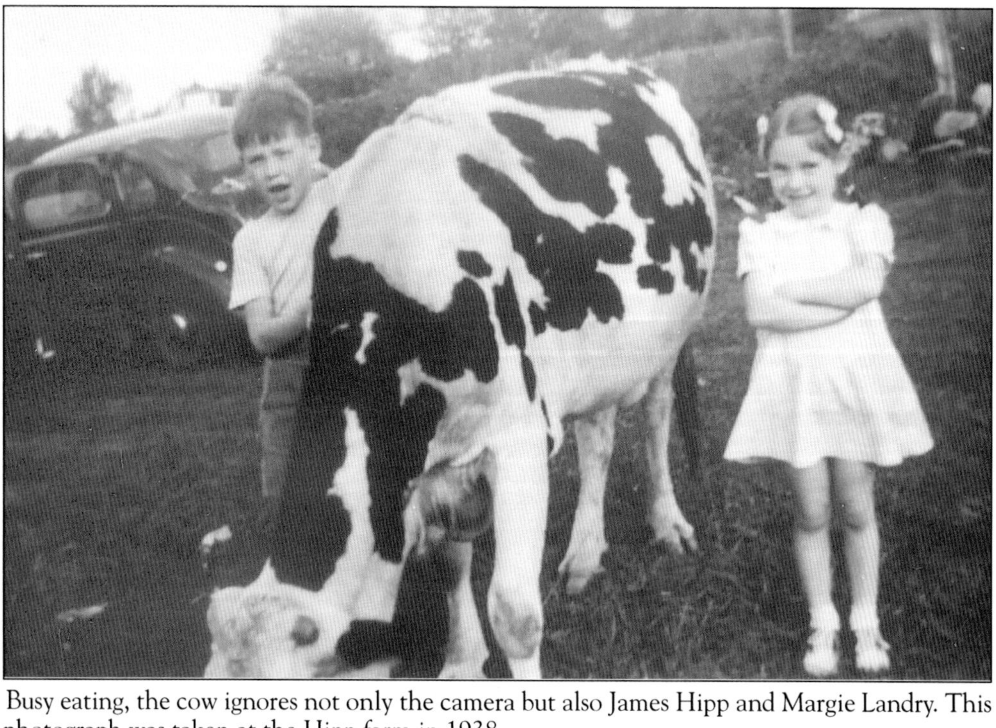

Busy eating, the cow ignores not only the camera but also James Hipp and Margie Landry. This photograph was taken at the Hipp farm in 1938.

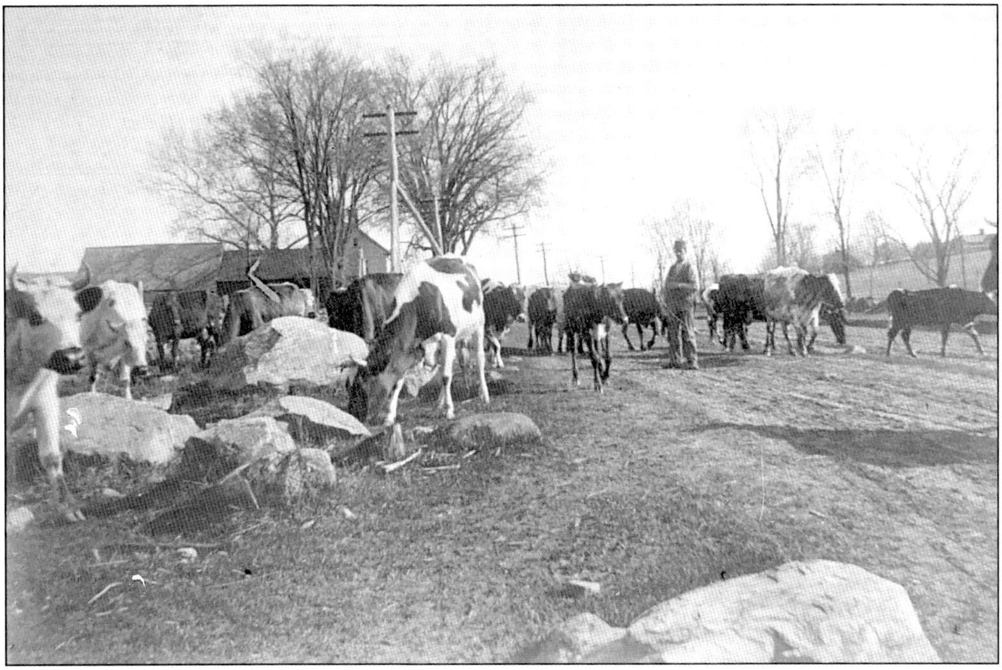

William Bostwick pauses as the cows wander in all directions along Park Lane. This photograph was taken looking south from the Bostwick Homestead in 1906. The old house was taken down *c.* 1906. The Howlands now own a home where the old house stood.

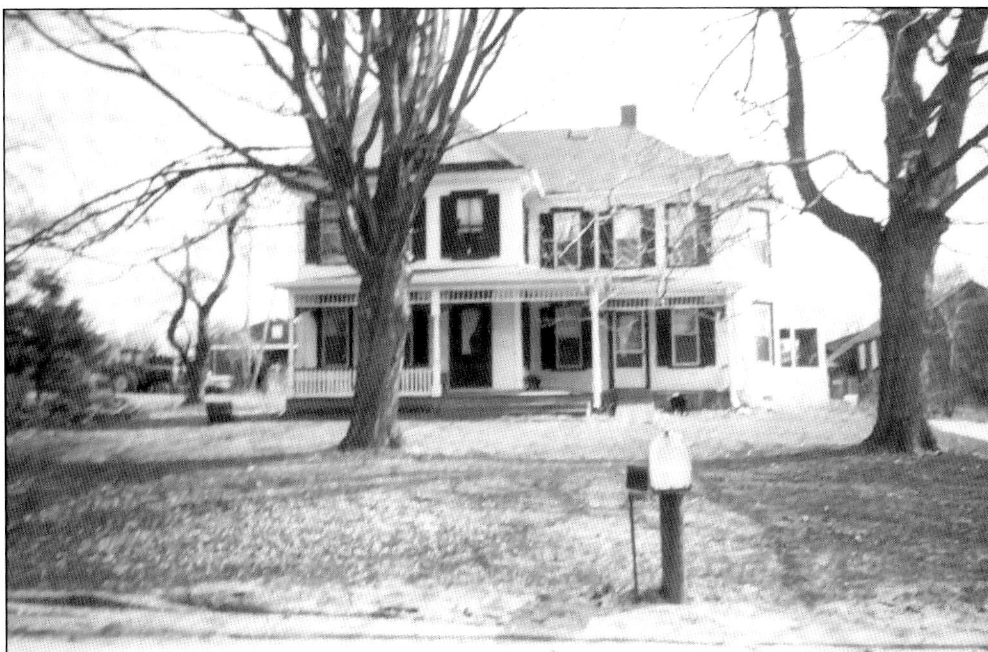

This is the Cobble Hill Dairy Farm, one of the last working farms in New Milford. Located on West Meetinghouse Road in the Merryall section of New Milford, the house was built by the Mr. Young who owned Young's Hotel on Richmond Street. The farm's present owners are Mr. and Mrs. Charles Flynn; they purchased it on July 4, 1955.

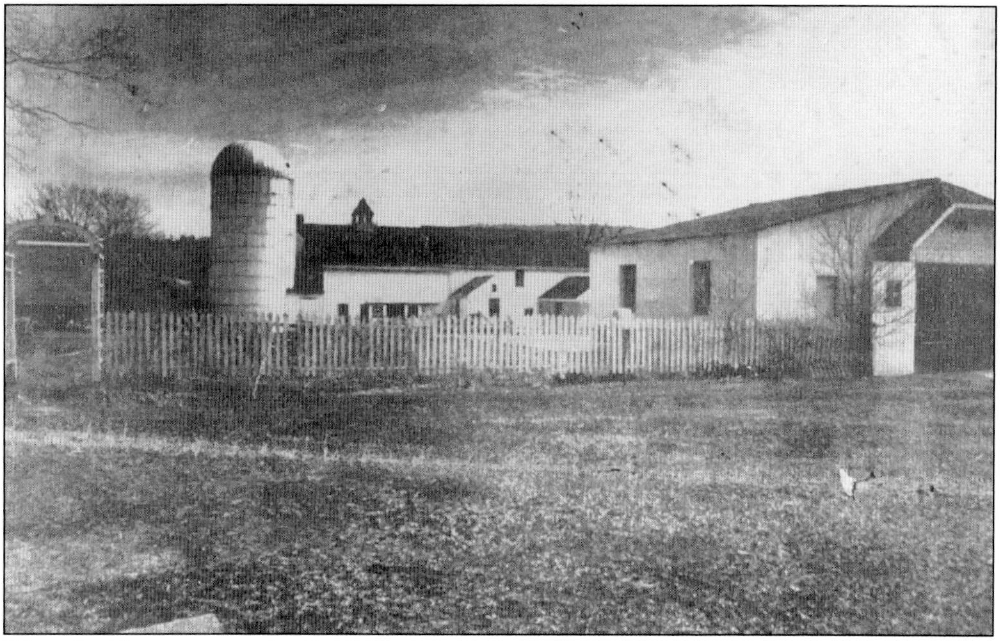

These buildings were at the Stack farm on Route 7. Robert Stack started farming in 1951. He ran the Stack farm as a milk farm. It is now a thing of the past. Today, only two working farms remain in the New Milford area.

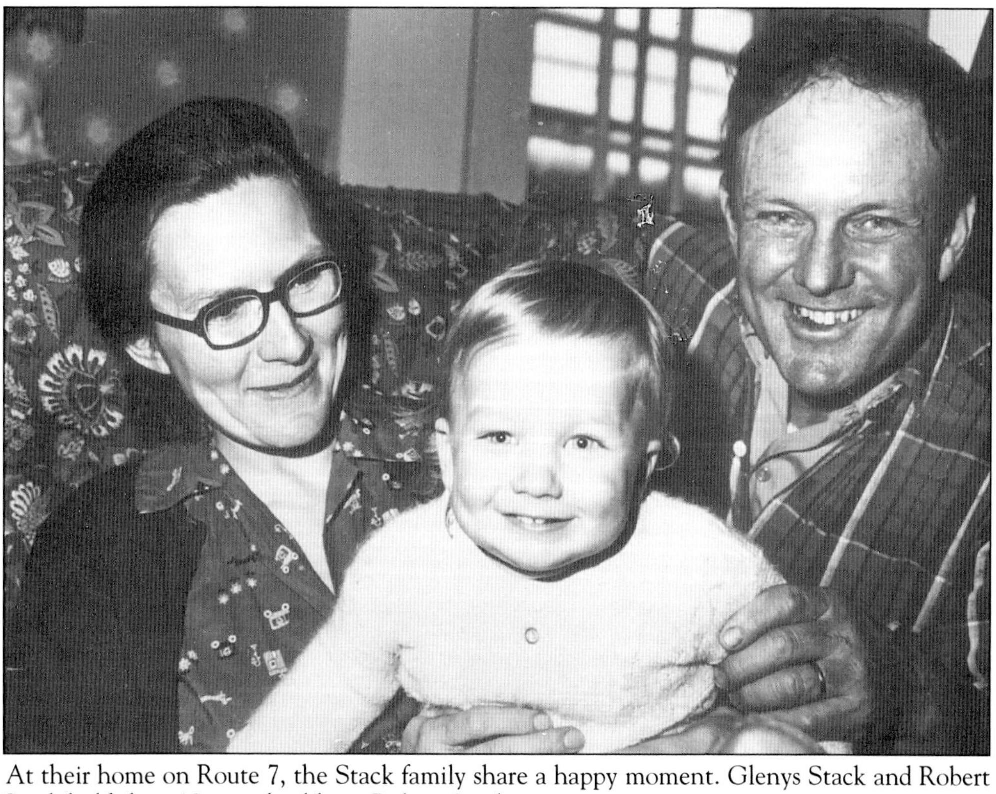

At their home on Route 7, the Stack family share a happy moment. Glenys Stack and Robert Stack hold their 18-month-old son Robert Stack.

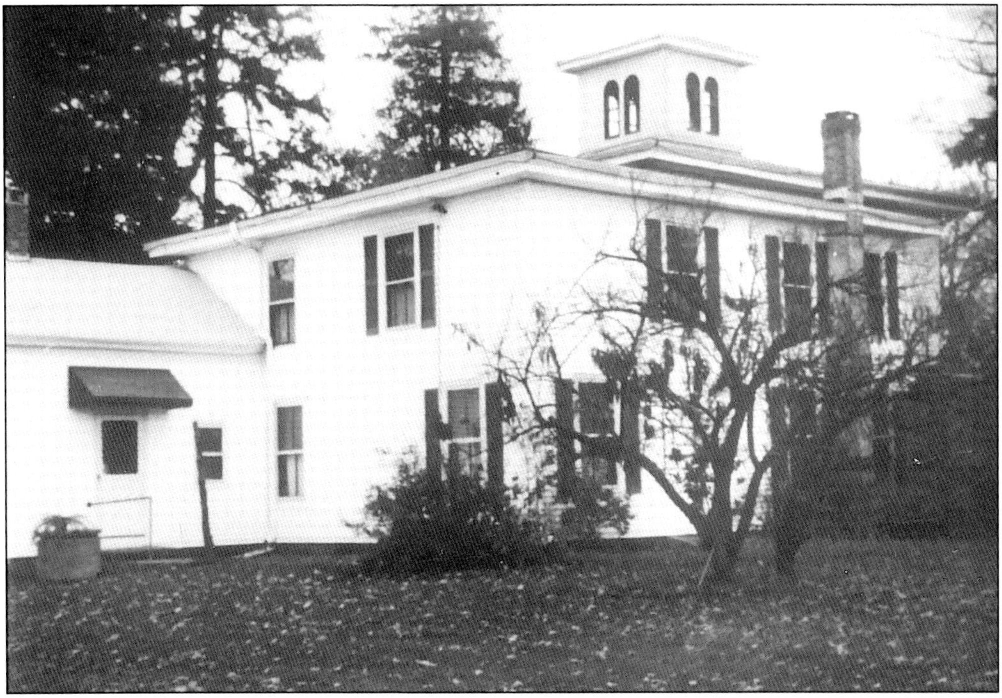

The Siskey farm was built in 1864 on Ridge Road. Loring Canfield was the original builder. The house contained wallpaper that dated from 1865, the year that Pres. Abraham Lincoln was assassinated.

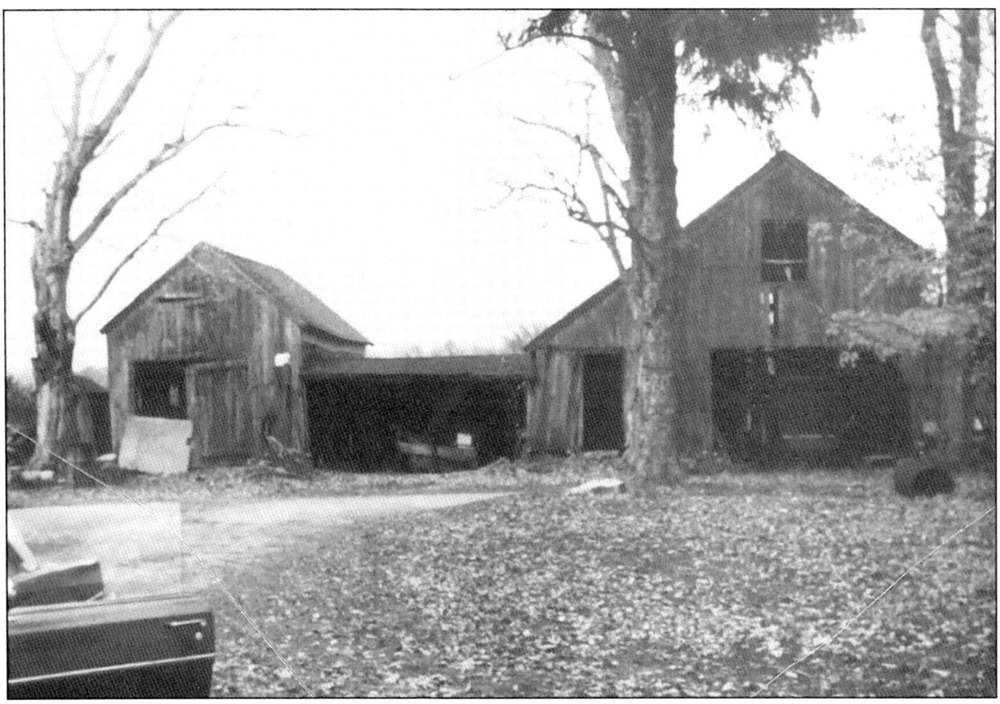

The barns on Siskey farm were built in the 1700s on Old Ridge Road. They were first used as a blacksmith shop. The barns were destroyed in a fire.

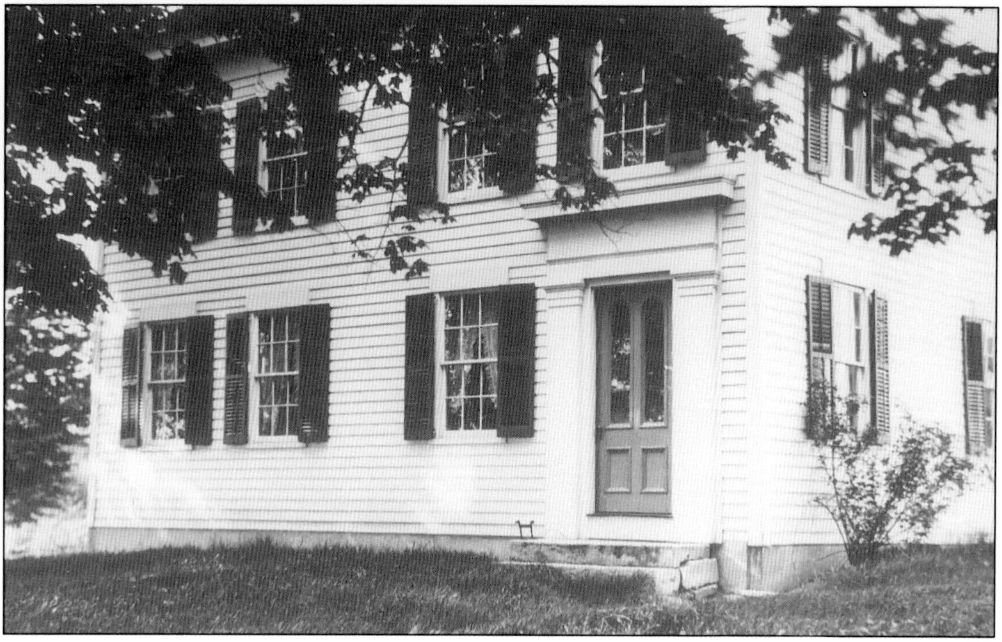

The Reimeridge farm is located on Chapin Road. For many, many years it was a working farm. Its chief product was milk, and the cattle were Holstein cows.

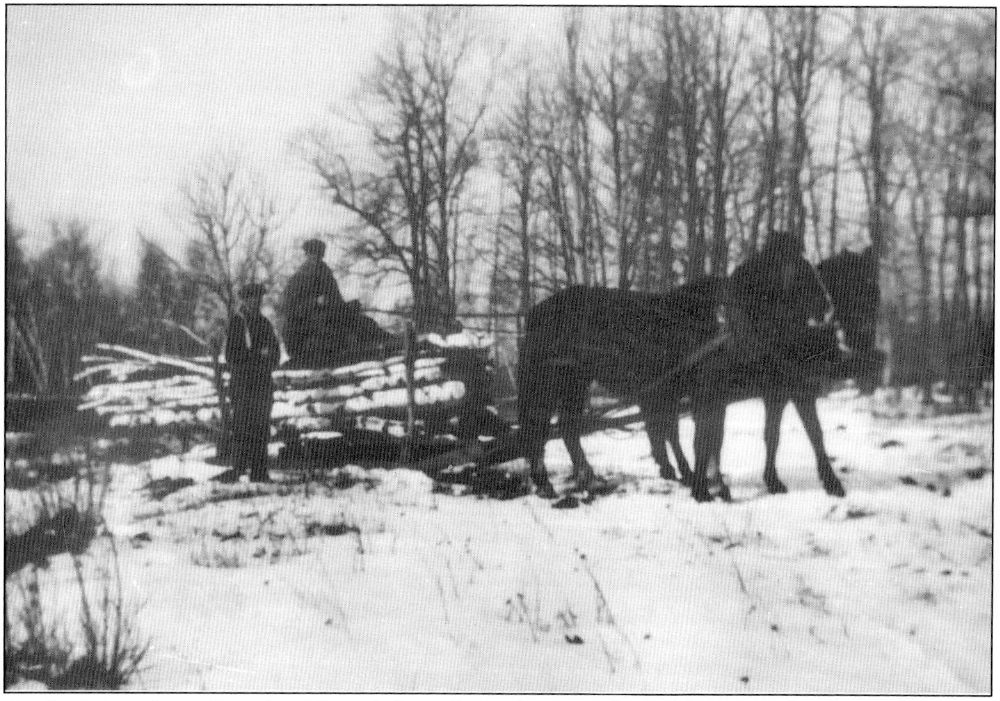

At the Hipp farm, Grandpa Hipp, left, and another member of the Hipp family load the cart with trees cut down either for wood burning or fence building. The photograph was taken in the early 1900s.

Seven

A Look Around

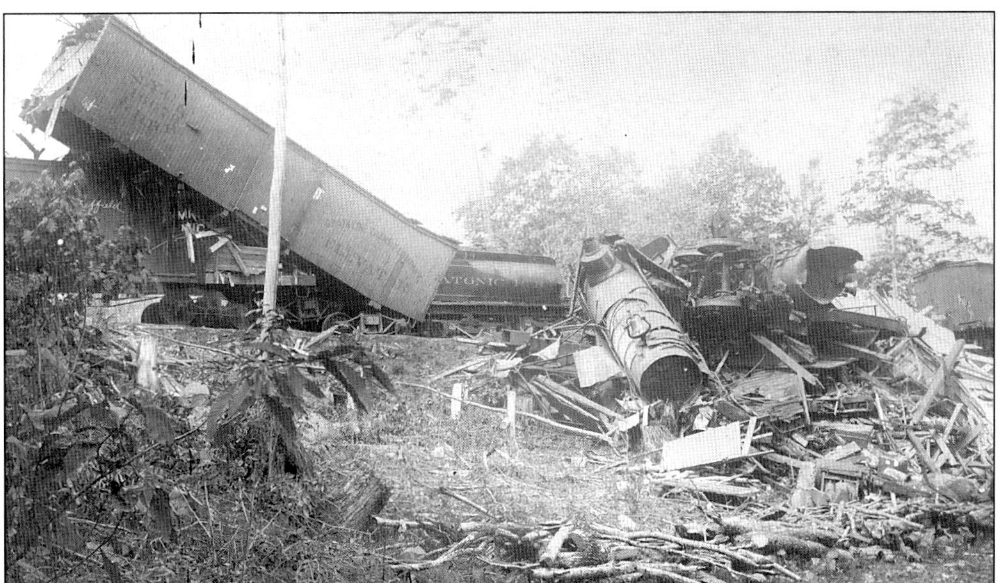

This train wreck occurred at Merwinsville (now Gaylordsville) *c*. 1910.

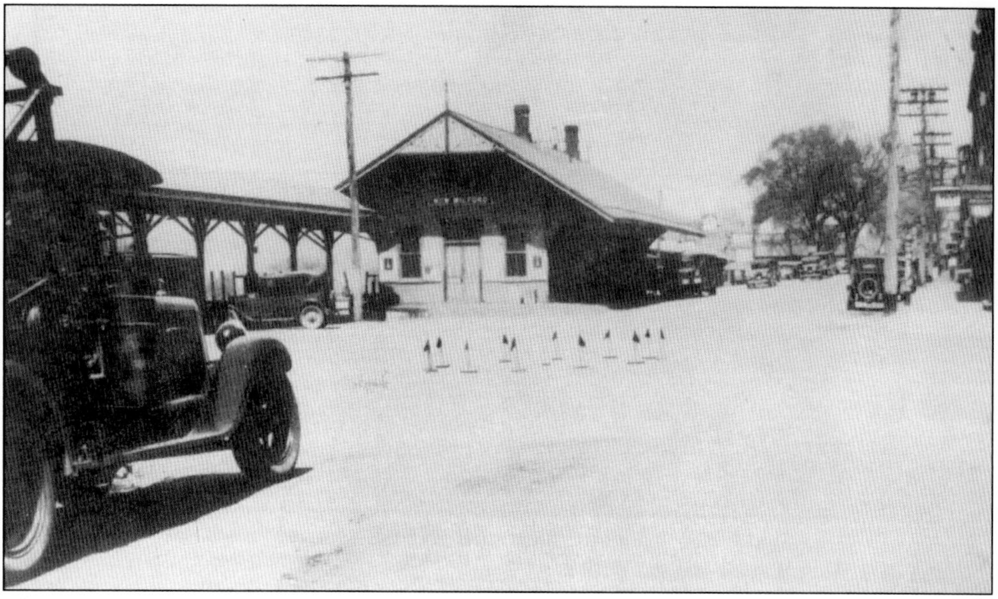

The railroad station is shown in this photograph taken looking north from the intersection at Bridge Street *c.* 1920s.

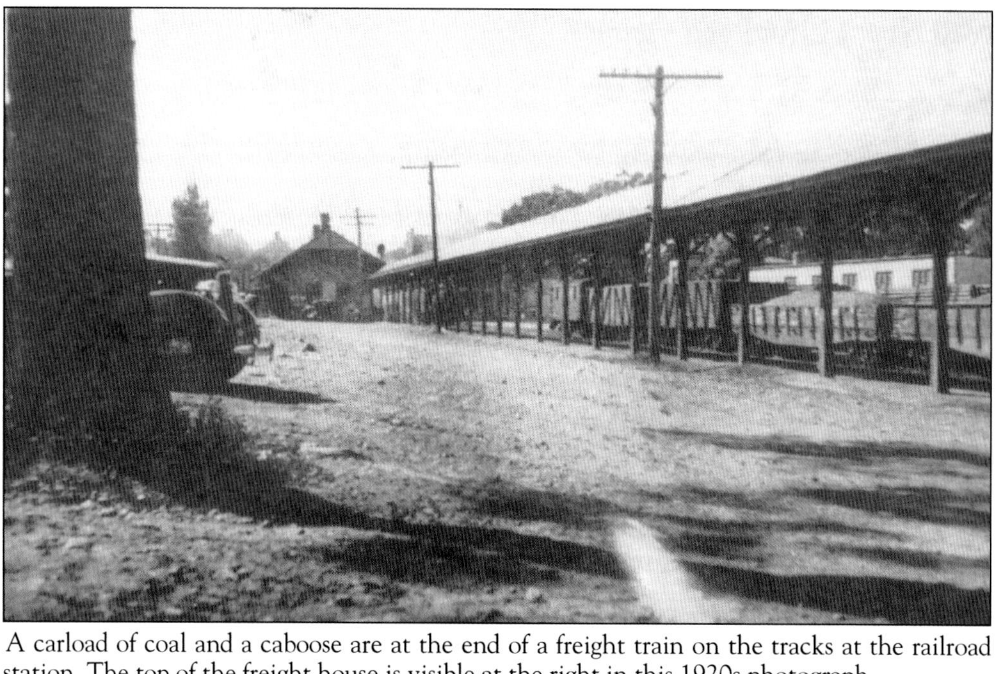

A carload of coal and a caboose are at the end of a freight train on the tracks at the railroad station. The top of the freight house is visible at the right in this 1920s photograph.

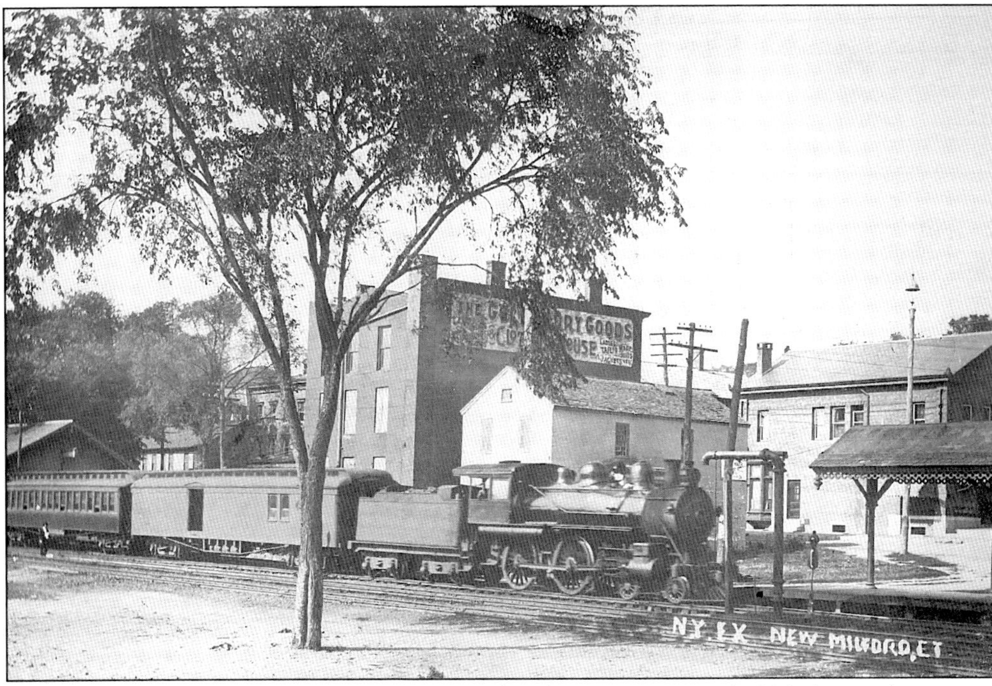

This photograph of the old freight depot was taken between 1902 and 1906. Across the street is Golden's Store and Albert Evitt's drugstore, which was Botsford's in earlier days.

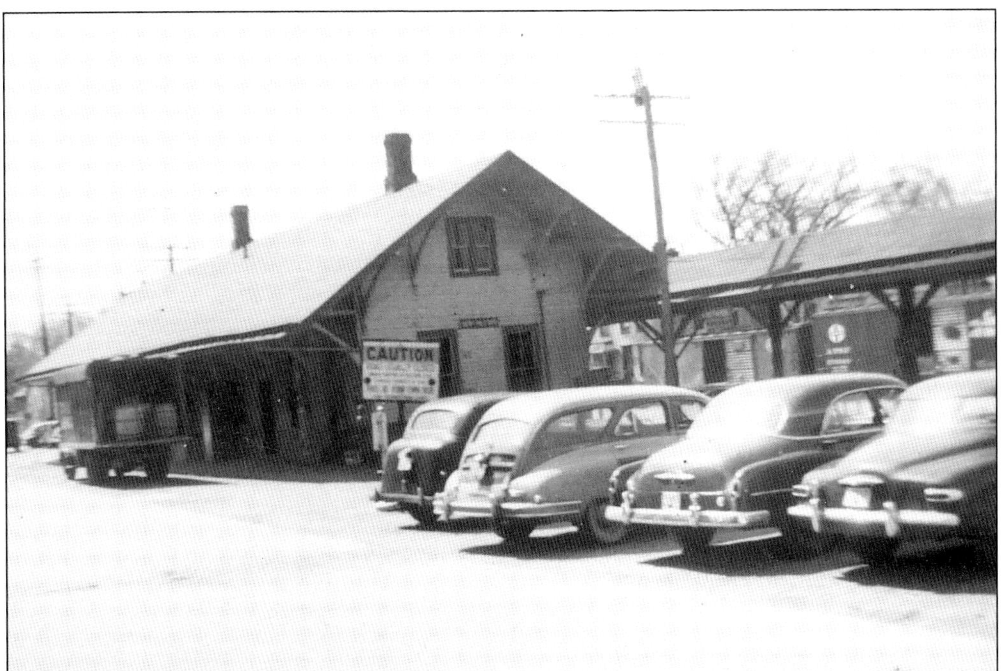

Parking space is pretty well taken up in this 1950s photograph of the railroad station.

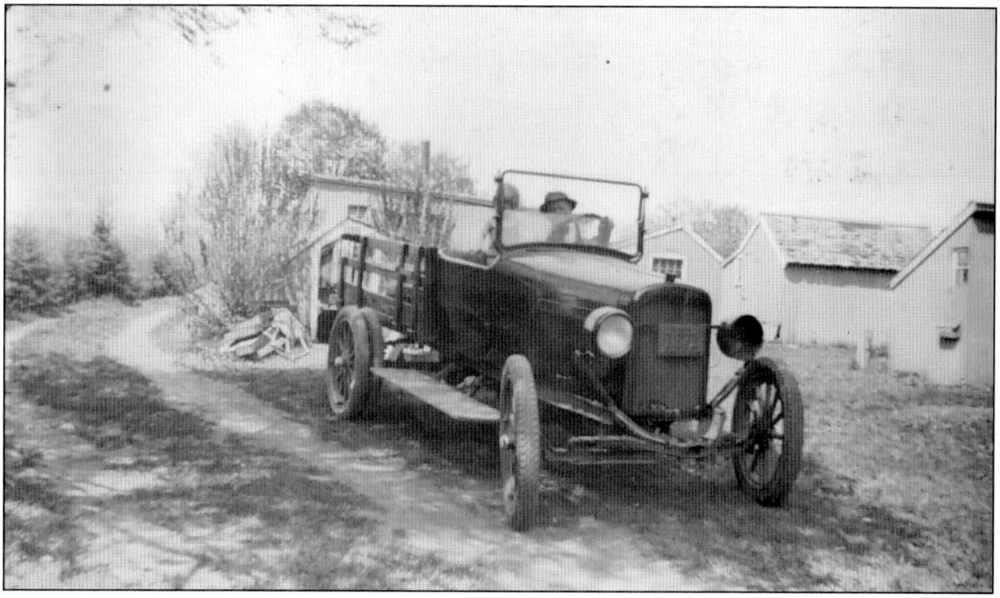

Driving the Model T truck tha he remodeled for apple picking is Edward Howland, at the Wayside Fruit Gardens in 1936.

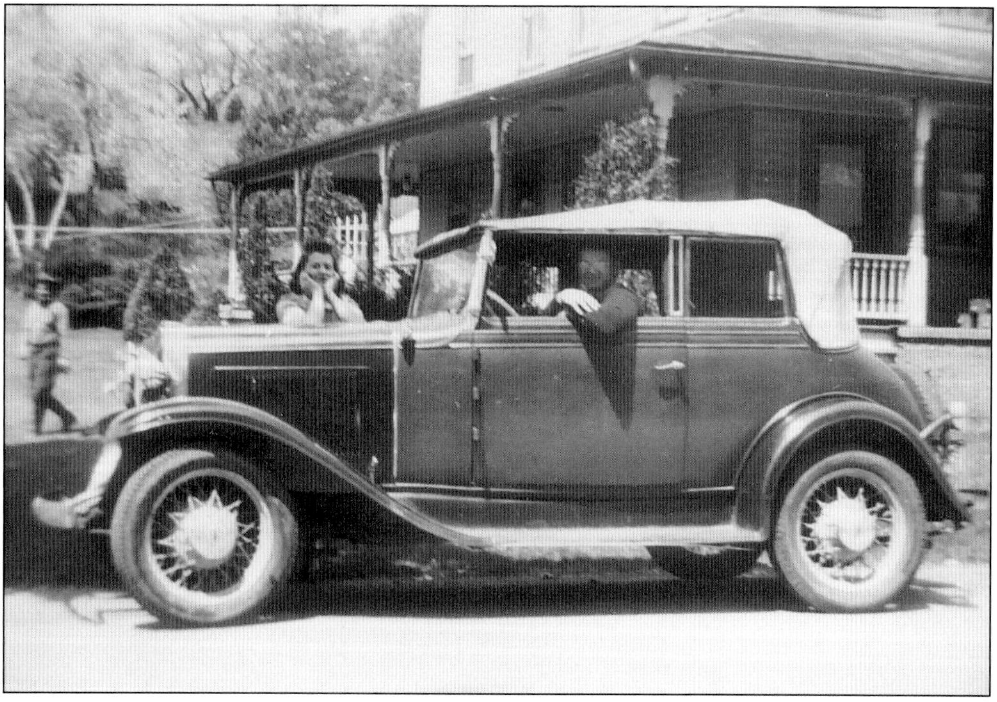

Truman Richmond, who had a passion for automobiles, sits in a 1932 Chevrolet. The picture was taken in Northville.

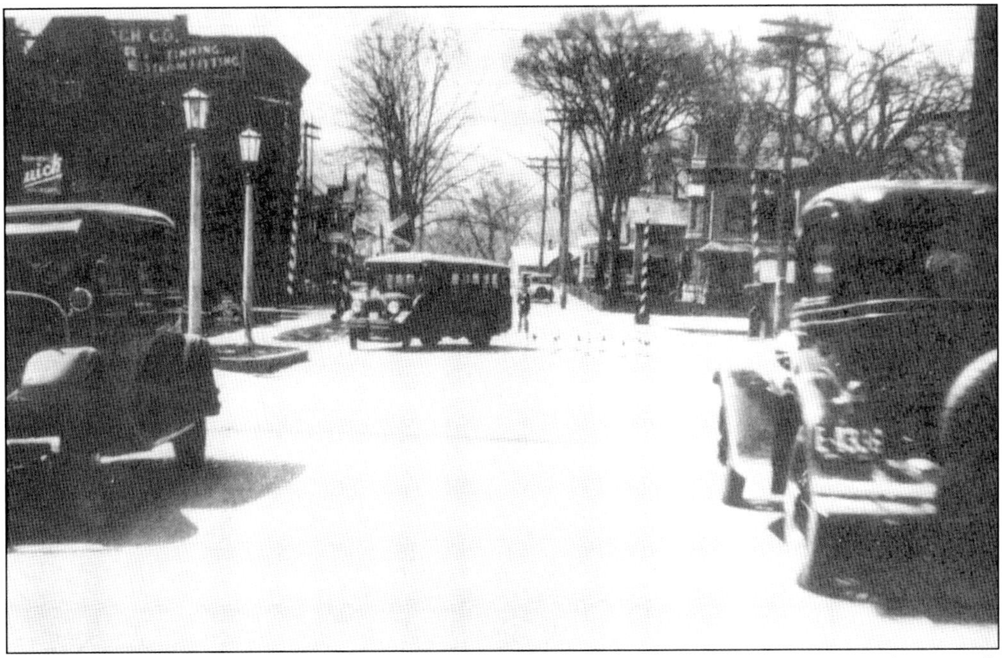

With a guard standing behind it, a school bus turns around on Bridge Street. This photograph was taken looking west across the railroad tracks. Notice the streetlights and the gatehouse on the right, past the tracks.

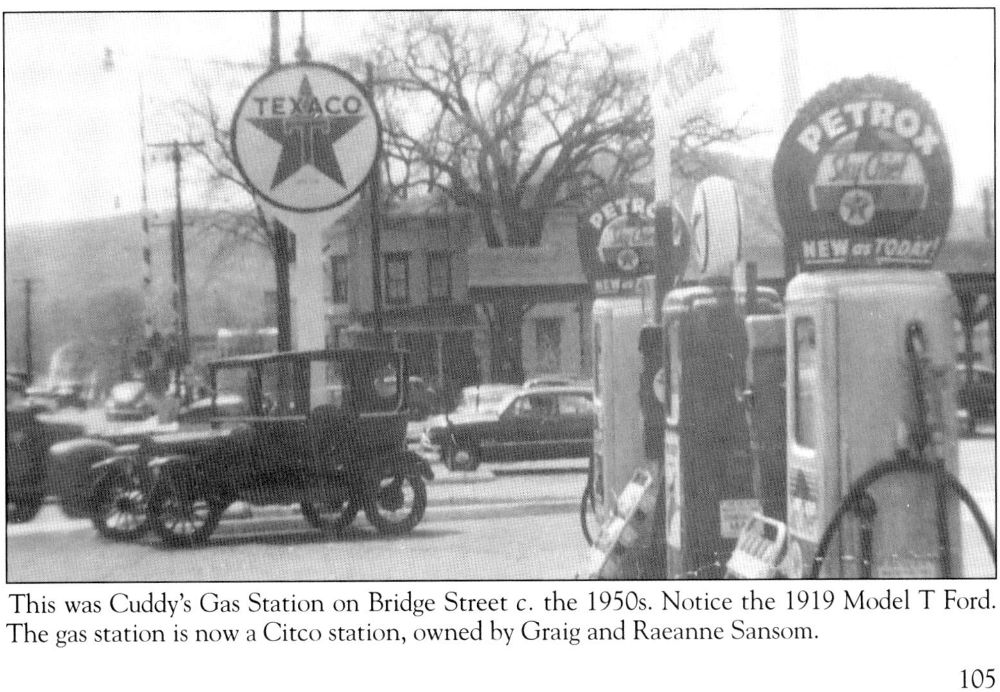

This was Cuddy's Gas Station on Bridge Street *c.* the 1950s. Notice the 1919 Model T Ford. The gas station is now a Citco station, owned by Graig and Raeanne Sansom.

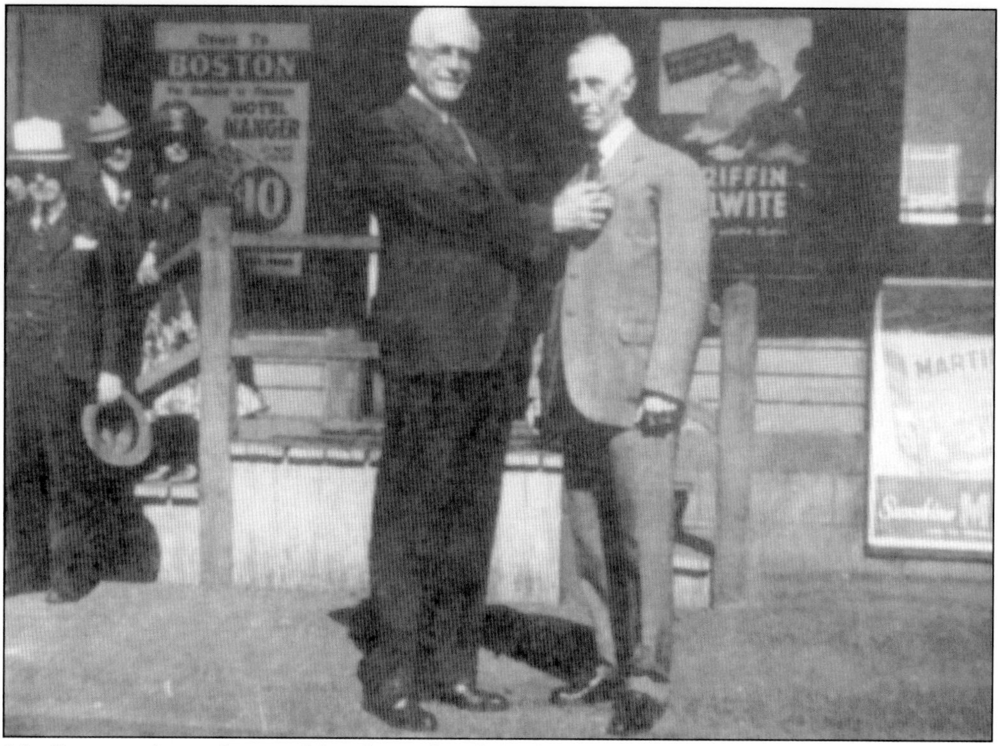

Mr. Percy, right, is honored by the railroad for his 50 years of service in the late 1930s. On the left are employees of the New Milford Hat Company who are waiting for the train.

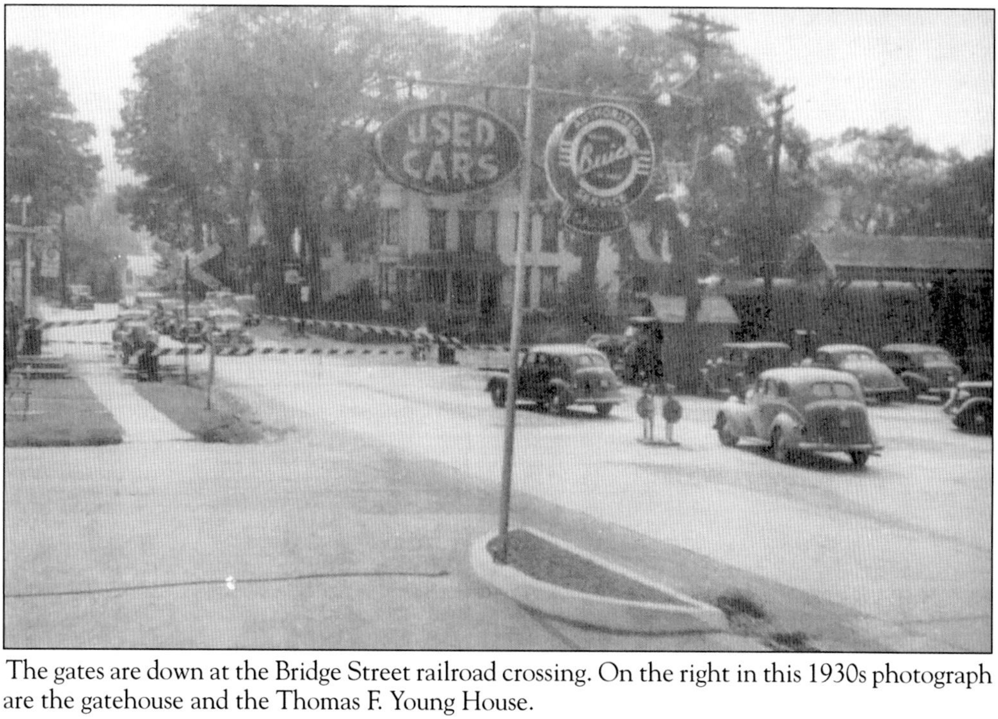

The gates are down at the Bridge Street railroad crossing. On the right in this 1930s photograph are the gatehouse and the Thomas F. Young House.

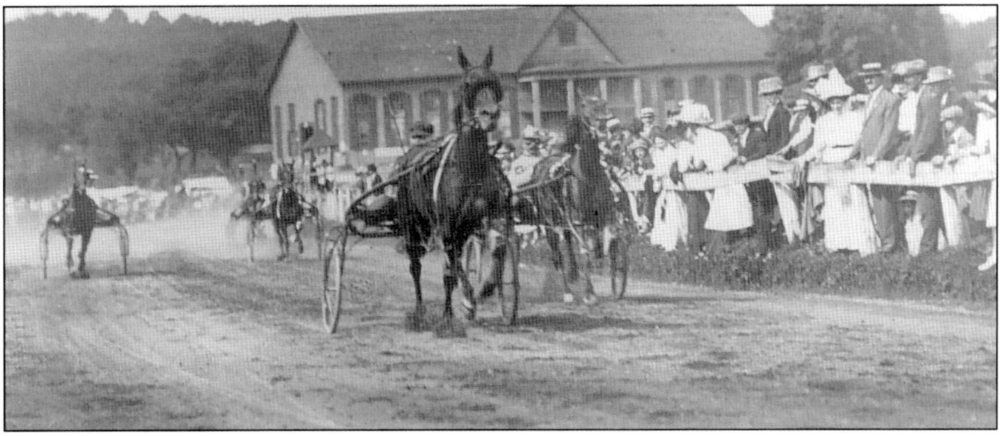

The race is on at the New Milford Fairgrounds Race Track, which was located at Fort Hill in the years from 1905 to 1910. These spectacular races drew large crowds.

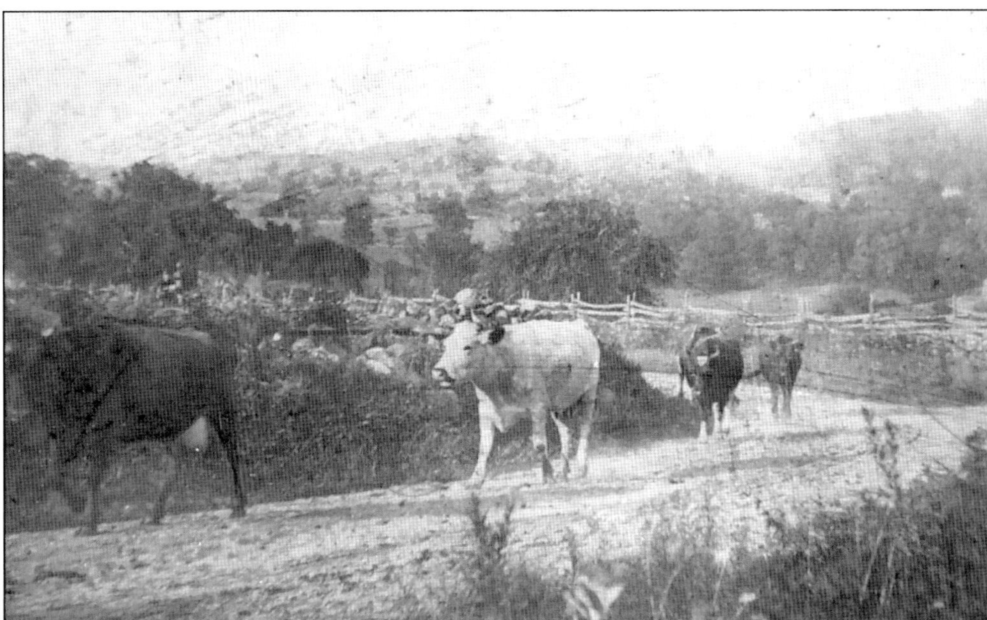

Cows come around to the square on Old Park Lane. Today, this area is occupied by the New Milford Family Practice, at One Old Park Lane.

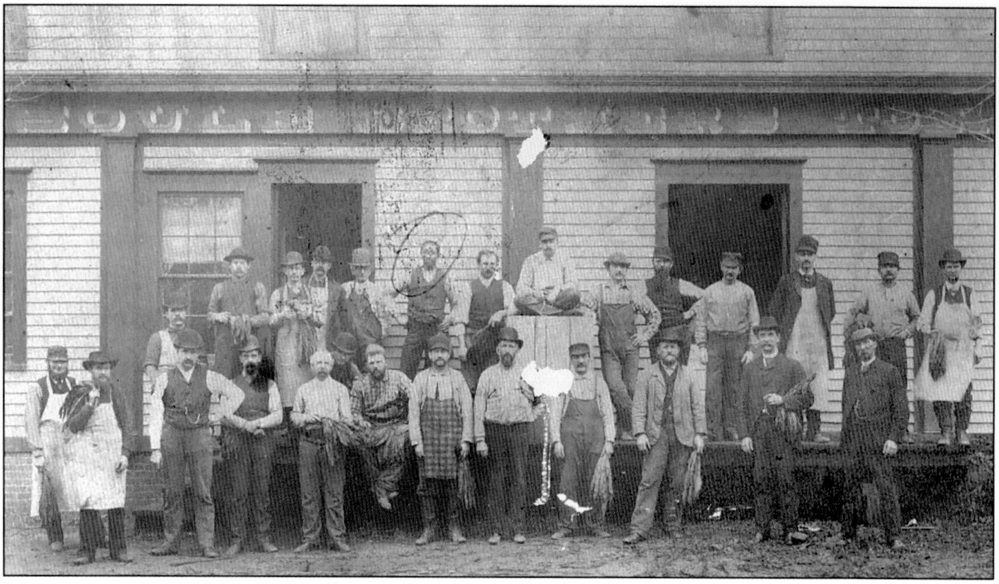

This photograph of Soule Brothers Tobacco was taken in *c*. 1886. Alfred Heacock, fifth from the left in the back row, was the shop foreman.

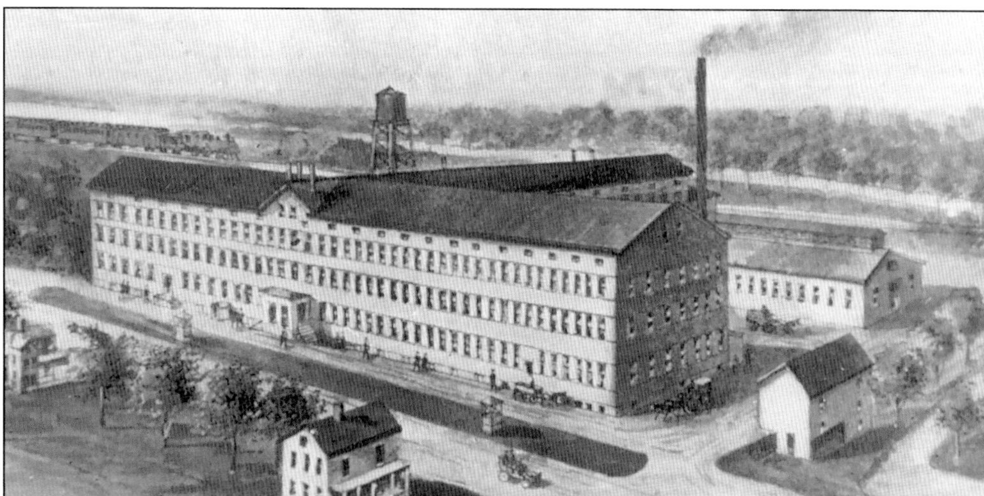

The New Milford Hat Company was located on Housatonic Avenue. Hats were manufactured there in the early 1900s. After the hat industry died out, the building became a fur-processing plant.

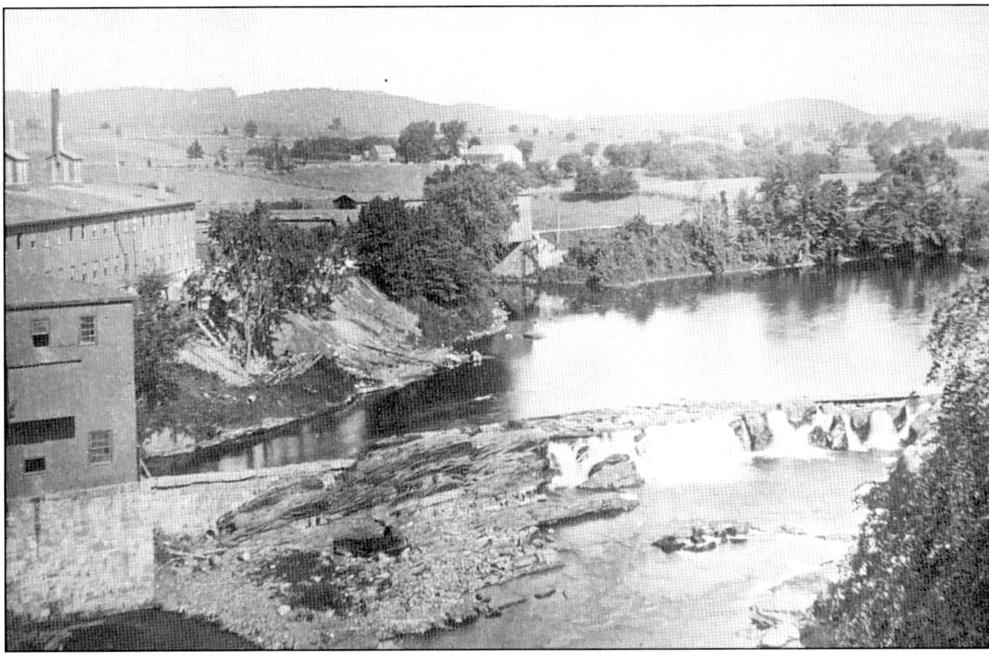

This view of the Still River and the valley beyond was taken from the bridge in 1898.

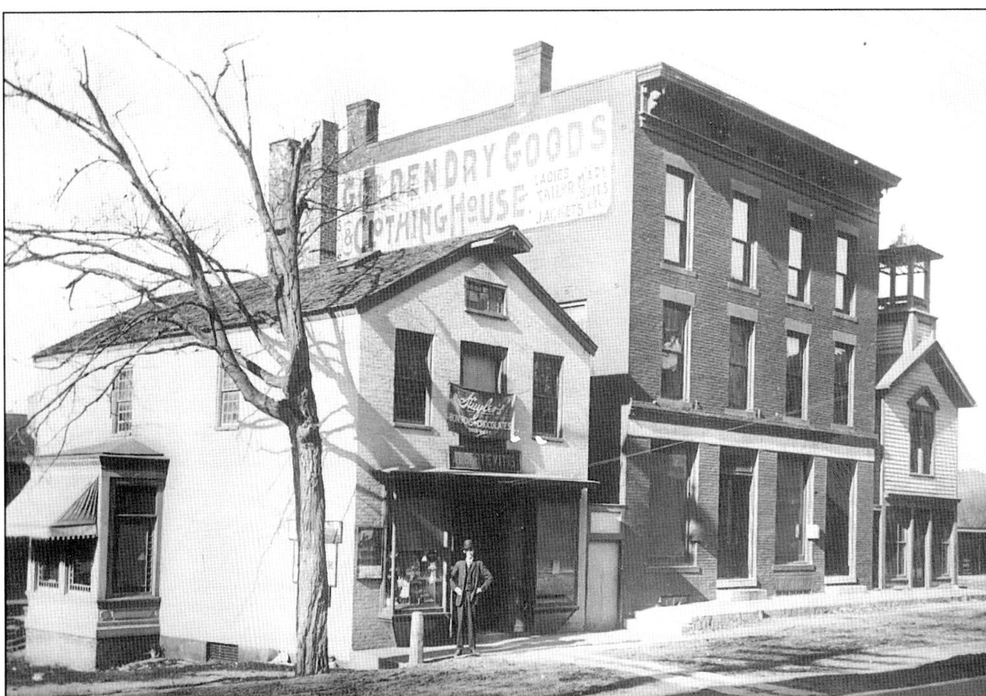

The building with a man standing in the front is Golden's Clothing Store. The picture was taken c. 1905 from the west side of Railroad Street opposite Bank Street.

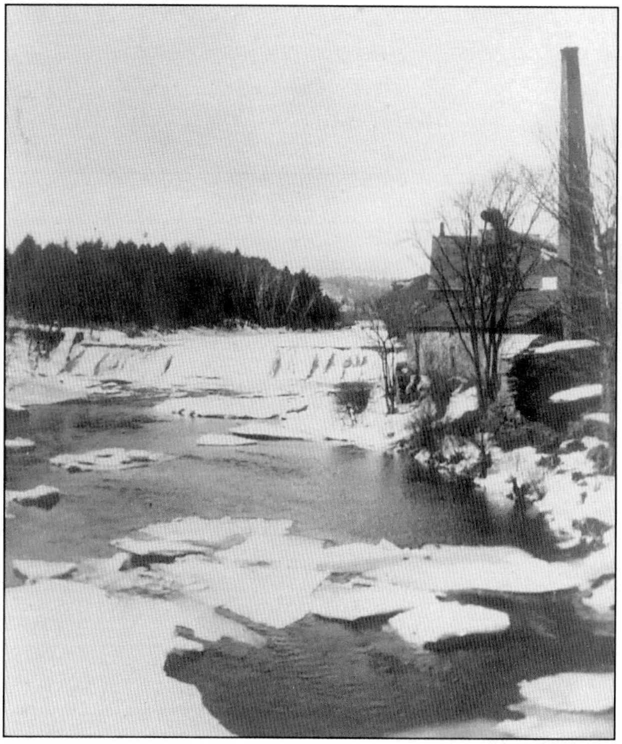

The first gristmill was built in 1717 by John Griswald and William Gauld at Lanesville. This mill also served as a sawmill, a dam-bolting works, a clothes mill, and an ironworks. In May 1789, Capt. Joseph Ruggles purchased Eli Dunning's half of the ironworks at Lanesville; Ruggles died in 1802 at 71 years of age.

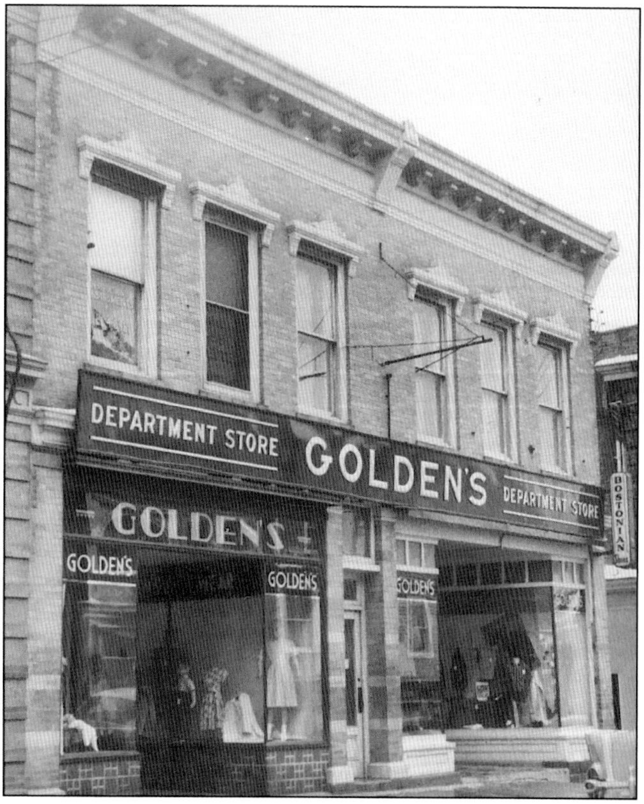

This March 1951 photograph shows Golden's Department Store on Bank Street. For many years the Goldens had a retailing business in New Milford.

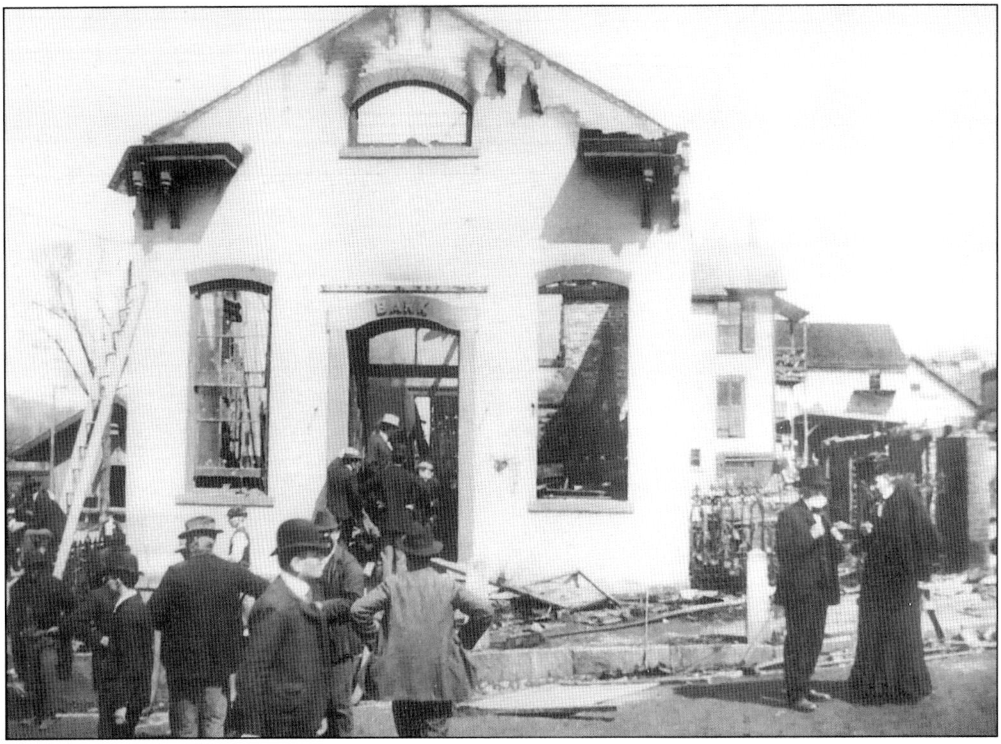

The fire of 1902 destroyed the First National Bank building at the corner of Bank and Railroad Streets. The bank was moved to a new location.

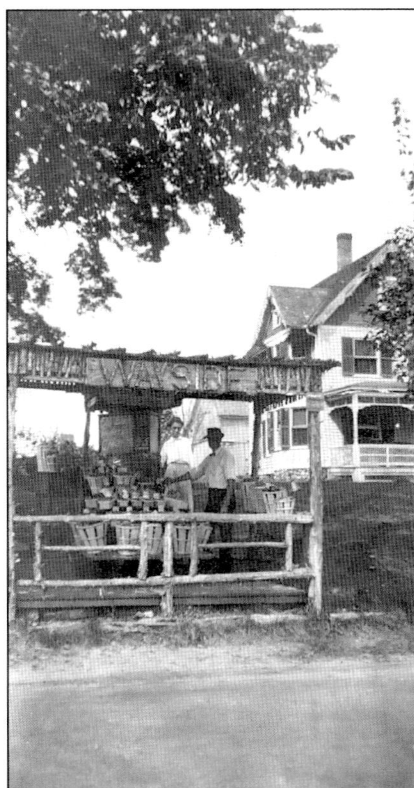

This was the original fruit stand at Wayside Fruit Gardens at 43 Park Lane Road (Route 202), which opened in 1899. The owners were Edward Clyde Howland and his wife, Annie Bostwick Howland. By the 1930s, the stand had expanded and had become popular with visitors from New York City.

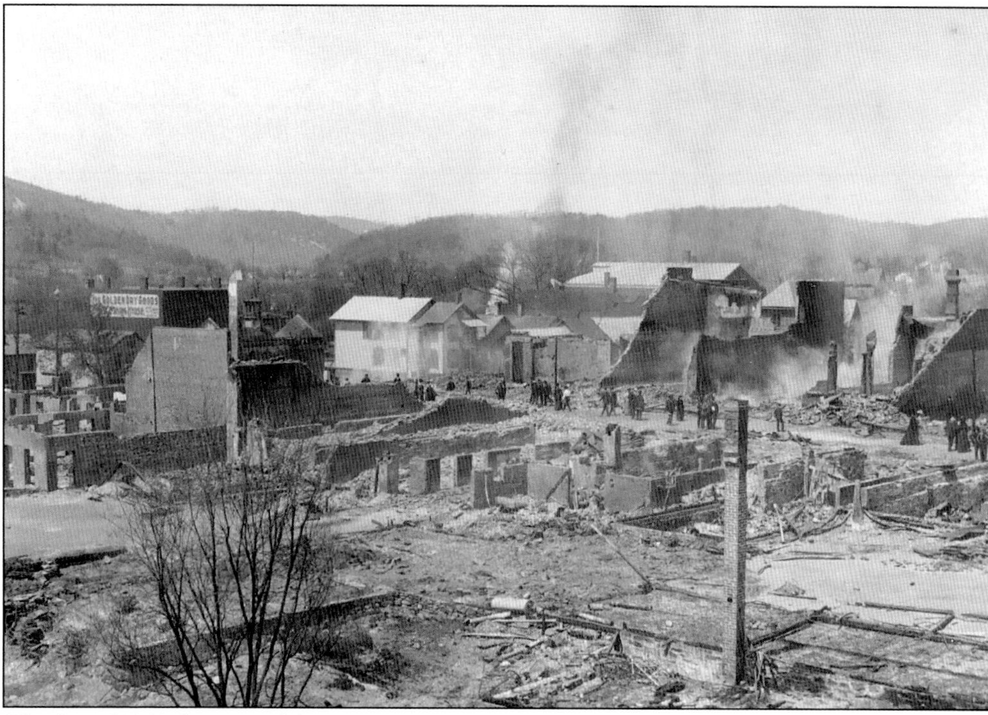

The fire of 1902 devastated the Main Street area of New Milford. Many buildings and businesses were lost.

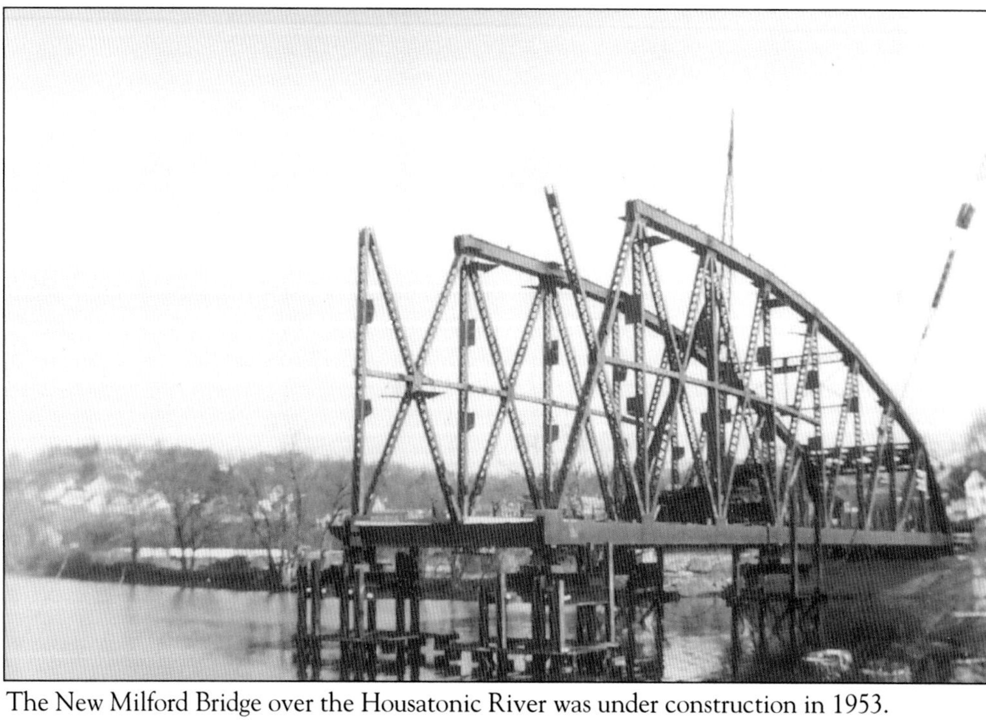

The New Milford Bridge over the Housatonic River was under construction in 1953.

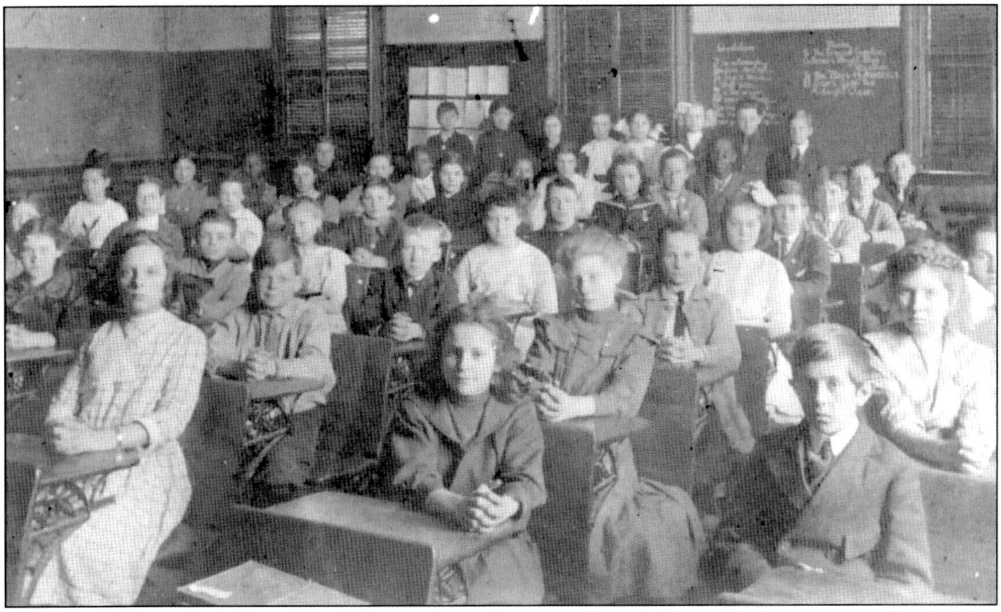

Ethel Worley, front center, was the daughter of Alfred C. Worley and Ada Worley, a family who had lived in New Milford since 1902. Her father bought the *Gazette* and the *New Milford Times*. In 1918, she married Percival Prince. Over the years, she was involved in many activities, such as the United Fund, the March of Dimes, and the Christmas lighting of the green. She was the founder of the Santa Claus Emergency Fund. She served on many town committees, including the Commission on Aging and the Board of Tax Review.

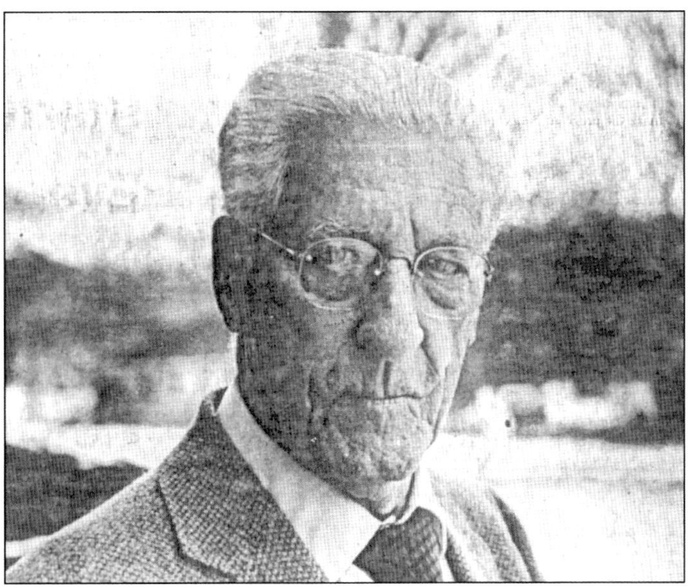

Howard H. Peck served as New Milford town clerk from 1938 to 1970. He was also the town historian. He was born on February 19, 1893, on Grove Street.

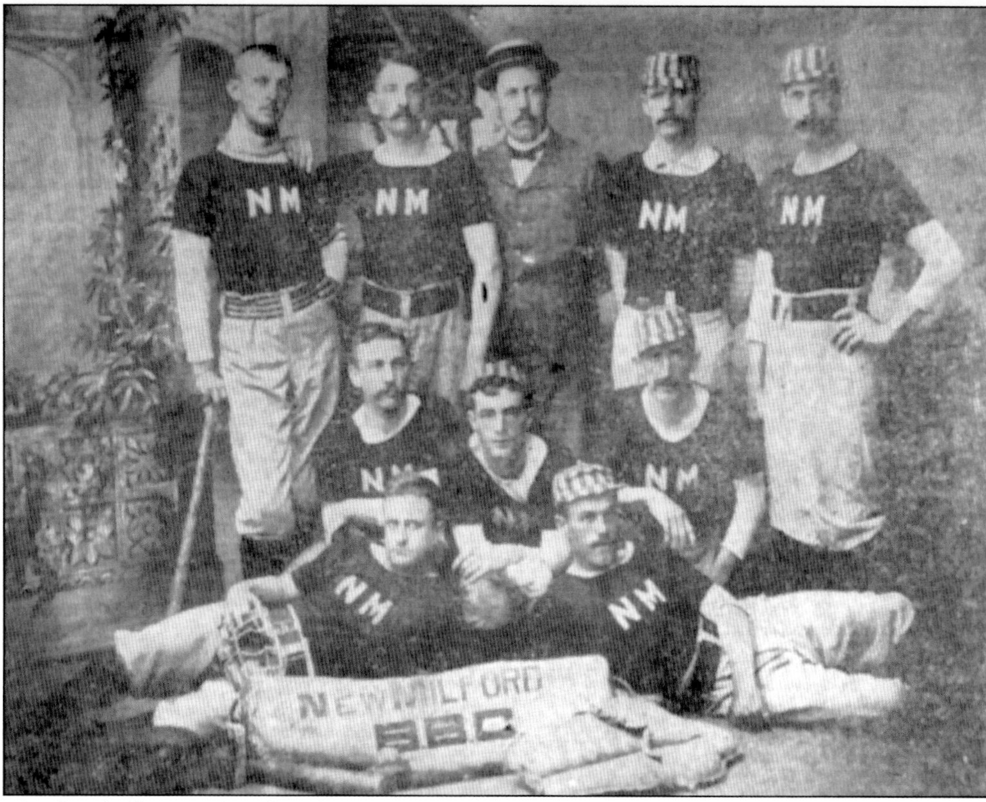

This baseball team played in the late 1800s. One member of the team has been identified: the late Judge John R. Addis, front row on the left.

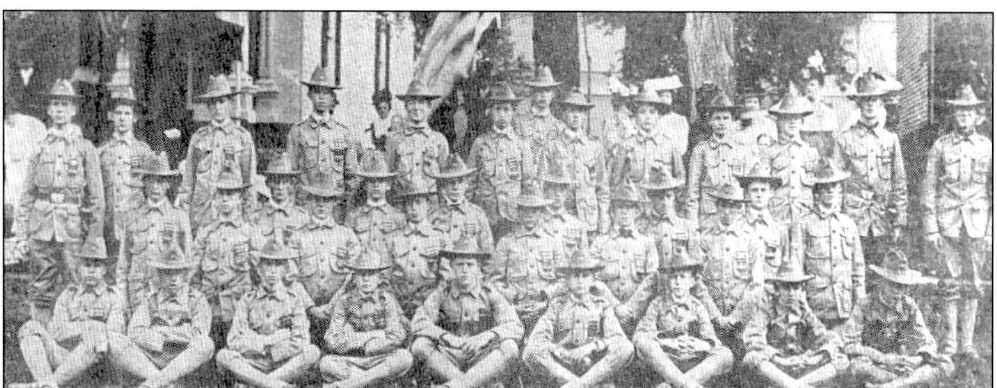

The Boy Cadets pose in 1907 in front of the C.M. Beach Home. Among those pictured (mostly by last name only) in the front are Sergeant Breining, Couch, Lathrop, Kyle, Captain Rettalick, Draper, Greining, Moore, Corporal Boyton, Knowles, Green, Halpin, Bouton, Hine, Mullins, Bray, and Beck. In the middle are Caldwell, Wesley Parcells, Corporal Barker, Clank, Mulchy, Halpin, and Corporal Barton. In the back are Capt. Clifford Noble, Lieutenant Noble, Hunt, Stone, Connors, Law, flagbearer Marcy, Howard Peck, Parcells, Warner, Hunter, Lieutenant Canfield, and Sergeant Robertson.

In the 1920s, the building on the south side of the New Milford Police Station was W. Oliver's blacksmith and wheelwright shop. Neither the building nor the business still exists.

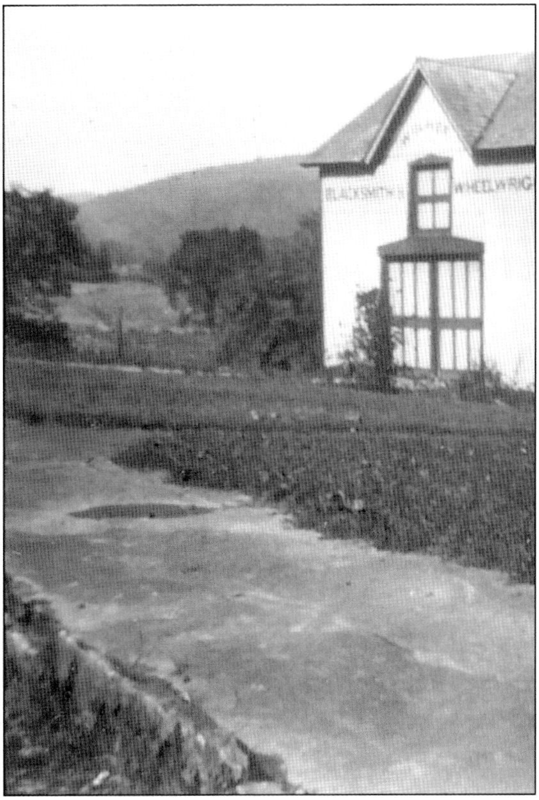

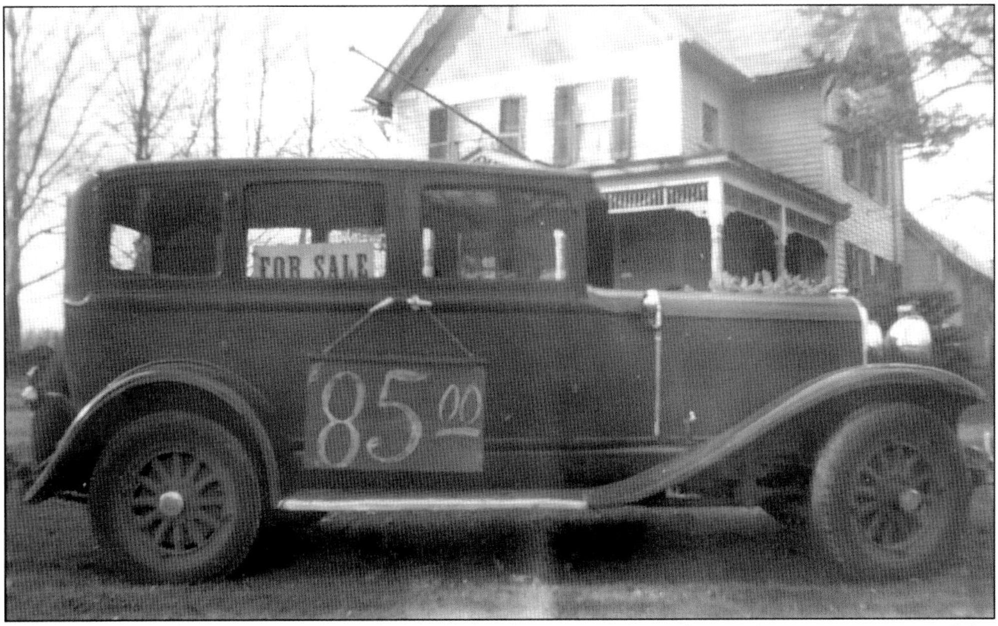

Pictured is a 1929 Chrysler four-door, on sale in 1929 for $85. The car was owned by Edward Howland.

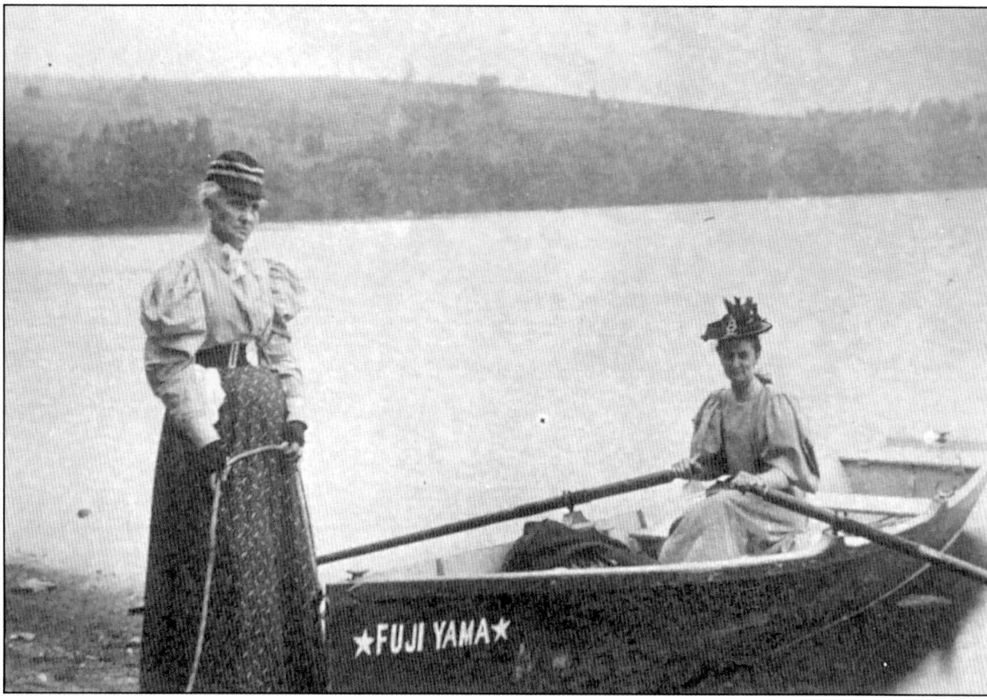

This picture was taken at Lake Waraumaug in New Preston in the late 1800s. Pictured is Mary Doty Bostwick, holding the rope, and her daughter Mary Bostwick Berry in the boat the *Fuji Yama*.

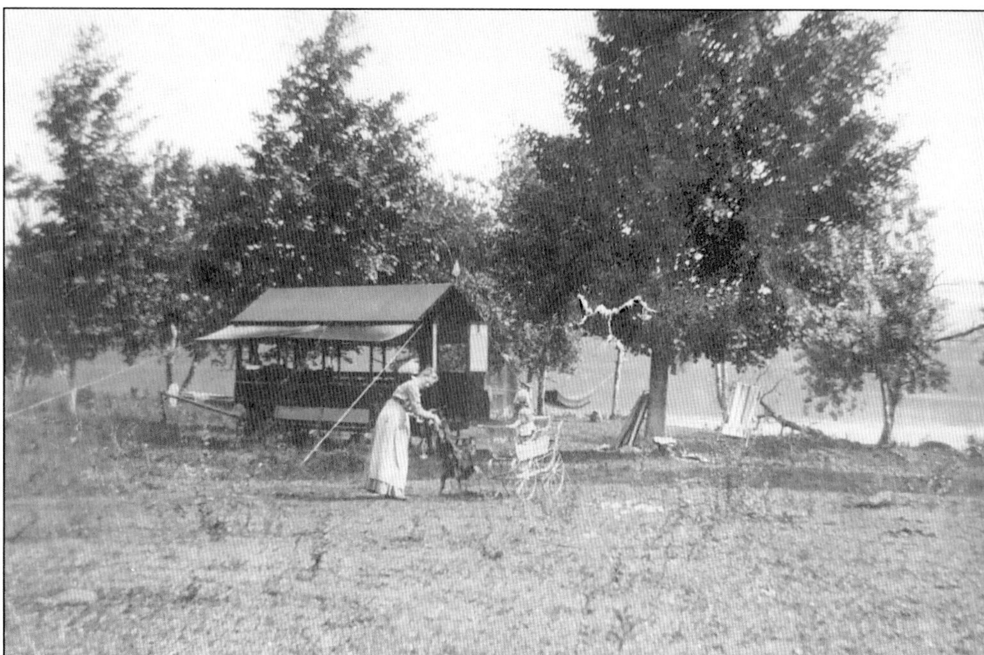

The Bostwick family camps out on Lake Waraumaug in 1902. Millie and Molly Bostwick are in the carriage. Members of the Howland family camped with the Bostwicks. Property at that time sold for only $100 an acre.

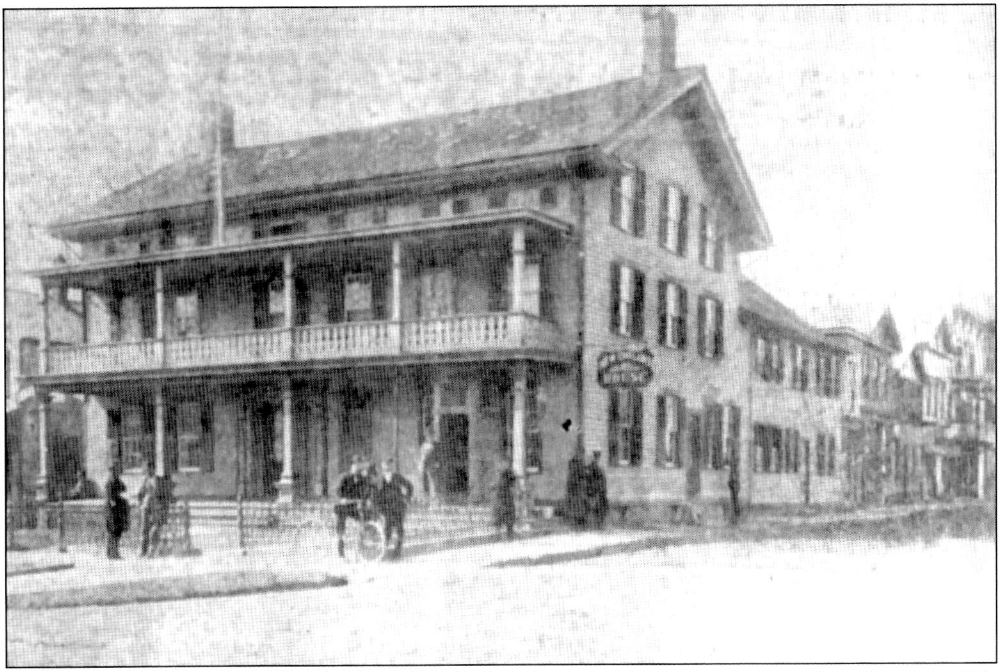

The well-known New England House hotel played an active part in the social and business life of New Milford in the 19th century. It was destroyed in the fire of 1902. Notice the overhanging balcony.

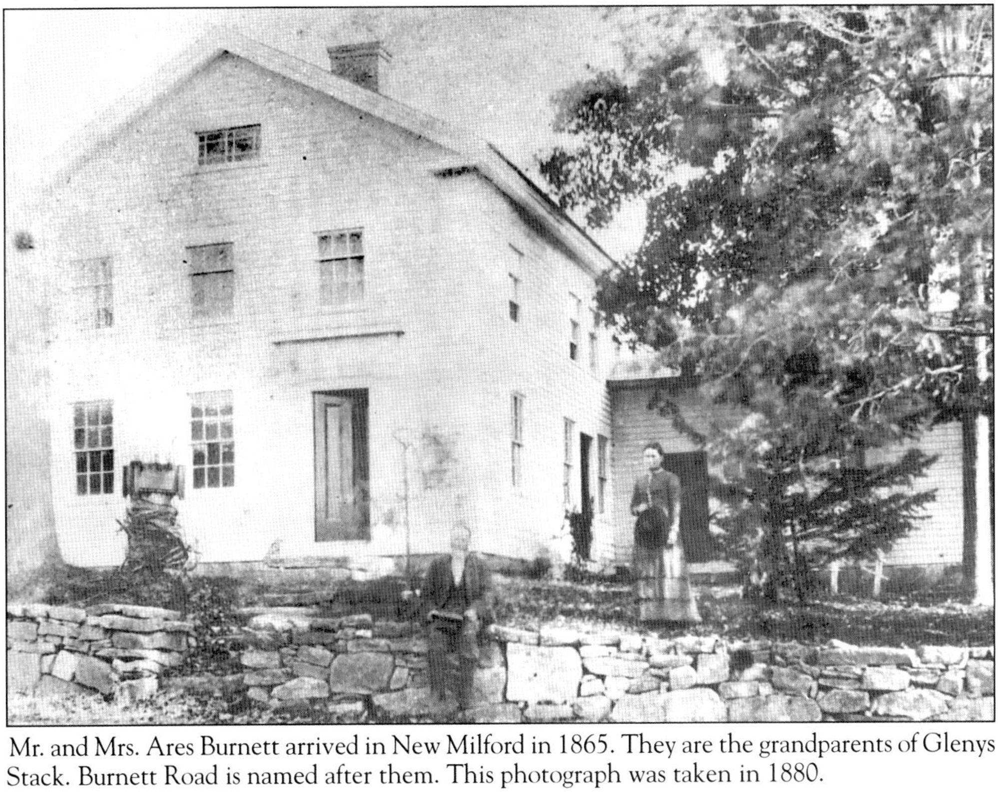

Mr. and Mrs. Ares Burnett arrived in New Milford in 1865. They are the grandparents of Glenys Stack. Burnett Road is named after them. This photograph was taken in 1880.

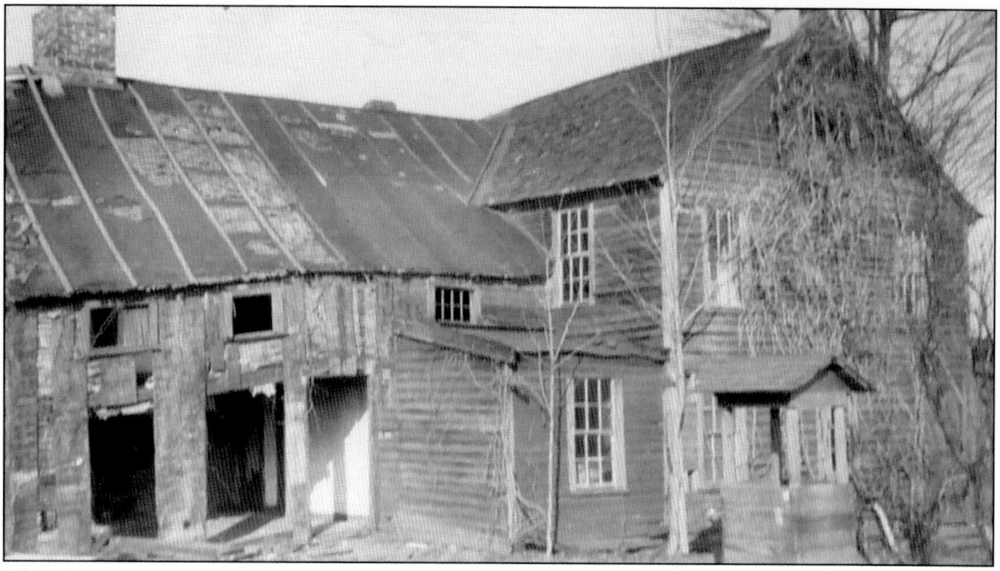

This house shown on Park Lane, pictured in 1919, was later remodeled as a tavern. In 1948, the Old Tavern was owned by Herbert Williams and it later became the Old Pug Tavern. More recently, it was owned by Ralph Baldwin, Fred Berry, Tanno ?, and Herb Williams. Today it belongs to Dr. Kreiger.

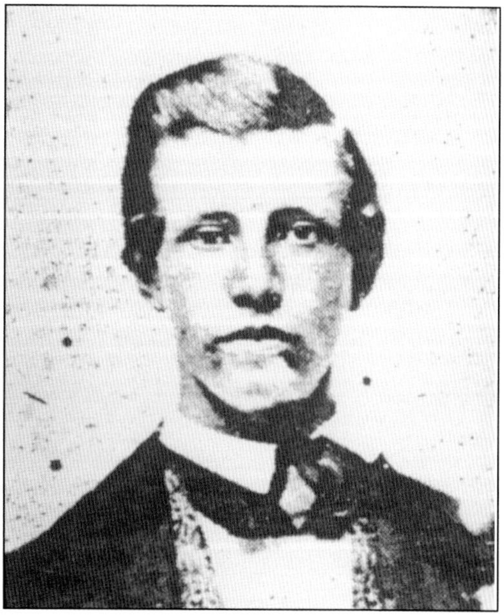

Charles Marsh was raised in the Lanesville district, not far from the bridge that was later named for him: Marsh Bridge. He enlisted in the Union Army on October 21, 1861. For outstanding heroism in battle during the Civil War, he was awarded the Congressional Medal of Honor. He died of tuberculosis at the age of 27 in Pawling, New York.

Thomas M. Stack Jr. of New Milford was a sergeant in the Corps of Engineers 102. He served in the Infantry, 26th Yankee Division, in 1918. He is the grandfather of Robert Stack of the Stack farm on Route 7.

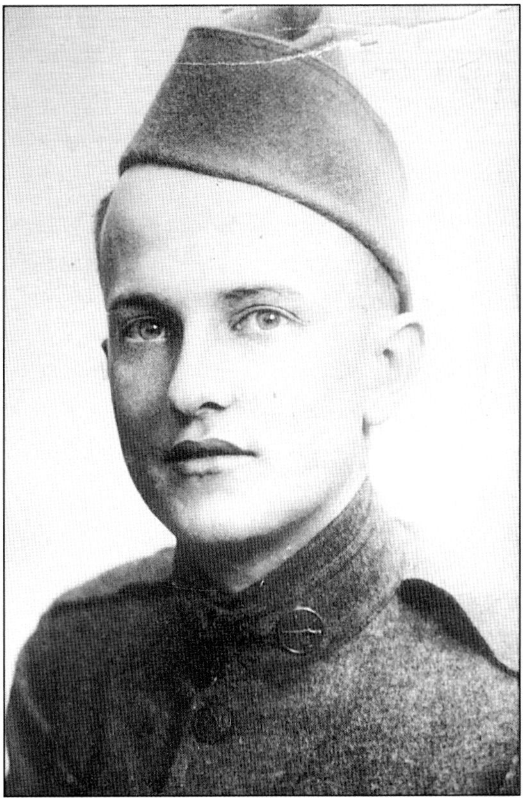

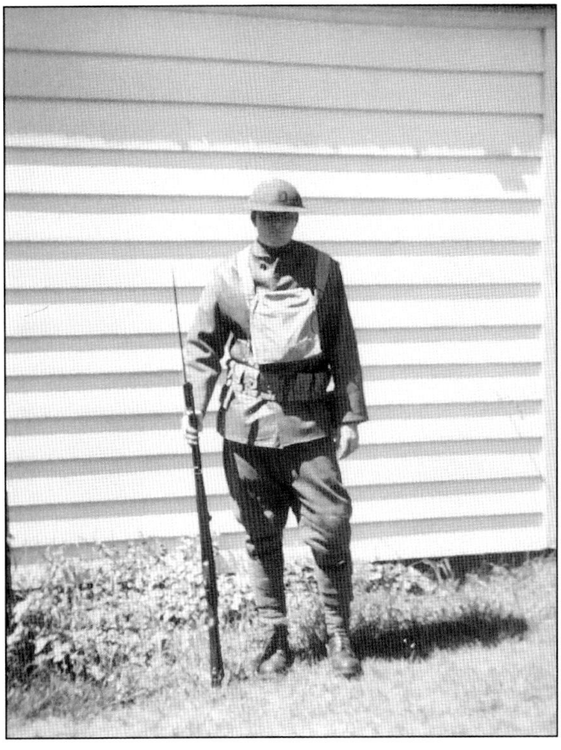

Robert Stack, the son of Robert and Glenys Stack and the great-grandson of Thomas M. Stack Jr., wears his great-grandfather's gas mask, helmet, and rifle. In 1991, Robert Stack received the Academic Excellence Presidential Award from Pres. George Bush.

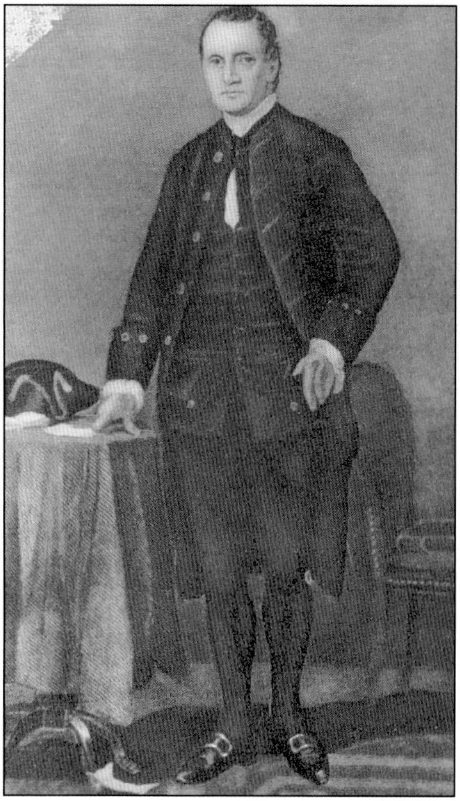

Roger Sherman was the only signer in the 13 colonies of the four fundamental documents: the Articles of Association in 1774, the Declaration of Independence in 1776, the Articles of Confederation in 1777, and the U.S. Constitution in 1787.

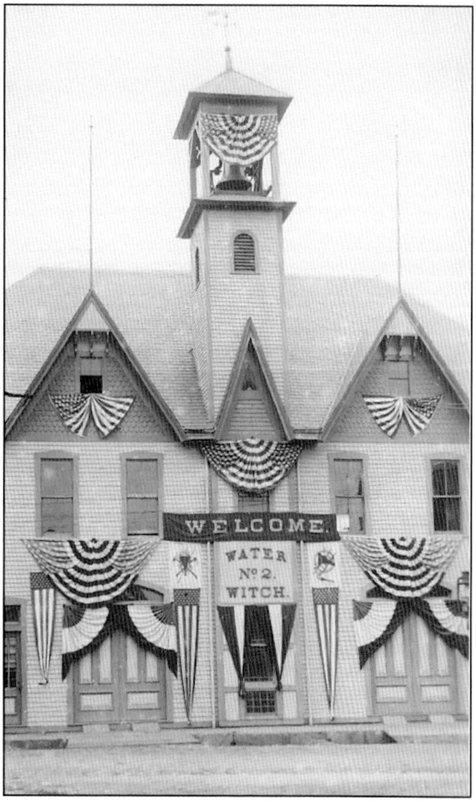

This firehouse was decorated for the Firemen's Parade in 1900. This is the Water Witch Hose Company No. 2. Notice the dirt street. The building still stands on Church Street.

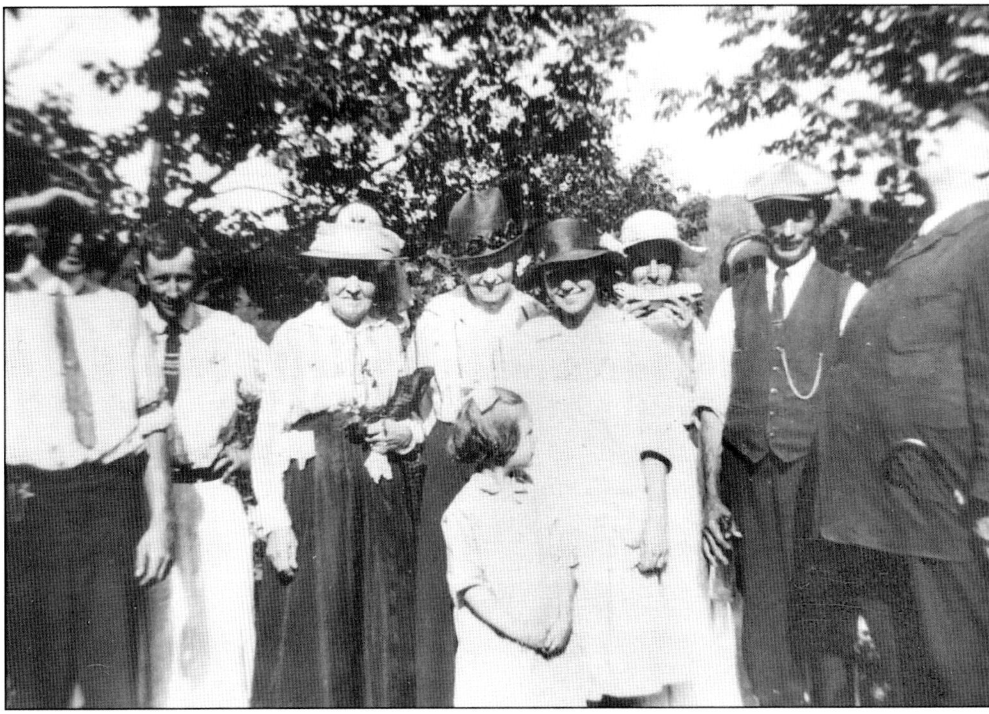

Posing for this 1916 photograph are Raymond Bostwick (holding his hand over his eyes), Mary Doty Bostwick, Sara King, Jet (standing and facing sideways), Harriet (in the black hat), Mrs. Emmons (eating watermelon), Annie Howland, Lottie (peeking over Will's shoulder) Will, and Dr. Frederick King (looking up and wearing a black suit).

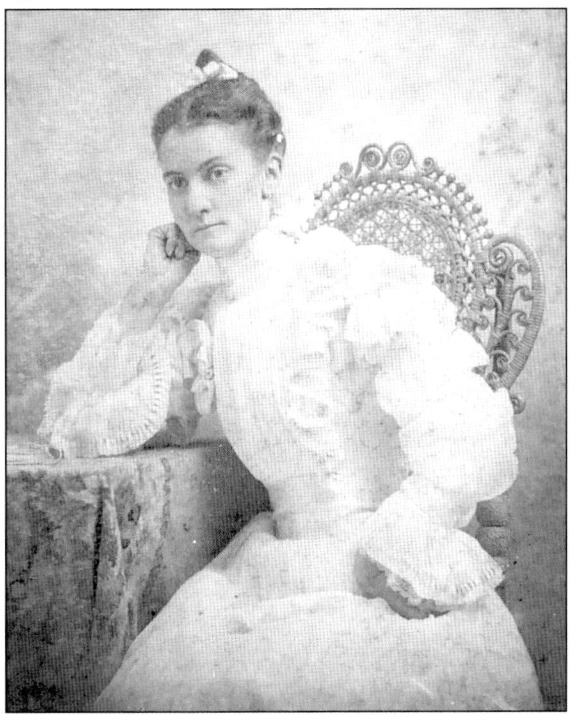

Mary Bostwick Berry, wife of Fred Berry, wears an elegantly styled dress. She lived on Park Lane.

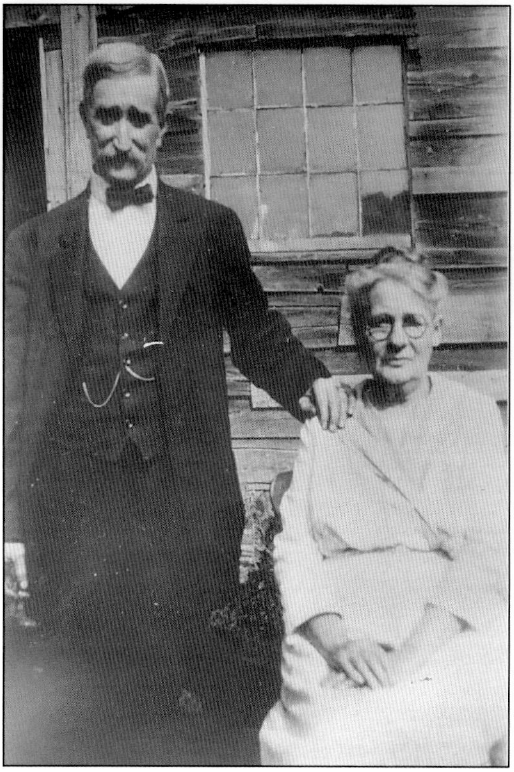

This man standing at the Merwinsville Hotel on Forge Road in Gaylordsville is believed to be a Merwin. The woman is unidentified.

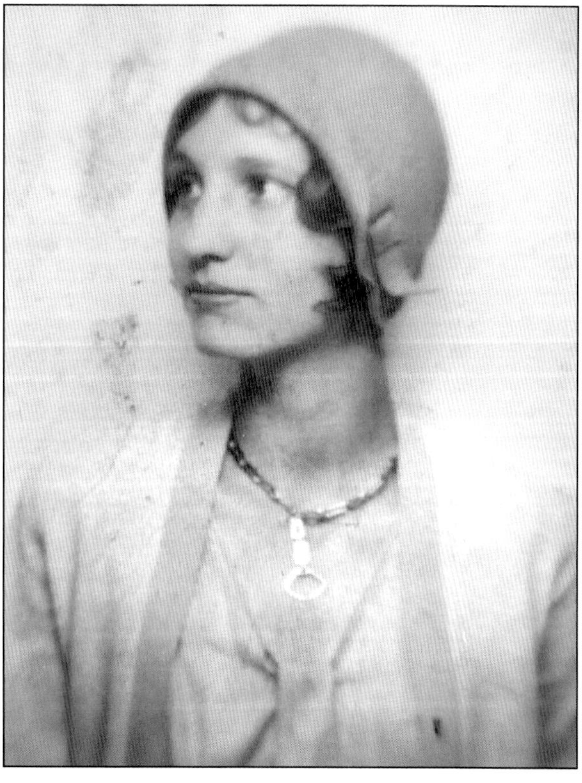

Pictured is Marjorie Merwin. The photograph was taken in the 1920s.

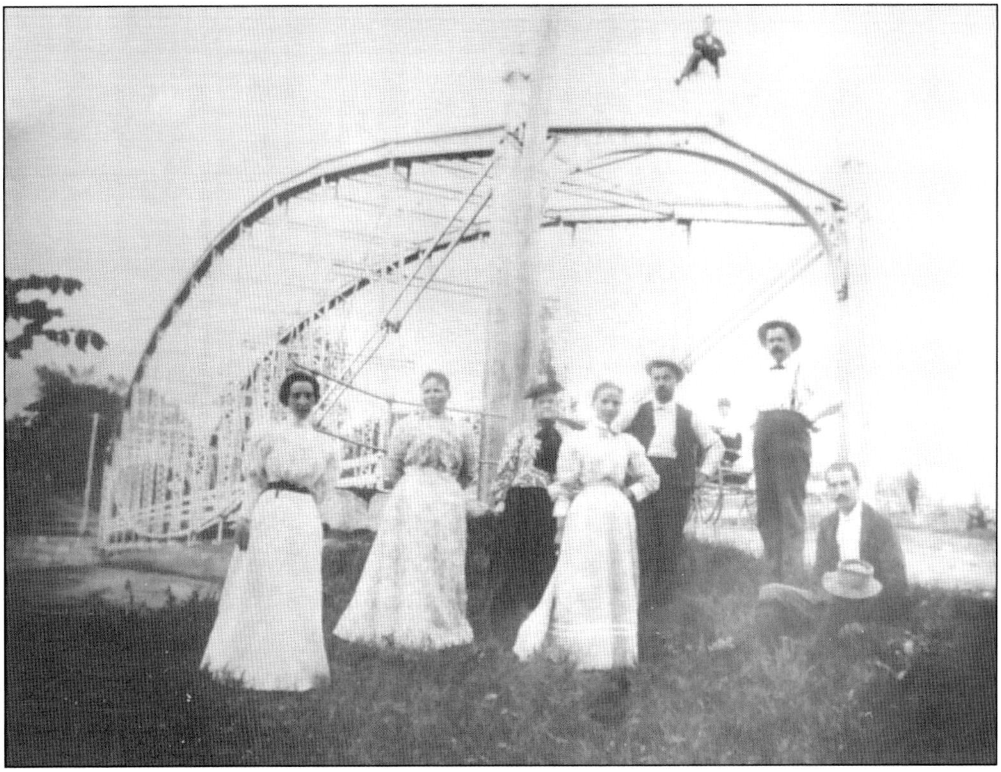

The Boardman Bridge was built in 1888. Notice the man on the top of the bridge and, third from the right, the man in a carriage.

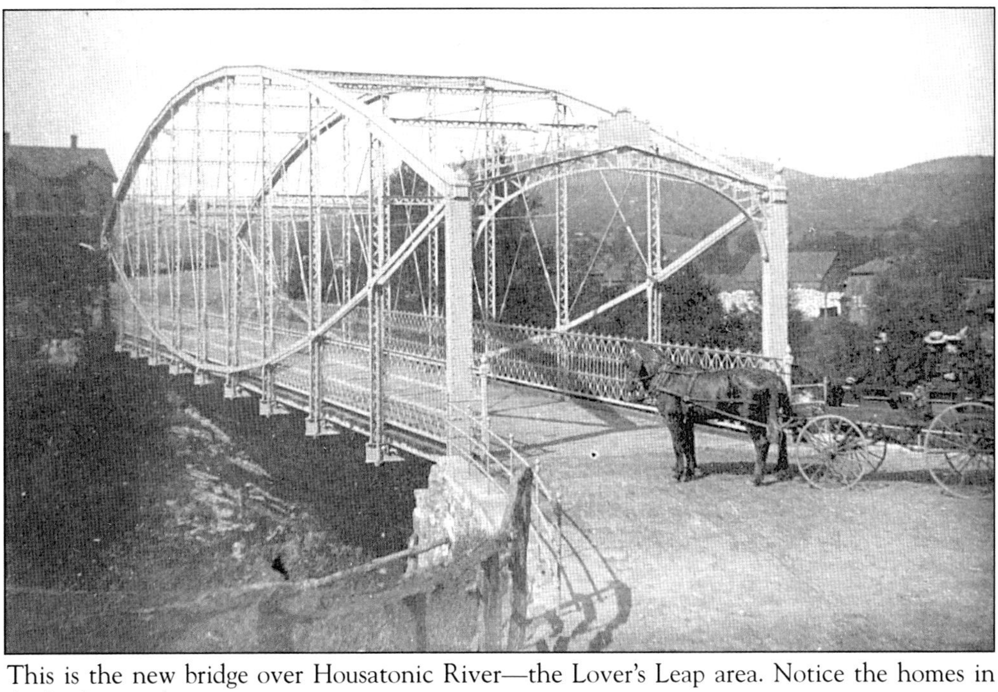

This is the new bridge over Housatonic River—the Lover's Leap area. Notice the homes in the background.

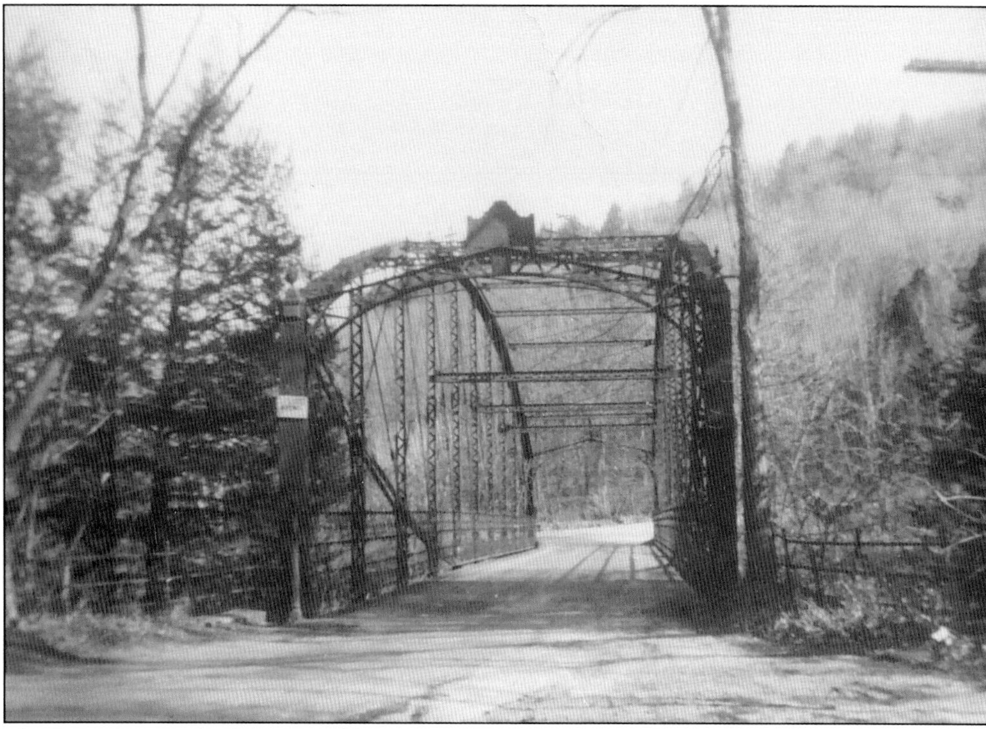

The Lover's Leap Bridge is a well-known spot in New Milford.

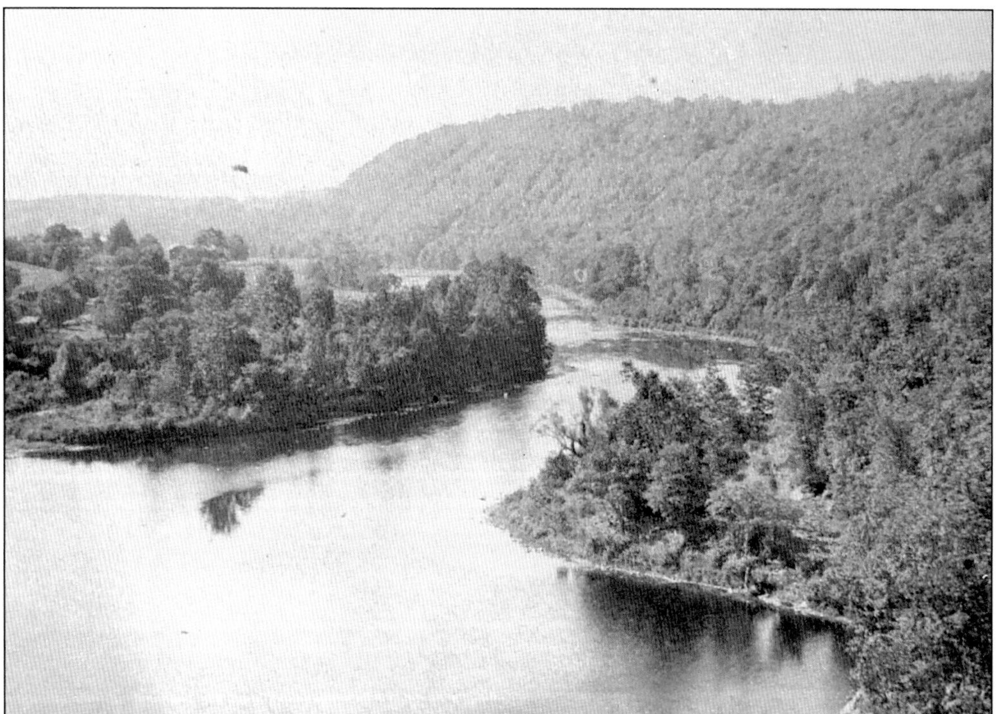

This photograph of the Still River was taken from Lover's Leap *c.* the 1890s.

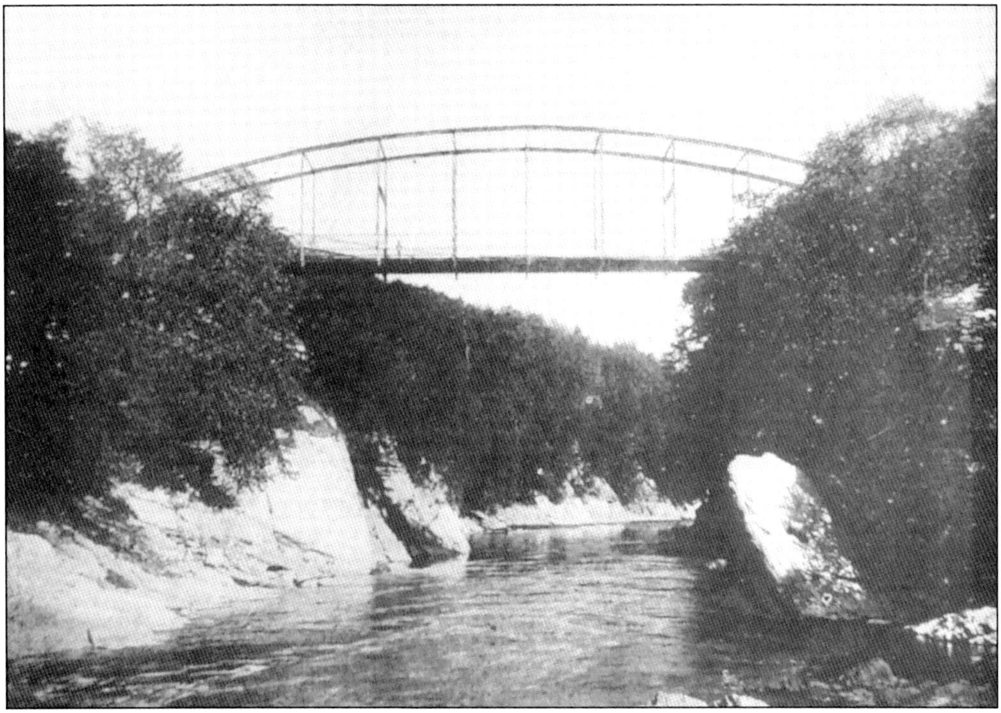

Pictured *c.* the 1890s is the Falls Bridge at Lover's Leap.

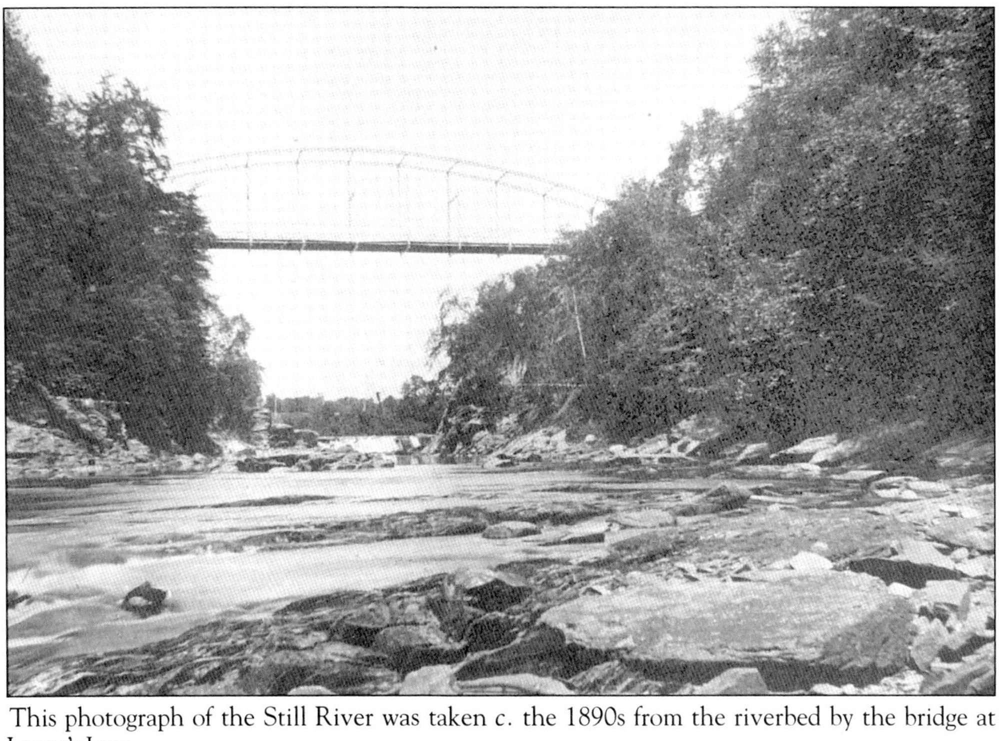

This photograph of the Still River was taken *c.* the 1890s from the riverbed by the bridge at Lover's Leap.

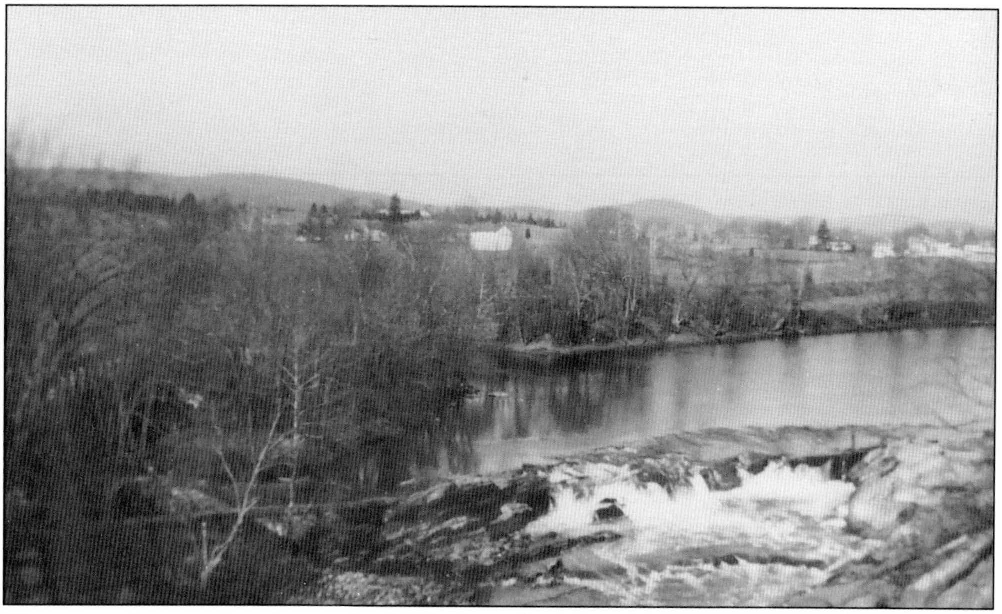

These two photographs taken *c.* the 1890s show the falls at Lover's Leap.

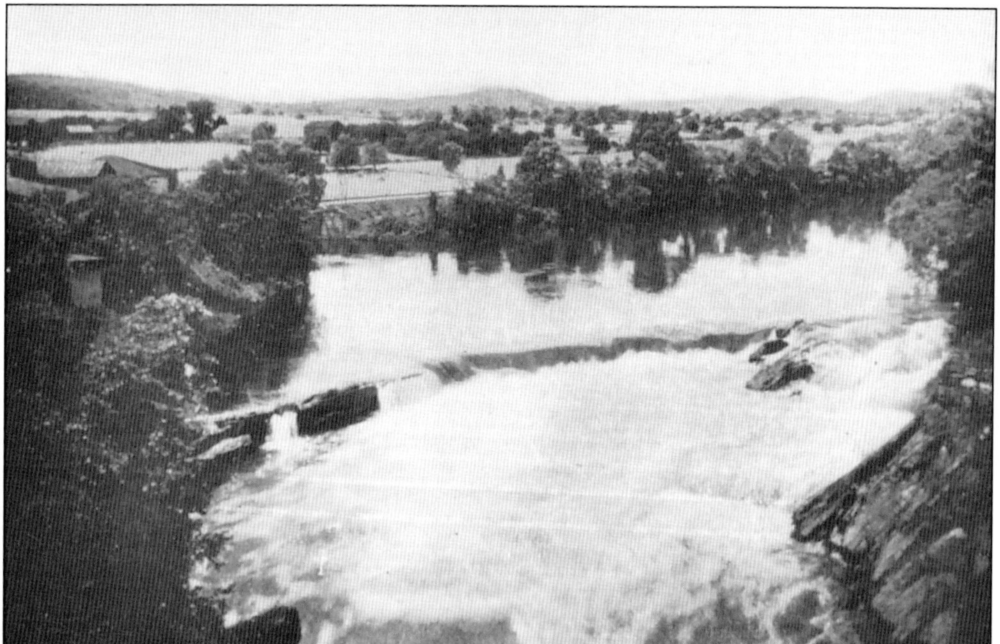

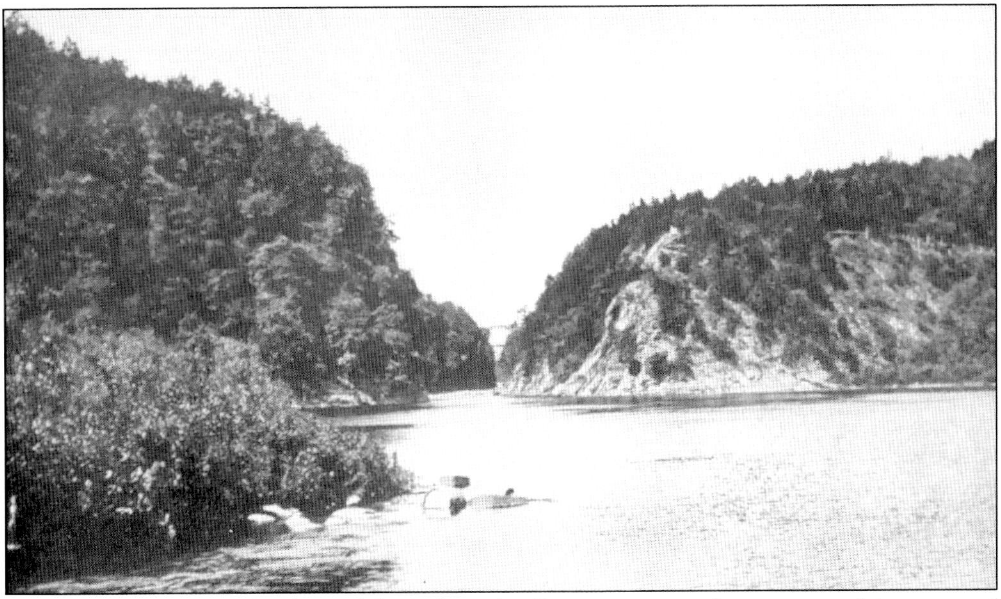

The legend is that the daughter of the Indian chief became attracted to a young white man and he to her. The match not being acceptable to the old chief, the lovers threw themselves off the point of rocks into the river and from this came Lover's Leap.

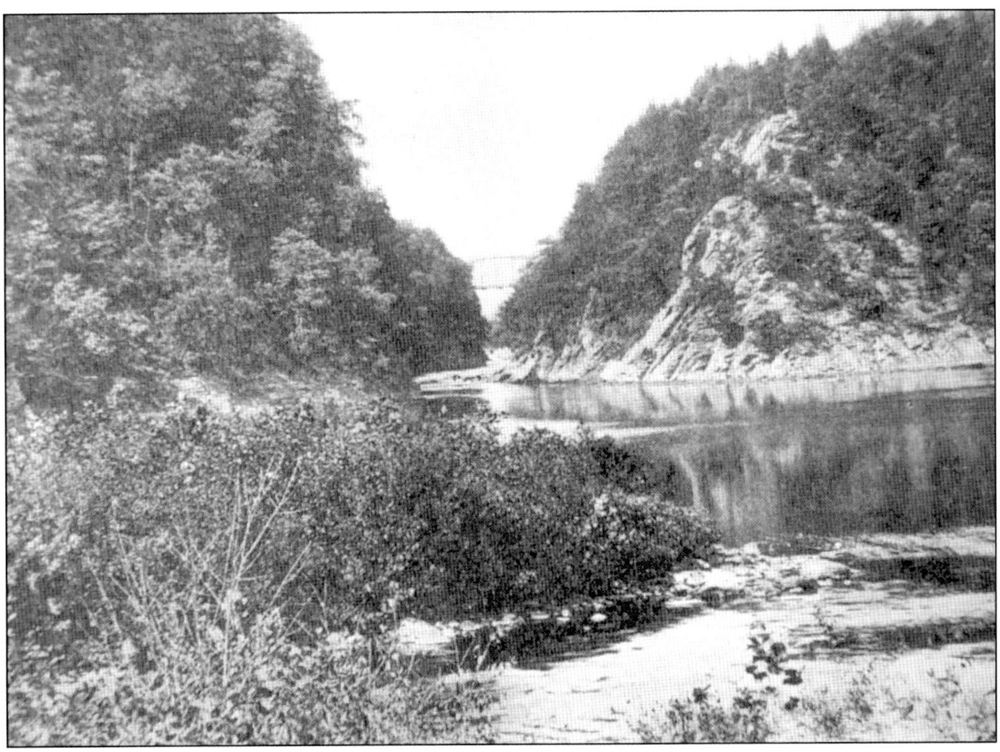

This 1890s photograph shows the cove at Lover's Leap.

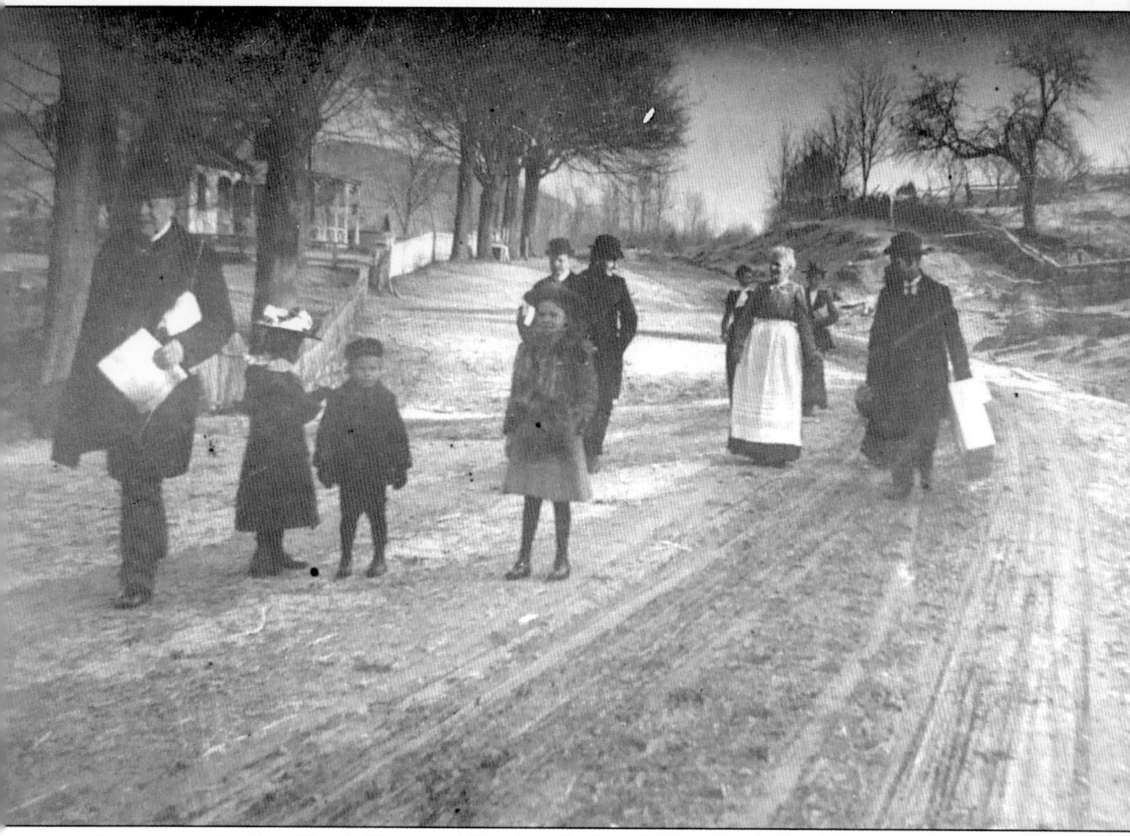

A party was held at North Kent in 1898. Dr. Frederick King leads the families, who are related. Pictured with King are Lottie and Raymond Bostwick, Eugenia King, Sarah King, Mary Doty Bostwick (wearing a white apron), Edgar Bostwick (carrying the box), Dewitt King, William Bostwick, and Em and Lottie Bostwick (in back).